The Waves

Sam's Story: Whistle Bay Book 1

By

Heaton Wilson

In the waves of change we find our true direction.

- Anon

Also by Heaton Wilson

Every Reason

Whatever It Takes

Retribution

Beneath The Surface

Chapter 1

The gull pecked and preened; titanium white against the burnt umber sand; its feathers flickering in the sharp salt breeze that cut in off the Irish Sea.

The September sun struggled over the castle ruins, fighting to be seen among crowds of clouds, valiantly throwing splashes of weak warmth onto the grey and foam flecked sea.

Fat patches of bloated seaweed wobbled at the water's edge, while their compatriots lay helpless on the gritty sand.

The gull was a regular visitor now. Sam called him Gary The Governor, for the simple reason that he was so bossy that no other bird dared come near when he was around. They hopped about hopefully at a distance, feigning interest in unappetising drifts of bladderwrack.

Sam took a handful of crumbs from the carrier bag. 'C-Come on then.'

Gary's head twisted questioningly, but he stood his ground. Sam held on until his legs started burning, then gave in and tossed the crumbs and watched them vanish into the camouflage of sand. He shuffled backwards, gouging channels with his bare feet.

Gary stepped cautiously forwards, and began tapping with his beak, sending up little explosions of sand.

'Suit yourself,' Sam grumbled as he stood, pushing on his thighs with both hands. He was only 25, but his knees had paid the price after a few seasons in the county league. He was a midfielder; good enough in his teens to have trials with Derby County, but Dad had needed him, so that was that.

He waited for Gary to finish: 'Got to get on now, mate -' he turned to scan the empty beach: '- before the rush.'

Gary squawked and hopped and bounced and flapped and flew; posing perfectly against a patch of blue sky before the upper current carried him out away.

Sam walked slowly to the hut.

1

He had plenty of time to sip tea and stare. He loved watching the sea shift from grey to blue to indigo; clockwork clouds in procession; the sun switching on and off; shadows moving like giant hands over the chalk hills.

Sam's father and grandfather used to get through the quiet times by reading charity shop Westerns. The books were musty and fragile now, leaning against each other in alphabetical order on stout planks.

Dad had always been a keen reader, but Sam preferred the view from the window. He'd told him so many times over the years, but towards the end the conversation seemed to be on a permanent loop. The doctor eventually confirmed what everyone had suspected: dementia was stripping his father's mind. It soon stole his love of books; then, just 18 months ago, it killed him.

The sky was blue on the day of the funeral, but everything else was black. Women in big hats leaned in awkwardly to kiss his cheek; men in dark suits and frowns shook his hand and told him: 'He was one of us.' Then, a doubtful look: 'I suppose you'll be takin' the business on?'

The stutter got worse for a time after Dad passed. He'd learned to live with the nickname. A few of the lads in the football team still used it now and again...*S-S-Sam.*

When Dad died, no-one expected he'd want to take on the deckchair business, or thought he'd be any good at it.

It wasn't as if he had a choice. Mikey, the eldest, was making enough money catching fish, so he wasn't interested. Sean, the youngest, had died of a heart condition before he'd made it to voting age; and Mum passed away five years ago. She'd never recovered from losing Sean; shut herself in the living room with her television and photo frames. Lived there, slept there... eventually died there.

So one day, near the end, Sam held Dad's hand and promised he'd take over. The hut had become his second home anyway. He'd run there after school, and sit in the highchair by the window to do his homework, while Dad slurped tea and read Zane Grey.

Soon, he was helping out: jumping down the wooden steps with the money bag to collect from a new customer or stomping importantly across the soft warm sand to show them to their deckchairs.

And now, it was his.

He made it his priority to repaint the sign: sky blue letters on a white board - BAY DECKCHAIRS est 1923.

Then he recoated the hut with creosote overnight when the pubs were full and the beach was empty. It was strong stuff, and banned for most, but Dad had a barrelful, and special dispensation from the council to use it. It stank for a while, but the hut looked good and nobody complained.

Trade ebbed and flowed that first year. Mainly ebbed. Easter was supposed to be the start of the season, but Covid kept people at home. Things picked up in May as the number of cases went down, but then the weather turned bad, and the beach was empty again. Sam strapped the chairs under the tarpaulin at the foot of the sea wall until the storms passed, and the beach finally came to life in July and August.

Sam laughed when a few of the locals wrote to the Recorder complaining about the crowds, and the rubbish they left behind. He and the other traders just counted the money, and Gary and the other gulls made short work of discarded chips.

A family from the Midlands told Sam they were sick of sitting at home, so they paid £20 for four all day chairs, hammered in a windbreak, and sat on the beach drinking takeaway beer and cider from plastic cups.

Many of them left the windbreaks behind. Some put up small tents for the kids to play in, and lots of them were abandoned, too. Sam collected them every night for a local charity and got himself featured in the Recorder for his trouble.

At the end of the busier days, he'd sit in the hut, enjoying the late sun turning the interior burnt orange, listening to country music on the cassette player, and looking back over the accounts. They were in Dad's immaculate handwriting, and Sam could track the development of his illness by the way his writing deteriorated.

But the short summer rush was over now, and there was no cash to add up.

Sam boiled the kettle and poured another tea.

3

He'd put a dozen chairs out today, and even that felt optimistic.

Jivin' Jack Deavers, the old boy with the dyed hair who owned the amusement arcade, came out for a smoke, leaned on the railings and raised an eyebrow: 'Bit halfhearted, Sammy.'

He could still strike a pose despite the arthritis. He used to be a ballroom dancer - mainly cruise ships, with a few national competition wins thrown in - and he always wore a suit for work.

Sam looked up. 'I could shut down completely, I s-suppose Jack, but if we all did that…'

There were a few signs of life today, including Mrs. Simpson, Mike the Meat's wife, who was plodding at the water's edge in the bob hat and wellies that she wore whatever the weather. She was shouting at her over excited German Shepherd - a fluffy bear of a dog that was grabbing mouthfuls of seaweed, dropping them at her feet, barking madly, and going back for more.

A hundred yards to the left, a young couple huddled together on the sand, leaning back against the sea-smoothed stumps of an old groyne. They had white earbuds in, blocking out the Latin American dance tune that wafted across the beach from Jack's arcade.

Sam smiled. They wouldn't have sat there a few years ago. They'd have been deafened by the screams of children on the red and yellow bouncy castle. He shook his head: was that only three years ago?

He looked to his right and watched the breeze catch the red white and blue striped canvas of the chairs.

His stomach rumbled: a sure sign of the need for food. Mum used to say he must have hollow legs.

He went inside to check the calendar. There were another six weeks before he'd be putting the shutters up for the winter. But they were talking about another Covid wave, so was there any point staying open till then?

Covid had depressed him. He'd had his jabs, but so many people seemed to think the government was drugging them into passive obedience. Yet people younger than him were being knocked out or even killed by it.

4

Sam shook his head. The virus had killed trade as well as people, but what chance did he have of making money any other way? How do you diversify from renting out deck chairs? A few of the pubs had done takeaways and put heaters under gazebos outside. No doubt brother Mikey would be under one of them at lunchtime, throwing his catch money down his neck. A couple of the cafes were offering home deliveries, but they - like some of the pubs - were finding it hard enough to recruit staff, never mind persuade people to spend money.

Jivin' Jack had opened a cafe at the arcade and his wife made cakes and waggled her bum to the bossa nova. He told Sam they took £4.20 yesterday.

Sam had laughed: 'You need to change the music, Jack.'

He waited for the one o'clock time signal, then locked up and walked into town in his uniform: khaki shorts, red t shirt, no shoes.

It was only a few yards across the narrow one-way esplanade to the sandwich shop. His cheese and tomato bap and slice of fruit cake was on the counter, as usual, in a white paper bag with 'Chair Man' written in blue felt tip.

Loud Louise was carrying a plate of something colourful and greasy to one of the tables at the back, so he left his money on the counter and called out, as he always did: 'Thank you, Lou!.

He heard her belated 'Thanks my luv!' as he stepped out onto the pavement.

By four o'clock he was packing away the chairs. He carried them two at a time, while the gulls cried and squabbled and the tide ran in, pulled back the tarp and stacked them against the others. He tied a string round today's chosen few to remind him to use a different batch tomorrow: to even out the wear and tear.

Dad used to tell him to treat the chairs with respect: 'Do that, and they'll outlive me, Sammy.' He was right.

A high-pitched toot on a car horn made him look up. A girl parked her car and walked quickly up to the railings. She was about his age, in a yellow waterproof and red leggings: much younger than your average day tripper, and, Sam thought, much better looking.

5

Her legs were at his eye level, and he tried not to look as she called out: 'Hello! Oh dear, I'm too late, aren't I?'

Sam smiled. 'Yes, s- sorry. It's pretty much closing time.' He turned and pointed across the sand. 'But you're welcome to sit on the s-sand. No charge.'

The wind wafted her long dark hair over her face and she swept it away, laughing. 'That's very kind of you. Tempting, but... yes, right. Perhaps not. Sorry! Erm ... silly question... will you be here tomorrow?'

'I will.'

'Oh good, lovely! I'll see you tomorrow then.' She waved and got back into her car. He climbed a couple of steps and watched her drive off. Possibly heading to the Best Western. Or the caravan park.

Her red car looked like one of those old Citroens that sounded like a lawnmower but lasted forever.

Sam finished fastening everything down, dropped the shutter over the window, and padlocked the door.

Mum's theory was that he stuttered because he was sensitive, but he was sure it was more complicated than that.

No point fretting, though; he wasn't expecting to see her tomorrow. There was a yellow warning of wind, and 80 per cent probability of rain.

Chapter 2

Walking home reminded him of that feeling when school was over, but without the chattering and chasing and laughing and satchel swinging.

He remembered running everywhere as a kid, eating everything put in front of him and asking for more, especially if it was mum's apple pie. They were happy times, and even though he'd get home feeling upset some days because the other kids laughed at his stutter, mum would always be waiting at the front door, ready to ruffle his hair; and he'd soon get over it.

Walking home these days gave him the chance to talk to people who, like him, had spent most of their day shut away in their shops, locked in by routine.

Dad would always make time for a chat, because he said traders in seaside towns needed to stick together. He told Sam the railways brought Whistle Bay to life, but the Beeching closures killed it, so it was important to support each other.

According to him, the town's fortunes were transformed when it found itself on a branch line with connections to Birmingham and Manchester. Dad could remember trains bringing in hundreds at a time, mainly from the Midlands. He took Sam to the library once, to show him old photos: men in dark suits, shirt and tie packing out the platform; women in smart dresses; and everyone wearing a hat; the beach thronged with people.

Trade was suffering now, though everywhere was taking a battering if the news was to be believed. Sam wasn't sure Beeching could be blamed for the current mess. According to the news, and people at the Chamber of Commerce who seemed to know a lot more about it than him, it was down to the government's failure to deal with the pandemic and its predictable aftershock. Sam felt it was too easy to blame the government for everything. Still, as he was always being reminded, he was only young, so what did he know?

Many of the traders were suspicious of him at first. But he knew he'd been accepted when he qualified for a nickname: The Chair Man.

Sam smiled to himself as he padlocked the hut. He'd hear that nickname more than once on his way home. Still, it was a lot better than the chants he got at school.

There was no sign of 'Appy Aaron at his kiosk on the esplanade, but Billy was there stacking metal frame chairs and tables at the side of the Whistle Cafe. Local gossip had it that he came up with that name simply because he whistled, rather than it being a nod to its location. Whatever the reason, most traders - and customers - wished he'd stop.

'Hey up Chair Man,' he called out, laughing. 'Rushed off your feet again today?'

Sam raised his baseball cap to a shopper before diverting across the precinct. 'Afternoon Billy Whistle. It's been mayhem. I ran out of deckchairs. Standing room only. What about you?'

Billy's eyes squeezed shut and his ample stomach vibrated as the laughter morphed into a fit of coughing.

When he got his breath back, he breathlessly ventured the opinion that the share price of coffee would probably go up because he'd served so much of it today: 'Queueing round the block, they were.'

Sam smiled. 'I bet they were. Anyway, keep smiling. I must be on my way. Get the tea on. See you tomorrow. You'd better grind another ton of beans before tomorrow's rush, eh?'

He heard Billy whistling his heavily embellished and extremely shrill version of 'My Way' as he walked away through Marine Parade. The high notes seemed to carry, bouncing off the metal shutters on the empty shops.

He exchanged banter with a few more traders who were carrying stock inside after a day of crosswords and word searches.

He reckoned he was the youngest by at least twenty years. Most of his schoolmates thought he was daft taking on the hut, but they were the ones living at home, drifting, eating fast food and drawing benefits.

8

That annoyed him almost as much as visitors who looked down their noses at the T shirts and the buckets and spades, the carousels of ancient greeting cards, and inaccurately named 'ladies' fashions'. It was too easy to take the mickey. These were the people he'd grown up with. Many of them went to the same school as Dad. As far as Sam was concerned, they chose to work hard, and they deserved respect.

The house Sam grew up in was a semi-detached at the end of a cul de sac that backed onto the park; close enough to the ring road to pick up the low hum of traffic heading to and from the supermarket, or by-passing Whistle Bay in favour of the bungalow settlements that were springing up all along the coast.

Sam had brightened up the frontage with cream masonry paint, and the red front door was open.

He pushed it slowly, calling out cautiously: 'Hello?'

Mikey's voice: his usual toneless greeting: 'In here.'

He was in the living room. Sam walked through quickly and leaned against the door frame.

'What are you doing in here, Mikey?'

'Nice to see you too.' His brother was ten years older but looked like he'd aged another decade. He was lying on the sofa, head on the armrest. 'It's bad news, Sam.'

Sam was used to his melodramas. He did his best to hide his irritation, but it still came out like a disbelieving sigh. 'Why, what's happened?'

Mikey closed his eyes and breathed deeply for a few seconds. Then, with his eyes still closed: 'Doctor says I've got to change me life.'

'Change your -? What do you mean? Change it how? Close the front door behind you?'

Mikey sniffed and sat up. 'Very funny. I've got to cut down the drink and change me diet or I'll be dead in five.'

Sam pointed to the can of lager on the coffee table. 'So, just the one can before your tea, then?'

Mikey sniffed again and went on the attack. His voice was high pitched for someone so sturdy. 'Yeah, go on, have a laugh. It's all right for you. Mr. Bloody Perfect. I like a pint and I'm not ashamed to admit it. All you have to do is put chairs out then sit on your arse all day. I work hard, and I've earned the right to have a few beers. You try fishing these days. It's like Tesco on a Friday out there sometimes, trying to find a bit of elbow room.'

Sam moved his brother's Sun out of the way so he could sit next to him. The headline shouted out: *COUNTRY IN CRISIS! AGAIN!*

'Yeah, ok, sorry. So, come on, calm down. What did the doc say? Did she give you tests and stuff?'

'Took blood, wired me up, blood pressure, bloody urine sample... I said to her, why don't you measure me inside leg while I'm here?'

Sam grinned. He could picture the resigned look on Dr Prakesh's face. She saw Sam queueing up for his booster jab a few weeks ago, and commented, as just about everyone did, on the contrast between the two brothers: 'Are you sure you are same family?'

Looking at Mikey, it was hard to believe. Sam was just over six feet and built like an athlete, slim but with a strong upper body; Mikey was a good six inches shorter and top heavy. He was carrying too much weight - most of it on his stomach. Sam was blond haired and blue eyed, Mikey was brown and brown, apart from the grey in his thinning hair. And he smelt of fish.

He patted Mikey's knee because he knew it annoyed him: 'I'll get you a few cans of that zero-alcohol beer, see how you like it. Anyway, what do you fancy for your tea? Egg and chips all right?'

Mikey shook his head. 'You can stick your zero alcohol. And anyway, no tea for me: I'm going to see my lady friend tonight. She's taking me down the club.'

Sam groaned: 'You're kidding? Mikey, you can't; not after this!'

'Stop fussing. You're not me bloody mother. Anyway, it's just for a couple.' He sighed like a soul in torment and pushed himself up off the sofa with difficulty, hitching his baggy jeans up as he stood. 'I'll start the regime tomorrow. Scout's honour. Don't wait up. I'll probably stay over. Ta ta!'

Sam waited till the front door slammed shut, then started tidying up. Mikey had turned his bedroom into a pigsty, but he wasn't going to wreck this room too.

He wanted to keep it as it was when Mum spent her final days here. It was the only time he'd spent with her after Sean died, binning her tissues, stacking her magazines, freshening her up with wet wipes. He was in the sixth form then, and he'd chat about his day at school; and how he was helping Dad down at the hut. She'd usually just listen, but one day she reached out for his hand as he bent down to pick something up.

'You're a good boy, Sammy. Look after them for me, eh?'

He couldn't think of anything to say. He remembered feeling scared and there was a lump in his throat. Her eyes were bright, and her voice was hoarse. She'd changed, and it felt like he was saying goodbye to a stranger.

Ten days later, he did say goodbye, standing by her grave in one of Dad's suits, trying not to cry as the vicar said something about people never dying.

They went to the White Hart for sandwiches and sausage rolls, as people got over their grief with the help of real ale and Asti Spumante, and the subdued conversations grew progressively louder. No-one noticed when Sam left his orange juice and lemonade on the bar and walked out. He pulled off his tie and sat on the bench on the Green where mum used to watch him kick a ball around.

Now it was just him and Mikey.

He carried old papers and magazines, the empty lager can and three unopened ones, out to the bins, then sat in the kitchen with a mug of tea.

He heard a football bouncing on the pavement: the local kids off for a game on the Green. More memories; more reminders…

Mikey had reset the old wireless to Radio 1, so Sam tweaked the dial to Country FM, and drowned out the news headlines by wrestling with a bag of oven chips that had decided to weld itself into the tiny freezer compartment.

There were only two eggs in the fridge, so it was just as well Mikey wasn't staying. He turned on the oven and waited for it to warm up, as the first spots of rain hit the window.

11

The DJ introduced Choices by George Jones. Sam sat down again and closed his eyes:

I've had choices since the day that I was born
There were voices that told me right from wrong
If I had listened, no I wouldn't be here today
Living and dying with the choices I've made

Two hours later, he heard the Eastenders theme tune on next door's television as he stepped out into the rain.

He pushed the key into his football shorts and set off at an easy pace onto the ring road; gradually increasing speed as he reached the discount store that sold everything from pans to watercolour paint, and never seemed to close. Then he pushed harder as he turned left onto Bay Road and relaxed his shoulders on the long descent to the Esplanade.

There were still a few boats in the harbour, including Mikey's. He'd bought it off a mate four or five years ago. He fished for mackerel and bought the rights to a string of lobster pots not far offshore. He complained about the time it took, but Sam knew he must be doing okay to afford to fill up with beer every night.

He was loosening up nicely now, feeling the adrenaline as he ran along the esplanade, savouring the freshness of the night air.

There were a few boats out at sea, their lights sparkling through the misty rain. Further out, a city of lights moved slowly - one of the cruise ships that passed this way.

Taking a left-hand bend, he saw the red Citroen, under the floodlights in the South View Hotel car park. He wondered what she was doing here. She seemed too young to come here for a holiday.

He thought about her again as he turned left again for the climb home, picking up speed to hit the sweet spot. It felt as if he was floating, breathing gently despite the effort and everything else was forgotten. It was just him, and the sound of his footsteps.

He slowed down about half a mile from home and she came back into his head. He'd assumed she was on her own, but she might not be. She could be visiting a relative, or her boyfriend, or working at the hotel - no, that's not right; her car would have been round the back. What else? A contract in town somewhere? Shop designer? Maybe, but her clothes… that funny old car…

The rain had stopped by the time he reached the end of the street. He walked, taking exaggerated long steps to stretch his calves. He stopped at the gate and checked his fitness tracker: four miles in 26 minutes. Not bad, but he'd run it faster.

He put his gear in the washing machine and ran a bath.

Another night alone.

He didn't mind normally. But if felt different tonight.

Chapter 3

Gary didn't show up next morning, much to the delight of a crying crowd of gulls that circled and swooped and beak-drilled the crumbs Sam was scattering.

Jack Deavers looked on, the cigarette stuck to his lips, as Sam walked across the sand to unstrap the tarp and pick out today's deckchair selection.

'Goin' for the blues and greens, young fella?'

Sam squinted up, the sun in his eyes. 'Anything for a bit of variety, Jack. Got to be done. Anyway, what about this weather? They s-said it'd be crap today.'

Jack nodded, looking moodily out to sea, his eyes narrowing. Dark grey clouds gathered on the horizon, sucking up the sea through menacing looking trails. 'Don't worry, Chair Man, it'll be coming our way before too long.'

Sam turned to look and nodded. 'Yep, I reckon. Got any plans today, Jack?'

Jack shook his head, peeled the remains of the cigarette from his bottom lip and flicked it onto the sand. 'Got a few machines want repairing. See you.'

He always was a man of few words. Sam shook his head, smiling, and spoke to his back. 'Have a good one.' He pinched the tip of the discarded fag end and put it in the bin at the side of the hut, then set the chairs out, grouping them in pairs to spread them out a bit.

The early morning sun was a bonus, and a reminder of Dad's first rule, always have the chairs facing the sun. He and Dad used to have such a laugh, watching people moving their chairs because they wanted to face the sea, or even the esplanade. They'd always end up snapping shut and some of them took forever to work out how to put them back together. Dad called it deckchair origami.

Sam could never sustain it on a busy day, but when it was quiet, he'd shuffle the chairs round to follow the sun every couple of hours.

On sunny days, everyone told him he was a lucky man. He did love being able to kick off his old deck shoes, feel the sand on his feet and the sun on his back; take the weight of the chairs, enjoy the exercise, savour that sweet salty air; and watch people enjoying themselves.

He'd remind them that the sun doesn't shine every day. But when it did, they were the best days: children squealing at the cold-water shock; giggling at dad messing up a football trick; the smell of sun lotion and cigarettes; excitement when mum opened the bag of food, or the ice cream van rang out from the esplanade.

Sam turned to the sun and closed his eyes. He could hear the tune now: Greensleeves. Why was it always Greensleeves?

Then, a voice: 'Oh, there you are! Hellooo!'

He opened his eyes, though he knew who it was straight away.

Most people look comical, walking on sand, but she floated elegantly - like a brightly coloured sloop in her bright green smock and yellow leggings.

She was barefoot, carrying a pair of trainers in one hand. The other was clutched round the strap of a large and heavy looking bag.

She was out of breath by the time she reached Sam's hut, and let her bag fall at her feet.

Sam nodded and she smiled, catching her breath. She seemed so full of energy. 'What a beautiful morning! I never expected this. It's perfect!'

'Well, I don't think it's going to last long.' He pointed to the horizon, regretting instantly that he sounded just like Jack, and hoping the stutter stayed away.

She turned to look, then laughed. 'Oh them! They're miles away. We'll be all right for absolutely ages!'

Sam shuffled his feet. He wanted to come back at her with the same energy and good humour but he didn't know what to say. 'Erm…'

She held out her hand. 'Sorry! I talk too much… Lindsay. Nice to meet you. You are..?'

He took a step closer and caught the scent of her perfume. 'Sam.'

'Hello, Sam.'

She took off her glasses and put them in her breast pocket.

Sam tried to be nonchalant but winced inside at his naff attempt at conversation. 'Is that a fisherman's smock?'

She laughed. 'This? Oh, no. I'm afraid I bought this at a charity shop in Marylebone. It's meant to make me look artistic. Epic fail!' She stopped. 'Why didn't I just lie? Yes, of course it's a fisherman's smock! Would that make me fit in more round here, do you think? They don't know what to make of me at the hotel.'

Sam feigned ignorance. 'Where are you -'

'South View. Do you know it?'

'Yeah, there aren't that many decent ones round here, to be honest.'

'Really? Well, South View is all right, if you like that sort of thing. It's a bit old fashioned, though, isn't it? The breakfast waiter was wearing a bow tie, poor man. He was wearing it last night, too. And they bring your coffee to you in this funny little sitting room.' She laughed. 'And… they've actually got a sideboard in there with board games piled up. I love it!'

Sam smiled, feeling overwhelmed: 'I've never been there, to tell the truth.'

She nodded, frowning. 'Well, you must be busy, running this place, I expect.'

Sam looked round at the deserted beach and smiled. 'Well, yeah, fairly.'

Lindsay laughed again, and this time Sam joined in. They looked at each other for a moment.

Sam chewed his bottom lip, then stopped himself. 'S-So… did you want a chair today?'

'Yes, yes, I do, please. Nearly forgot. Chattering away. Sorry, no-one gets a word in when I start. How much do I owe you for a morning?'

'Just pay me at the end.' Sam smiled. 'I trust you.'

'Thank you. I'm glad. Any one I like?'

16

Sam waved an arm. 'Take your pick.' He stepped in as she leaned down to pick up her bag and their hands touched briefly. 'S-Sorry. Erm… would you like me to carry that over for you?'

'Oh yes, please. It weighs an absolute ton.'

Sam walked behind her as she picked the nearest deckchair and stood behind it, looking round. 'Ok if I move it?'

Sam nodded. 'I'll do it, if you like. Just tell me where you want it.'

She pointed to the east, where the sun was projecting a warm tint onto the stark white of the chalk cliffs. 'Facing that way, please. I just love that view.'

Sam lifted the chair and put it where she wanted it: 'Right, well… I'll leave you to it.'

He watched from the hut as the kettle boiled. She was balancing a sketch book on her knees and holding two pencils in her mouth. She seemed frozen in position for a while, gazing intently, then her hand moved quickly, backwards and forwards over the paper, as if she was scribbling.

The hut was full of steam by the time Sam remembered to switch the kettle off.

The day was getting better by the minute. He'd rented out another half dozen chairs by 11.

Sam tried to make his mind up whether it was because the sun was shining, or because Lindsay was there.

She was certainly attracting attention. Old boys in windcheaters and sensible shoes stopped to look down at her as they slurped on Aaron's 99 cones from the kiosk.

Lindsay just kept drawing, her hands moving swiftly. Her action reminded him of a drawing gadget he got for Christmas a long time ago; what was it? Etch A Sketch?

He took more money that morning than he'd taken over the whole week. He even had to put out a few more chairs just after 12.

If he'd had more confidence, he would have offered her a free chair for the rest of her stay. He wanted to see what she was working on, but he felt awkward, and he couldn't even find the courage to ask if she wanted a cup of tea because she might take it the wrong way.

17

He didn't want to be accused of treating her differently just because she was young and good looking. He'd never hear the last of it, especially if Jack or Aaron spotted him. More importantly, he was pretty sure she'd think he was a creep.

He checked the clock. It was near lunchtime, and his sandwiches would be waiting on the counter, but he was happy to wait.

He'd done a web search for *Lindsay artist Whistle Bay* but nothing came up.

When the town clock struck its melancholy one, he was sitting at the hut window rehearsing how to ask for her full name: *'excuse me for asking, but what's your name?'*; *'are you an artist Lindsay? what's your second name?'*; *'I'm not being nosey but...'*

It was no good, they all sounded wrong. Awkward. She'd just think he was pestering her and he'd never see her again.

There was a knock on the door, then it creaked open.

'Sam? Sorry to disturb, but I've finished. Thank you so much. I've really enjoyed it. Got some good sketches done, so I'll be able to turn out some nice new paintings. Awesome! Anyway, how much do I owe you?'

Sam checked the clock on the back wall. Dad was so proud of it; told him it was atomic - accurate to one second in Lord knows how many hundred years.

Lindsay seemed to understand. 'Is that clock a bit of a family thing? It's lovely.'

'Oh yes. My Dad got given it by the town about ten years ago.'

'Wow, really? Was there a special reason?'

'What? Oh... I don't know. I was a bit younger then.'

She laughed. 'About the same age as me, I guess. Are you...' She looked him up and down, playfully. 'Hmmm... 28?'

'26.'

'Not bad. Guess how old I am.' She saw Sam's discomfort. 'No, that's not fair is it? A lady's age.... I don't mind telling you, though. I'm 25.'

He helped her up the esplanade steps with her bag after he'd locked up and watched her walk slowly away.

18

She turned and called out: 'Bye Sam. See you tomorrow, OK? Save me a chair!'

He grinned. 'I will. I'll put your name on it, if you like!'

He could hear her laughter as he headed off to the sandwich shop, a big smile on his face.

The clouds rolled in, darkening as they got closer.

Aaron closed the kiosk and Jack put the shutters up soon after two.

But Sam resolved to see it through, just as Dad would have done. He'd once thought about adding a strip of wood under the sign to say *We Never Close,* but Sam talked him out of it with cold logic: 'Yeah, but we do close, Dad.'

He turned up the heater and washed out a couple of mugs.

He'd watched Aaron step down from his kiosk, his Liverpool shirt stretched across his beer belly, and the old jeans cut off at the knee. He never wore anything else. There was much debate about whether he had a few identical items in his drawer at home. But it was all conjecture: and his new wife, always immaculately turned out in dress and cardigan whatever the weather, refused to divulge.

Sam watched him hitch the kiosk to his old Transit and drive off, bouncing noisily over the speed bumps on the esplanade.

He liked Aaron. Others saw him as a figure of fun, but he took his work seriously. Sam sent his customers to Aaron if they wanted an ice cream or a bag of jam doughnuts. He could often hear his chatter, which always began with '*Right me darling*' or '*Greetings young sir.*'

The customers loved it and the way Sam saw it, anything that gave them a better day was good news for the town.

The change in the weather made no difference: he'd not had a customer since Lindsay left anyway. But there had been a buzz on the beach this morning, and he had some takings to add up later, just for a change.

Lindsay had left him with a feeling inside that he'd not experienced since he met Sally all those years ago.

He remembered Sally so well. It felt like nothing could hurt him, everyone and everything was wonderful, and the sky was always blue. He was so far gone he'd even written some soppy poems.

They called her Silly Sally at school, because she spoke funny and lived in her own world. She'd lie on the grass at break times, staring at the sky, winding the end of a pigtail round and round her fingers, while everyone else was either playing cards or sitting in circles talking about sex or television, or both, or like Sam, playing football.

He went to retrieve a ball after it landed near her one day. He said sorry and she sat up and took her glasses off and looked at him with her ice blue eyes and smiled. He'd never seen her without her glasses before. She didn't say a word: she didn't have to. He didn't take his eyes off hers until he was roughly dragged back into the game by one of the other lads.

Even now, he couldn't explain what happened. He only knew he couldn't get her out of his mind, and that when he was thinking about her, he felt happy inside.

To him, at the age of 15, Sally and Sammy were meant to be: the dream team.

He kissed her for the first time one day after school. They'd taken the path through the woods up to the Green to get away from the others, then lay on the grass looking at the clouds, giving them names, holding hands.

She turned to look at him. 'Do you love me Sammy?' She said it strangely. It sounded like *luff*.

He didn't need time to think it through. He pushed up onto an elbow. 'Yeah, I do. Do you luff me?'

She put her hand behind his neck and pulled his face down to hers. Her eyes closed and her lips opened and they were so soft and wet and warm and he'd never done it before but somehow he knew what to do and it felt amazing.

It was just a kiss but he felt different after that. He didn't see her often, what with his football and her dancing classes, but Sam recognised it now as the time when he knew what love felt like. It wasn't anything like loving mum or dad. He knew what it was but he still didn't understand it.

Was it so long ago? He could taste her on his lips as he relived that kiss. He could see the sandy freckles on her cheek, feel her soft skin, her warmth…

Sam twitched back into the here and now as a gust of wind shook the hut window. The rain had started, pockmarking the sand where the outgoing tide had smoothed it out, and tapping heavily on the roof.

He slid open the drawer Dad had made to fit under the window shelf, with its plywood compartments for notes and coins. It had been a while since he'd seen £5 notes in there. The thought came from nowhere: how was he going to survive if this pathetic amount counted as a good day's takings?

It wasn't as if he needed much to live on. He didn't spend much: never bothered with video games; didn't smoke or drink; avoided using the car to save petrol. He'd even cancelled his Sky Sports subscription because he could listen to radio commentary on the football for free.

The money Dad left in his will had subsidised him up to now, but it wouldn't last forever. Mikey never offered any money. He didn't know what economising meant, and he was hardly ever there, so he was no help. The house was an asset, but if he sold that, he'd still have to buy or rent something else.

He threw the money back into the drawer and slammed it shut.

The tapping of the rain became a drum beat and he knew it wouldn't be long before it found the gaps and began dripping down into the corner.

Chapter 4

The beach had that undiscovered look.

It could have been a million years in the past: the sand smoothed by the firm hand of the sea; as if life was waiting for its evolutionary moment; its one glorious chance, the first footprint. Just the sigh of the tide and the call of the birds. Timeless but hinting at the start of something.

Lindsay loved moments like this: up and outside before before the sun was up, breathing the fresher air, soaking in the silence that was only broken when the birds began to sing.

It was a ritual, wherever she went. She told friends it didn't have anything to do with being an artist; it had everything to do with belonging.

She once tried to put it into words in her blog: '*Roam Alone! You can't know a place until you see it empty of people and traffic; you can't know yourself until a new day begins and there's just you.*'

It worked just as well in London. Always an early riser, she enjoyed sharing Paddington Street Gardens with birds that sang just for her. It was about the only time they were audible.

She sat on the worn wood steps of Sam's hut.

A gull hopped down from the esplanade railings and gave her a look. 'Hello darling. What are you planning today, hmmm?'

She leaned back to watch as it lifted off with hardly a movement, spiralling effortlessly above her, carried by an invisible force. Did it choose where it went, or just follow the wind?

Lindsay breathed in deeply, then stood and watched as the dark grey of pre-dawn slowly give way to beige/blue, coral and orange, streaking across the palette of the sky. As the colour came, the birds sang.

People always described it as the cry of the gulls, but Lindsay preferred to think of it as calling, sending messages to loved ones: 'good morning!' 'have a nice day!'

She made herself laugh at times. Most of her friends thought she was from another planet.

The rattle of a diesel engine broke the spell. She looked to her left. A bakery delivery lorry. Just beyond it, the sun was lifting itself to peep over the hilltop.

She'd chatted to an older couple over coffee in the hotel last night. She told them she used to come here on holidays with mum and dad, catching the train from Warwick, and changing at Birmingham, and how she wanted a change of scene to get over a relationship and freshen up her art.

They told her it was a nostalgia trip for them. They came here on honeymoon more than 40 years ago.

They were friendly and polite, but she could tell they were bemused as she chattered about everything from why the sun always rises in the east to the importance of negative space in art.

Lindsay was always being told as a child that she talked too much. She'd answered back: *'what's wrong with having plenty to talk about?'* But in her quiet moments she suspected it was her way of coping with insecurity. She'd noticed Sam at the deckchair hut had a slight stutter. Maybe that was insecurity, too.

She took her beanie off and shook out her hair as she walked along the water's edge back towards the hotel, her sneakers leaving prints that slowly melted in the wet sand, as if she'd never been there.

She hoped coming here would give her new inspiration. She'd felt for some time that her paintings were just brush strokes on paper.

She'd specialised in botanical and still life after graduating from UCL. Sold quite a few, too. Made her name and a decent income; enough to rent a studio with accommodation in Marylebone after a few years. Her exhibitions were popular with collectors, and if she'd wanted to impress her fellow guests last night, she could have name dropped a few celebrities.

But the city had begun to feel claustrophobic and it was getting harder to coax herself onto the Tube to go sketching at Kew Gardens.

She was surprised how quickly she'd relaxed here, and thrilled with her first crayon sketches from the beach: the way light and shadow played out; the colour somehow accentuated and distorted at the same time; the spectacular greens and chalk whites and dollops of yellow on the hills that sloped steeply down to the sand; the shingle; the gulls; the sea...

She loved the Bay, too. It was as she remembered it 15 years ago. It looked just as old fashioned even then. Now it felt as if the last 30 years of progress had passed it by. From what she'd heard, attitudes and lifestyles were just as antiquated.

Sam was intriguing, though: out of place in a pension age town. He was young, blond, well built, good looking, and so attractively gauche. She smiled as she walked, remembering his awkwardness, then smacked her thigh and told herself not to be patronising.

He'd probably hate her for even thinking it, but he was such a nice change from the wine bar bores of London.

She jogged up the stone steps up from the beach to the hotel terrace, counting as she went: 26! That was his age, wasn't it?

0645... The clock radio glowed harsh blue. The thin curtains rolled smoothly from top to bottom in the draught from the sash window.

Sam pulled the duvet over his head and turned on his side.

He usually slept well, but rest was hard to come by last night. He'd sat up later than usual and drank coffee while he listened to the shipping forecast.

Then he woke up at just after 1, convinced he was late for work.

He'd been lying there ever since, worrying about money, about why he felt so isolated when everyone knew him, and why he was so nervy and awkward with Lindsay.

It would help if he could talk about it, but who with? Mum and Dad would have listened, even if they hadn't understood, but there was no-one now, and it didn't matter how many times he told himself to stop being so soft, he still felt cut off.

24

Dad once told him all the lights went out when Mum died, and Sam had never forgotten how broken he looked after the funeral.

In his half-awake state, he imagined the happiness seeping out of him like sweat; leaking into the old, thin sheet, dripping slowly into the worn carpet; through the floor and into the foundations; soaking into the earth to wash away the soil until the whole house came crashing down.

0652… He tore the duvet off and waited until the coldness of the draughty room gave him a good reason to get up and get dressed.

Gary hopped about on the hut roof, then glided down onto the sand.

Sam crouched down and held his hand out, palm upwards: 'Come on Gary. I got up specially for you today.'

Gary hopped once, then again. 'Come on, I won't hurt you.'

A voice, behind him, laughing. 'Talking to the bloody gulls now are we?'

Sam dropped his head in exasperation as Gary flapped away.

He turned and threw the crumbs onto the sand. The anger was a tight knot inside. He looked up at Aaron. 'Thanks a lot. I've been trying to get him to trust me for weeks.'

'Ooooh, pardon me, Doctor Doolittle… You wanna watch it. Too much time on your hands; it sends you loopy.'

'You'd know all about that, wouldn't you, Aaron?'

Aaron looked away. Sam moved towards him: 'I'm sorry, Aaron. That was a stupid thing to say.'

He shrugged his shoulders. 'True though, innit?'

'No, it isn't. You got over it.. You've been out of there for years, built up a good business. Take no notice of me. I'm having a bad day. Didn't get much sleep.' He pointed to the hut. 'Come and have a tea with me, yeah?'

Aaron followed him without a word.

Sam talked about his money worries and they began to bond again.

They shook hands and Aaron headed back to his kiosk. He turned and waved: 'Get to work Chair Man, and don't forget to send me all your customers.'

25

Sam promised he would, then went into the hut and punched the wall. How could he have been so cruel? Everyone knew what Aaron had been through... a messy divorce, then a breakdown. He was shut away in hospital for months and came out looking like an old man.

Sam had heard the chants in his final years at school but never joined in. Dad had been close to Aaron and often talked about him. He'd become a family friend, invited round for meals, and slowly, so slowly, he'd put weight on and got his smile back.

And knowing all that, Sam had one sleepless night and lashed out at one of the few people who'd stood by him from the start.

He looked out onto the beach. Mrs Simpson was waving her arms about, trying to keep her dog in check. He heard a scrabbling sound outside and wearily opened the door to look down.

It was Gary. Standing in profile on the step, his yellow eye unblinking.

'Come back for more?' He grabbed his bag and sat on the top step with his hand out, coaxing: 'Come on then...'

Gary slowly moved his head, left and right as Sam kept talking... 'C-Come on, you know you want to'... 'Hop up here mate'... 'It's your favourite'.

Then, in a noisy flurry of grey and white and yellow, Gary flapped up to Sam and pecked out of his hand.

He was unfolding the 24th and last of today's deckchair selection when he heard her.

'Sam!'

She was impossible to miss in pink shorts, yellow sweatshirt, and a straw hat. The shorts were short, her legs were tanned, and it was hard not to stare as she dropped her bag on the sand at his feet.

'Right! Choose a chair!' She laughed: 'Sounds like a game show, doesn't it?'

A few onlookers had already gathered at the esplanade railings. Sam checked his watch. It would be another half an hour till Billy started serving, so they'd decided to fill the time gazing at Lindsay.

He positioned her chair - a green and yellow stripe - facing the hill. He'd been tongue tied yesterday, but today felt different. 'Can I get you a cup of tea or coffee? I'm making one anyway.'

'Oh wow! Really? Gosh, thanks! Yes, erm … coffee please… Oh! Do you have soya milk? I don't do dairy, sorreee.'

'Oh, no, I don't. But I could go and -'

'No, don't worry. I'll have it black, please. Perfect! thanks so much, that's so sweet of you.'

He lowered his voice: 'Do you mind coming to collect it in a few minutes? It's just that -' He nodded slightly in the direction of the people leaning on the railings.

She hid her face as she snorted with laughter. 'God yes! Don't want them thinking you run a cafe! Why not put it in a paper cup, then it'll look like it was my own takeaway or something? Do you think that would fool them?'

Back in the hut, he watched her unpack her bag. She turned to her audience and said something, and there was much pointing and shaking of heads.

A minute later, she walked in with a tote bag, laughing again. 'Give me an Oscar! They think I've got a flask in here. What a liar! I asked if any of them had a spare paper cup and one of them said I should ask in here. Isn't that just perfect?'

Sam was conscious how close they were: him with his back to the window, her right in front of him. Her skin looked soft as butter and her scent was of the sun and the sea.

Just one move and his arms would be round her… He'd not been this close to a woman for months.

She must have caught the look on his face because she stepped back slightly.

He turned away quickly to pour the coffee. She took the cup and stopped at the door.

'Thanks, Sam.'

Sam's face felt hot. 'Oh, that's ok, you're welcome.'

'Right. Great.' She turned quickly and was gone.

He heard the soft scrape of her bare feet on the sandy steps, and then voices.

She was standing by her chair, sipping coffee, looking to the west, holding up a stick as if she was measuring the view. And a dozen people were settling into the chairs closest to her.

Sam grabbed some change from the drawer, tossed it into his bum bag and hurried down the steps.

She was still there at four, bent over her drawing pad, biting her bottom lip.

Most of her hangers-on had gone, apart from an older couple in beige who were staring at the sea, arms folded.

That's how it had been with Mum and Dad towards the end. It was like Sean's death had killed them, too. The result was that Sam and Mikey were left to themselves, most of the time. Mikey looked older than his age, so he took full advantage and started boozing at an early age.

Sam thought of himself as the lucky one. He loved being allowed to run down to the hut to be with Dad; watching people, learning. He remembered telling Sally once that the business would be his one day, but she didn't seem too impressed.

The main attraction was that he was with Dad. But as he sat by the hut window now, counting up, he wondered whether his mates had been right. They were always telling him he needed to get out and do new things. *Get a life.* But he couldn't imagine what else he'd want to do that could be better than this.

Looking back, he'd known before Dad died that this was going to be his life. He'd keep the business going for Dad, and he'd keep the house nice for Mum.

It gave him a reason to get up in the morning, but he still got laughed at. It was one of the reasons he didn't turn out for football so often. They made a big thing out of earning a few quid at the bakery, or the engineering plant, or living on benefits - sharing tales, cracking jokes. Sam just had his chairs and the beach, and Gary, to talk about.

He glanced to his right. Lindsay had put on a brown jacket against the late afternoon chill. He sensed she was finishing off by the way she was holding her pad at arm's length, her lips pursed.

Sam wondered about her pictures. Would she let him look?

He loved the beach and the views. Knew the place as well as anyone. It would be interesting to see what she'd done. But what would he say if he didn't like them? It's not as if he was any good at it. He remembered his art teacher sighing a lot and smelling of mints. 'Why don't you try abstract art, Samuel? I think that would suit you more.'

He only got good marks for woodwork, maths and geography, and dreaded Mum and Dad reading his school reports. But they never made a big deal out of his Cs and Ds, and he loved them for that. 'You don't need letters after your name,' said Dad. 'You need to know how to treat people; show kindness; take pride in the simple things; work hard.'

Sam wondered what Dad would have thought of the way he'd behaved with Aaron today.

Gary had cheered him up, but Lindsay had made him laugh, brought in some customers, and made him money. And she was someone he could talk to.

The least he could do would be to say a polite good evening and show interest in her pictures.

Chapter 5

Lindsay was paying an extra £15 a night for a room with a sea view, despite the fact that she needed to stand at one side of the bay window and develop the neck of a giraffe.

If this was London she knew she would have stamped her feet and demanded a move, or compensation, but there was something about Whistle Bay.

So much so, that she immortalised it in her new Instagram page: *'I love Kathleen Frank and James Abbott McNeill Whistler - but not as much as I adore the gorgeously quirky art paradise that is Whistle Bay'*.

She sat at the oak table facing the window, studying one of her sketches; still relishing being out of her artistic comfort zone.

Everything she'd done up to now had been about close observation and the delicacy of fine detail. As she wrote on her Insta page: *'Sitting in the open air and allowing emotion into my work feels like finding freedom.'*

She'd been inspired to try landscape painting by the American artist, Kathleen Frank. As she told her followers, Lindsay had been *'blown away by her bold use of colour, and the joy of life and nature that shouted from her work.'* Frank was once a costume designer, and she felt it showed in the way she found simplicity of form in the bewildering detail of a landscape.

There were some excellent landscape artists, but Lindsay believed that many of them may as well have been photographers. She wanted to scream sometimes: where was the interpretation, the emotion?

It was a criticism she'd thrown at herself in the few weeks leading up to her escape to Whistle Bay. She'd started comparing her flower studies to *'staring down a microscope and copying what I see.'*

The crayon sketch on the table in front of her was the first opportunity to show what she was about: a chance to add her love of life to a natural landscape and turn it into something uniquely her own.

But looking at it now, it was just a view of the hill that sloped down to the sea. She'd been pleased that Sam had picked this as his favourite, but it was nowhere near ready yet.

She moved from side to side until she saw the problem. The focal point was in the wrong place, and she'd crammed in too much detail. Her intention was to draw the eye to the vibrant yellows about a third of the way down the hill, but the clouds hogging the horizon were too busy and distracting.

She chuckled to herself as she scribbled a pencil note in the corner of the picture: *Frank would have been frankly unimpressed.*

She looked again...*not bad apart from that... the rocks and the groyne in the foreground led the eye into the picture, and the perspective was okay.*

Frowning in concentration, she tied her hair back in a band and bent over the drawing. She rubbed out a few notes on the paint colours she wanted to use, and added Prussian blue, alizarin, and cadmium scarlet to the list.

Her tea had gone cold, but she drank it anyway. She looked out. The light was fading from sunset red to twilight grey.

She yawned and stretched. It was hard to stay awake and there was still an hour to go before they banged the gong for dinner. She smiled. A dinner gong! It was so Agatha Christie.

The soft fat green sofa began to look irresistible. Her eyes felt heavy as soon as she stretched out. She was drifting... remembering...

...the sound of the sea, gently whooshing; the seabirds wheeling and wailing; the old folk staring down; Kathleen Frank dabbing even more colour onto Cotton's Morning; beautiful Sam, with his blond hair and broad chest and innocent eyes, standing close, looking intently at her sketches...

Karen Madeley was immune to disapproving looks.

Why should she worry: no-one would complain about men in shorts and a vest, would they?

She'd worked hard to lose weight after being fed a diet of burgers and chips by overweight parents keen to mould her in their own likeness. People used to point and laugh in those days, but now they point and tut instead.

She kept in shape by working the weights and running to and from her tattoo parlour in Hightown. It was an eight mile round trip, and she did it whatever the weather.

Most men just stared but women had to make their feelings known, as if anyone actually cared what they thought. The ones who gave her the most lip were the ones who were overweight and ugly, anyway.

Mum and dad had disapproved, of course. It was an easy decision to leave home ten years ago, and she never regretted it. She'd got her self-respect back and it didn't matter what anyone else thought.

She was buzzing lately because she was running at just over six minutes a mile. But she ran even faster today. It had been a good day all round - two new customers and a five star rating on Google.

She jogged up the stairs to her flat above the greengrocers: 'Mikey! Guess what?'

No answer. Where the hell was he? He'd be back from the pub by now, surely? She checked the bedroom in case he'd crashed out in there.

Then, in the kitchen, a note, folded in half, propped up against the red teapot.

Gone down to the boat. See you later. Mikey

Karen shrugged and shivered slightly as the sweat began to cool on her skin. She peeled off her vest and shorts and pulled the cord to get the wall heater warmed up, then turned on the shower and stepped back before the cold water hit her.

Sitting on the loo with a towel wrapped round her, she wondered about Mikey. He was always here when she got back; sometimes he'd have a cup of tea ready.

She tested the water and stepped in, and took her time over it. She dried her hair, pulled on her blue shorts, her favourite Harvard sweatshirt and a baseball cap, and walked down to the harbour.

Once a smelly, seaweed riddled swamp, it had been updated four years ago with a new sea wall and a dredging contract, thanks to a pile of European grant money. Locals were less than impressed mainly because only three boats used it.

She remembered Mikey cursing: 'If they've got all that spare cash, why aren't they supporting British fishing? Then there'd be more boats in here.'

She counted as she walked along the pontoon. There were six tied up now.

He was slumped in his chair in the wheelhouse. She caught the smell of cigarettes a few yards away and called out: 'You alright Mikey?'

'Come in here and I'll tell ya.'

She stepped onto the deck. 'I can't. It stinks of fags. I thought you'd given up. What's going on?'

'All right…'

He stepped out to join her. Karen put out a hand to balance herself as the boat swayed: 'What is it? You look terrible.'

He threw a cigarette over the side and pointed to a stack of lobster pots. 'Let's sit over there.'

They'd been together for three years and she'd never known him look so beaten. He drank too much but he was one of the only men who'd ever treated her as an equal. He'd never shown any interest in sex and that suited her. Mikey respected her. His mates thought he was a pisshead, but they didn't see the gentle, kind man underneath.

She knew it was going to be bad news, but what? Too many bad days at sea, run out of money, lost his licence…?

'Mikey, what is it? Come on, tell me and we'll sort it out.'

'We can't sort it.' He sobbed once and somehow choked it back. He looked into her eyes. 'I've got cancer, and they -'

She put her arms round him: 'How far gone are you?'

His head was pushed into her chest and his shoulders were shaking.

'I've only got a few months, Karen.'

Sam went through the ritual with Gary but couldn't coax him this time. He jerked his head, clacked his beak, hopped back and forth: everything except tap into his hand.

Sam even wondered if he was doing it to wind him up.

Aaron was watching from a safe distance: 'Maybe tomorrow, mate...'

Sam gave up on Gary and made tea. They sat on the step, laughing at Mrs Simpson's dog. Aaron nearly spat his tea out when it jumped up at her with a mouthful of seaweed.

'She won't like that. Getting her new coat wet.'

Sam laughed: 'How do you know it's new?'

Aaron winked: 'Got nothin' else to do but gossip. Now then, here's one for you: did you hear about Billy Whistle?'

Sam felt faintly aggrieved. 'No. What?'

'He's carryin' on with that woman from the hardware shop.'

'What, the new woman?'

'Aye. DIY Doris, we call her. Can't blame him either. She's alright, she is.'

Sam blew on his tea and chuckled. Another nickname to remember. He felt a bit out of it, tucked away in his hut on the beach, but maybe it wasn't such a bad thing if this was the level of conversation.

A tea break with Aaron was okay, but he had a sense of purpose today, despite Gary's crushing rejection. Today's forecast was for a fine dry day with sunny spells, and temperatures up to around 19. Not bad for September.

He'd got up with the alarm and was at work by 7.30. By 8, he'd swept the steps and laid out twice the usual number of chairs.

He chose the red and yellow stripes today. Lindsay said she'd be back and he kept the best one aside for her: the one with arms and a canopy. There were only six of them in the whole stack, and Dad always said it was best to save them to give the regulars a bonus towards the end of their week away.

'Makes 'em feel special, you see. Might even see 'em again next year.'

Lindsay was certainly special, but he didn't want to make a fool of himself. He'd been edgy yesterday, when he bent down next to her to look at her drawings; so close he could have kissed her...

She'd told him not to expect much because she was only using crayons and the colours would be different when she painted it, but they were beautiful. She'd asked him which one

34

he liked best, and he was surprised how quickly he picked one out, and by how pleased she was.

'That's the one I like. Didn't know you were an artist, Sam.'

He'd laughed but it had made him wonder.

He remembered he was supposed to be chatting with Aaron: 'Fancy another?'

He made an event out of checking his watch. 'Aye, go on. I can spare another ten minutes out of my busy day.'

'Sure about that? I'm surprised you're not trying your luck with DIY Doris.'

Aaron lifted his Liverpool shirt and scratched his belly elaborately. 'Nah.' He waited till Sam came back with another mug of tea. 'Are you and that artist girl a thing then? Have you – you know…?'

Sam nursed the mug in both hands. 'Nope. I'm not in her league.'

'Shame. She's a stunner.' He paused, chuckling to himself. 'You'd better stick to DIY then.'

Sam nearly choked on his tea.

Chapter 6

The late September sun was obliterated by easterlies that blew in dark mountains of cloud and sent the last holidaymakers scurrying home.

This was a surprise to Jim, Billy, Aaron and the rest, because OATs - old age tourists - were renowned for their ability to survive hostile conditions. The most reliable survival technique was to spend hours in cafes but spend as little as possible – usually on TATs - tea and toasted teacakes.

This got to Billy last year, so he retaliated by doubling the price. But they simply moved ons to a more understanding establishment. Billy was soon forced to admit defeat but it proved costly because he won them back by offering TATs at an even lower price.

Sam tried to stay positive, but it was obvious that even cutting prices wouldn't help now. The town was empty as October arrived, and the RETAIL PREMISES TO LET signs were even more noticeable. The sea picked up on the mood. Its sullen rollers thudded onto the smooth sand; plume spraying angrily off the whitecaps, soaking the esplanade in a cold mist.

Traders had even more time to spare, and so did the gossips. News filtered through to Sam that Billy was finding consolation in the arms of a regular visitor by the name of DIY Doris, who had – purely coincidentally, said Jim - announced she was shutting her shop early from October.

Sam kept himself busy. He coaxed the old calor gas heater into life and got on with some jobs. He hung up a few old photos he found among Dad's things and put down a rug his next-door neighbour was throwing out. He kept up with the weather proofing, too, when the conditions allowed… a fresh coat of marine paint to the frontage, and new felt for the roof.

And he always made time for Gary, who was regularly feeding out of Sam's hand without too much fuss. He knew he'd end up on the receiving end of town gossip, but he confessed to Aaron he'd happily adopt Gary: 'I could spend all day feeding him, chatting to him. He's like a mate.'

The days ticked by and the off-season jobs kept coming: sealing the gaps round the windows, sweeping out from under the bookshelves, fixing a wonky step and varnishing the older deckchairs.

There was plenty to do at the house, too. The garden needed tidying and the lean to at the back was leaking water.

The evenings dragged: a blur of tv detectives, country music, long runs, and thinking about Lindsay.

She hadn't been to the hut since the bad weather moved in, but she turned up one morning when the sun was trying to break through. Sam made tea and blurted out his news: 'I've been thinking… when I get all these jobs done, I'd like to have a go at painting.'

'That's fantastic, Sam! I'm so pleased!' She told him to practice every day if he was serious about it, and not get discouraged if things didn't go so well at first.

He tried to sketch as she'd told him: 'Draw what you actually see, not what you think it should look like.'

His back ached after two hours sitting still, and he wasn't sure the pain was worth it. The hill looked too big, the clouds were too small, and the sea was just wiggly lines. He tried sketching Gary instead, but he wouldn't keep still. He was embarrassed, but she was kind: 'Don't get down. It's just practice. Make the most of the free time.'

He signed up for the online class she recommended; bought a book in the charity shop for 50p; tried tracing pictures. But he couldn't get his head round perspective and focal points. He came to the conclusion that he was crap at school and he was crap now.

He just wanted to do what Lindsay was doing. She made it look so easy, sitting in the open air, or looking out of the window, drawing what she saw and looking totally relaxed.

She said she'd come to see him again in a day or two and Sam made her smile: 'Oh that'll be good; I don't get many visitors.'

He realised she thought he was joking. But it was true: he rarely saw anyone, even on the walk home. It was like the world had moved inside, hibernated. Apart from his regular cup of tea with Aaron, the only conversation he had yesterday was a phone call from Mikey, who said he was still staying with his girlfriend; the mysterious Karen.

Sam had never met her and was beginning to wonder if she really existed. 'How's it going? Still seeing the doc?'

'Yeah. No change there. I've cut down the booze and Karen's put me on a high vitamin diet. It tastes like parrot food.'

'That's good. She's doing you a favour. Don't knock it.'

'I know she is. But you don't care: it's Friday tomorrow; you'll be having fish and chips out of the paper, won't you?'

'I can't lie. Yeah. Anyway, promise me you'll look after yourself.' There was a pause. 'Mikey?'

'Sorry, got a touch of the sniffles. Yeah, I'll be fine. Thanks... you know.'

The call made Sam feel unsettled. Mikey never phoned unless he wanted something. He seemed friendly, which was equally unusual. Ah well, maybe Karen was having a bit of influence. Normally, you'd be lucky to get anything more than a yes or no out of him.

He often wondered why they hadn't bonded. Mikey had never joined in the chat when they sat down for tea as a family. He just ate quicker than everyone else and went to his room, which meant that Sam and Sean would be left to do the washing up and tidying away. Not that they minded very much: it became a fun competition, like everything else they did - one washing as fast as possible, trying to get ahead of the one who was putting the dishes away.

Sam looked out across the beach. The wind had dropped, and the low grey cloud was pressing down, flattening the light, smoothing out the sea.

He sat on the bottom step, remembering the breathless laughter and wide-eyed gulps of air as he raced Sean from groyne to groyne. 'There and back three times. Loser buys ice cream... Go!'

Sean won every time. He was a good six inches shorter, and stocky; perfect for sprinting on sand.. Sam was a slow starter, and although his long stride helped him catch up towards the end, Sean always found a sprint finish, and they'd throw themselves onto the sand laughing, gasping for breath.

He was good at everything, Sean: football, tennis, science, art. He used to bring his pictures home and mum would stick them on the kitchen cupboards. Sam never felt jealous. He told everyone Sean was not just his brother; he was his best friend, and he still felt that no-one could ever replace him.

A few of the traders talked about him occasionally; how he used to run errands for them, do odd jobs after school. He had a paper round, too, for a while. Sam was reminded of it when he went into the newsagents at the top end of Marine Parade a couple of nights ago. Baldy Blake was behind the counter with his nicotine stained fingers, and as soon as he saw Sam, he talked about Sean.

'That boy,' he said, 'was the fastest paper boy we ever had. Sunday papers done in an hour! Lovely, lovely, lad' -

An idea suddenly clicked into place. Sam climbed the steps to the hut, pulled the sketchbook out of his bag, rested it on the window shelf and picked out a pencil.

'Lindsay Ferris?'

The estate agent flicked her blond fringe off her face and held out a hand. She was a few inches shorter than Lindsay..

She smiled and held onto her hand for a few seconds.

'I'm Grace. You'll love this place.' She giggled. 'Sorry about the poetry. I swear I get more excited about viewings than the clients.'

She led the way up three steps to the white door and fiddled with a bunch of keys before opening up.

Lindsay turned to look at the view. The Bay looked different from here. The hill she loved painting was directly behind her and the whole sweep of the beach stretched away to the right. The clouds were tinged pink, and she wanted to paint them straight away.

She'd found the flat on the web. Grace King Property described it as 'a delightful ground floor apartment; immaculate; superb sea views; short term let.'

Grace was enthusiastic without going over the top, showing off the kitchen and the bathroom, pointing out the 'luxury wet room' and the induction hob.

Lindsay had made her mind up by the time they got back to the kitchen.

'When can I move in?'

Grace perched on a kitchen chair, her skirt riding up her thighs. 'Oh! Well, if you're keen, you could be in by the end of the week, subject to all the paperwork; you know, the usual stuff.'

Lindsay sat next to her, their knees almost touching. Grace looked so perfect; it was hard to believe she wasn't wearing makeup; not even lipstick; though maybe just a trace of mascara?

Her mouth felt dry. She licked her lips. 'So… I can pay you a deposit now, if you like?'

Grace leaned forward to take a folder from her briefcase. 'Well of course you can! But are you sure you don't want time to think? You don't need to hurry; it only came on the market a couple of days ago. The landlord lets them out for the holiday season, so …'

'Oh no. I've always done too much thinking.' She paused, leaning forward, her hand on the table: so close she could touch her. 'I just want to go for it. I love it. It's perfect, and thanks so much for showing me round.'

She could tell that Grace was feeling it, too. Their eyes kept meeting, then flicking away. Lindsay had that slightly short of breath feeling that she recognised only too well. She told herself after the last time that she should think of it as a red light, not green.

She hoped her time away from London would clear the fog in her head after she broke up with Molly. It did, for a time. Now, though, she was missing the close contact, the smell of a woman's skin, the warmth of her body, the soft words in her ear…

She forced herself to break away and walked to the window. 'I'm an artist, you see, and this is such a perfect location, especially after two weeks at the South View Hotel.'

Grace laughed. 'I see what you mean. South View… it's a bit antiquated, isn't it?'

'I know. I loved it, though. It was cute. But I need my own space for a while, so I can, you know…'

'Are you famous?'

'I wish! I used to do botanical painting, but I need to do something new, and I love it here.' She turned and looked into her eyes. 'I needed a fresh start.'

'Well, you've come to the right place. It's a bit special. So, you're feeling inspired by the Bay?'

'That's it, yeah. And the people, of course.' She turned to face her, smiling. 'What about you Grace. What inspires you?'

Her forehead crinkled as she thought about her answer. Lindsay noticed a slight flush on her cheek, as their eyes met again. 'You might think this is a bit daft, but I actually adore opera.' She laughed: 'Not that I ever get to see any round here.'

Lindsay put her hand on her arm. 'That's not daft at all. I love it too. You should come with me to the Royal Opera House.'

Grace didn't pull away. She spoke softly, almost a whisper. 'I'd love that more than anything in the world.'

Her first painting, *Whistle Bay Morning*, sold through her London gallery within an hour for £1,200, and her Instagram page hit 9,800 followers.

She and Grace shared a bottle of champagne at the flat, giggling as Lindsay replied to social media comments about groynes.

Grace told her that her pictures were putting Whistle Bay on the map. 'Just key Whistle Bay into a search and you'll see. I'll soon be putting my prices up.'

The owner of the gallery in Soho had called three times asking when she would be ready to stage an exhibition. 'You'll sell out, darling,' he assured her.

Lindsay laughed as she described Sam's face when she'd told him the asking price. She told Grace he was still trying hard to learn, and she was running out of constructive criticism. 'He could make a fist of drawing a rock at the base of the hill, but can't get the hang of working on a big scale.'

They lay on the sofa, light headed after fizz.

Lindsay's voice was slurred: 'The more I think about him, the more I see everything that is uncomplicated and unsophisticated. I love him like a brother, but I know he's fallen for me, and I don't want to hurt him. I look in his eyes and it's obvious he's been hurt enough. Do you know him?'

Grace yawned: 'Oh yeah. All the girls fancy him, but he's never shown any interest.' She laughed throatily. 'We used to walk past the hut and hitch our skirts up on the off chance he'd be there.'

'You tart.'

'I know.' She went quiet for a while. Then she sat up with an effort: 'Maybe you could invite him round here for a drink. I bet he doesn't get out much, and he'd probably relax after a couple.'

'What? Are you mad? You'll hitch your skirt up and he'll fall in love with you. Come off it!'

They dozed on the sofa, then Lindsay made coffee. She couldn't get Sam out of her head for some reason. She wanted to find something that would unblock him, allow him to make progress, feel positive about himself.

The next day she had an idea, and went to the hut to see his latest drawings. He made tea and told her that she was the only person he talked to these days. He wasn't looking for sympathy, it was a statement of fact.

'You can't rely on me, Sam.'

'I know. I'm sorry, I didn't mean -'

'No, don't apologise. I think you just need something new. Something that will give you a bit of energy, take you out of yourself, you know?'

'Erm... yeah?'

'Yeah! There must be something! Come on, make me another cup of tea and let's think!'

She went outside and did circuits round the hut to warm up while he boiled the kettle; pacing, thinking, shivering.

It was on her third lap that she convinced herself the idea could work.

She ran up the steps, and Sam said later the whole town would have heard her: 'Sam, I've got it!'

'You've got to tell him sooner or later.'

Mikey groaned as he pushed himself out of the chair. He swayed slightly and Karen held his arm: 'Come on. You can't go on like this. He's your brother!'

'I know. I will. I just -'

'What?'

'I don't know. I've treated him like shit for years. We never talk. He says I'm always complaining about something.'

'So what? Do you really think he's going to think you're making it up? Christ! You're terminally ill.' She sat down and held his hands. 'Talk to him, Mikey, please. If you don't, I will…'

She saw his eyes misting up again and turned away to butter the toast. Tears were never far away but she told herself he didn't need her sympathy, he needed normality; to make the most of what was left. They both did.

She put on a smile and made coffee for him; green tea for her.

He smiled his thanks and took a small bite out of a slice of toast and jam. 'So, what are you up to today?'

'Oh I'll stick needles in people and make them look beautiful, I think. You? Got the energy to go out in the boat?'

He nodded. 'Yeah, I'll give it a go. See what's crawled into the pots.'

'Yeah, you don't wanna leave it, otherwise someone else will move in, won't they?'

'Too right. Put me on a drip and I'll still be out there.'

They laughed.

Karen felt better about leaving him today. The run to work had taken on even more significance now. It was a chance to clear her mind, think about nothing other than stride, breathing and pace. Some people run with music blasting through their ear buds. She just wanted the sound of her steps, her breath and the rush of air.

She was reconciled to living alone. It felt like the story of her life, though she wasn't one to wallow in it. She'd walked away from her family with no regrets, but Mikey still had a brother.

And if he didn't tell Sam this week, she would.

43

Chapter 7

Sam bought a ruler from Baldy Blake and a tin box for the crayons and pencils Lindsay had given him. She told him to get a board to rest his sketch book on, too, so he'd cut a piece out of some MDF.

He checked everything. All set.

The weather forecast was ok for a few hours and there was no-one around. Mrs Simpson's dog had taken her for a walk, and - as Dad used to say with a chuckle: 'the coast is clear'.

He'd got a simple shape to draw and then he could use whatever colours he liked. He smiled as he remembered Lindsay's chatter. She was so lively. She made more noise than the gulls. 'Go wild!' she'd said in that posh voice of hers.

He put one deckchair by the hut for him to sit in, and a blue and green one a few yards away. That was the one he was going to draw.

Lindsay said the important thing was to get the proportions right, so he should draw a box first. 'That'll be the size of your drawing. You just fit the deckchair into that box, ok? Then all you have to do is look carefully and pick the right colours.'

It took a while to sink in, but it was obvious really: the chair is a few yards away, so it's smaller than if it was right in front of him, smaller in height and width, and - everything, really.

He tried her suggestion of holding his pencil up and adjusting his thumb so he could measure how big each bit of the chair should be in his drawing.

He'd had a go at it using photos, but it hadn't really worked because they were too small.

He felt a bubble inside at the thought of doing it for real, right now, out on the beach. Just like Lindsay. 'Plein air,' she called it.

He picked up the ruler, chewed his bottom lip, and faced his first dilemma: should the paper be long ways up or across? She called it landscape painting and he'd checked online about portrait and landscape formats, so he opted for landscape and carefully drew the box, counting the centimetres so he got a proper rectangle shape.

Good.

It sounded easy when she explained it, but the deckchair suddenly looked complicated with its odd angles, and the bit that leaned back looked further away than the bit you sit on, and the stripes weren't straight lines because the canvas was being blown a bit by the wind.

He puffed out his cheeks and tried to relax his shoulders.

He'd told Lindsay he wanted to dedicate his first 'proper' painting to Sean. She looked teary: 'Awww, that's so lovely.' Then she'd put on her bossy voice: 'Right, that settles it. Next time I see you, I want to see a lovely colourful deckchair. And you have to sign it!'

He'd watched her carefully as she worked. She drew the outline quickly and she told him to do the same: 'Be confident. You're in charge, and you can always rub out and start again, but at least you'll have some shapes to work with. You'll know when it's right and you can worry about colours and stuff later.'

He studied the deckchair for a moment, trying to ignore the clouds and the sea and the seagulls.

He could sense Sean watching over his shoulder, and the bubble inside subsided.

He chose a 2H pencil, and began to draw.

Sam picked at his nails as Lindsay opened his sketch pad.

'Oh my God, Sam!'

He laughed as she punched him on the shoulder: 'Ouch, what's that for?'

'This is fab-u-lous! You see? I knew you could do it.' He looked doubtful. 'Sam, seriously, this is good. You should be proud.'

'You're not just being nice, are you?'

'God no! Me? Nice? No, Sam, let me tell you, I am properly impressed. You've got form, colour, light and shade, all spot on. And look! You've been confident enough to add a splash of sea and sky as a backdrop. Wow! So, promise me, you'll carry on?'

He nodded.

'And will you sign this one for me to keep?'

'Seriously?'

'Yeah, seriously. I don't care what my landlord says, it's going on my wall. You should sign your pictures anyway. It shows pride in your work. I know you don't quite believe it yet, but you're good, Sam. It doesn't matter what other people say, apart from me, obviously. You're not doing art to be famous. You're doing it for the love of it, like me.'

Sam nodded. 'I did love doing it. I did it for Sean, but -'

'I know... You did it for yourself, too. And that's ok.'

He looked down at his feet. 'Thank you...'

Lindsay took his hand and held it in both hers. 'It's been a pleasure. I hope it'll change your life like it changed mine. I know you think this is just a drawing of a deckchair, but it's the first step on a journey.' She laughed and hopped as she tugged her shoes off, then pulled him towards the sea. 'And you are going to love it!'

Sam laughed. 'What are you doing?'

'Going to get my feet wet.'

'It'll be freezing in there!'

'Come on, coward!'

'Coward? Really? Right, come on then!'

He pulled his t-shirt off and ran straight in, diving into the first wave, gasping and laughing as the cold shock hit him. Lindsay was hopping and screaming: 'You are insane! My feet are frozen!'

'Now who's the coward?'

She shook her fist at him, and he waded nearer, scooping up water in his cupped hands. The look on her face reminded him of the games he played with Sean - scared and excited at the same time.

Lindsay was laughing, but she was backing away, her hand out in front: 'Stop right there! Sam. Do not do this! I'm warning you...'

He lifted his hands to throw the water and she instantly turned and ran up the beach, with a high-pitched squeal.

Aaron, Jack and Billy watched from the esplanade in their big coats.

Jack shook his head: 'Bloody idiots.'

Aaron smiled: 'Can't blame him, can you? The lad deserves a bit of fun.'

Jack lit another cigarette: 'Maybe, but she's not going to be sticking around, is she? She'll be buggering off back to London, you'll see.'

Billy nodded: 'Aye, that she will. It'll end in tears. Always does, doesn't it?'

Aaron winked at Jack: 'How's Doris, Billy?'

Sam sat in Mum's room with the pad on his knee, wondering what to draw.

He was buzzing after Lindsay's reaction, but it felt different now, sitting at home in the quiet, looking at a blank page. He'd put so much effort into that picture, and now it was gone.

It was like it never existed. It felt weird that something that belonged to him was on someone else's wall: Lindsay's wall - Lindsay, the artist who sold pictures in London!

He'd been to art galleries on school trips and never taken much notice, but he was preoccupied with art now. Questions kept popping up from nowhere: like, was that guy happy with his painting of that sunflower; did Mona Lisa really look like that or was it a made-up face; why did some landscape paintings look nothing like real life?

He'd found Lindsay's Instagram page and couldn't believe she'd got 26,000 followers. He scrolled through the images: the sketches were incredible enough, but her paintings made him realise how much he had to learn.

Sam had picked at his tea - pizza and a salad from the supermarket. He couldn't understand why he felt so … jumbled up.

She was famous and must have loads of money, but she liked him enough to spend time with him and to help him. But was that it? She just did it because she liked him? He didn't know what she did with the rest of her time, or where she went. Was she helping other people or was it just him?

She'd changed his life and he was happier; but life felt more …complicated now. He didn't know how to behave when he

47

was with her; much like it was when he was going out with Sally.

He tried to remember how that had felt. His schoolwork had gone down the pan, he knew that much. Mum and Dad went mad when he came second from last in science. He could still hear mum: 'You've let that girl turn your head. Don't throw away your future for her. She's not worth it!'

Now he was picking up the same kind of comments from some of the traders. They wanted to know about 'the fancy girl' and have a sly dig about the amount of time he spent with her. He could tell the way the chat was going and made excuses about having to get home early.

Sam went in the kitchen to make coffee, and imagined what Dad would say if he was there right now; paper spread out on the table, crossword pencil behind his ear, big mug of tea, doorstep sandwich.

He could picture him, in his shirt sleeves, filling the room with his big voice…He knew what he'd be saying, too: 'She's a lovely lass, but don't take your eye off the ball. You've got a business to run, a reputation to uphold.'

That was it… the thought that had been scratching away, trying to be heard. He should be down at the hut, fixing, cleaning, painting, coming up with ideas. It was only a few weeks ago that he'd been fretting about earning enough money to survive…

The kettle whistled and the steam was forming clouds, but he ignored it.

He'd promised Dad he'd look after things, build up the business. He promised he'd stay close to the traders who'd stuck with Dad.

So why was he larking about on the beach with a girl and pretending to be an artist?

Lindsay bought a pair of skinny jeans, and was goaded into lashing out on a sparkly top that showed a bit too much for her liking.

Grace pulled back the changing cubicle curtain to have a look and told her she looked gorgeous. Lindsay pouted and said she was self conscious about her small boobs.

48

Grace put on a serious face and mimed inspecting them with a magnifying glass, getting frosty stares from the prison warder who was on changing room duty today.

Grace gave her the eye and sounded like a head girl at Roedean: 'We'll take these if you'd be so kind as to show us where we pay. Thanks awfully.'

They laughed all the way to the till.

Lindsay dozed off on the drive back. Grace woke her with a kiss when she dropped her off at the flat: 'Come on, beautiful. You're supposed to be at the hotel in an hour; wakey uppy.'

Lindsay opened one eye: 'Are you that handsome princess I've been dreaming about?'

Grace winked: 'No. More of an old queen. Now go and get glammed up, paint your face and knock them out. Or something like that.'

Lindsay promised she'd call later and got ready for her meeting at the South View Hotel with Mr Matthew. She told Grace he was a work of art from a different era., in a black dinner jacket with jet black gelled hair; brilliant white shirt with a yellow carnation in his buttonhole; and a red bow tie.

It was topped off by his mournful face. The unkempt eyebrows, saggy eye bags and thin lips made him look like he'd been painted onto the wrong head.

This impression of a hotel manager built from spare parts was reinforced by his hands, which were as soft and pale as a baby; and his impossibly small feet were clad in pointed patent leather tie ups.

Lindsay chose a charcoal jacket she'd bought from an Oxfam shop in Camden, black jeans, her favourite Adidas trainers, and a quick spray of Calvin Klein Obsession. The sparkly top stayed in its carrier bag.

Mr Matthew always smelled of mothballs, and she picked up the aroma again when he walked up to greet her. She had him down as a secret drinker, but he was all smiles and offers of tea when they met in the reception hall.

It sounded vaguely creepy: 'I've found us a little corner where we can have our chat.' He pointed towards the main entrance. One of his porters was pushing two big old armchairs into a window bay, with a coffee table between them.

49

Mr Matthews led the way. 'The tea things are already laid out for us,' he said.

It was good to be back but hard to keep a straight face: tea things! But he'd told her he was sure the hotel would be willing to host her event, so...

She undid her jacket and put her bag on the floor. 'Thanks so much for seeing me, Mr Matthew.'

'Simon, please.'

'Oh, yes, Simon... I'm really excited about - you know... Erm... I brought along some of my work so you could see the sort of thing I am talking about. I thought it might -'

He held up a hand: 'Please, there's really no need. I found you on Instagram, and we all love your paintings. I've consulted the owners, and we'd be honoured to host your first exhibition in this part of the world.'

'Gosh! Really? Thank you so much.' She laughed. 'Well, that was a lot less stressful than I imagined. I've been getting tips from my - friend... on how to present myself.'

'No need, no need at all. So, shall I?' He made pouring tea look like the most important thing he'd done all day, and Lindsay studied him again. He looked and acted older, but something about the easy grace with which he moved, made her wonder if she should knock 20 years off his age. She found herself wishing she was a portrait painter.

She took the cup and saucer and turned down a chocolate biscuit.

He leaned back and crossed his legs. 'I suppose we should deal with the basic questions then.'

Lindsay smiled, still getting over the fact that he'd checked her out on Instagram: 'What do you mean?'

'How much space you would need, for example, how we go about inviting people - do you have a list you'd want to invite? and also, of course, when...'

He showed her the ballroom after tea and shortbread, but that was too grand. She said she liked the light and the neutral wall colour in the conference room better, and he approved: 'I so agree. And it would be much easier for us to manage bookings here, and to make space for you, so that's a good choice. I'm happy if you are.'

Lindsay was, especially when he confirmed he wouldn't charge. 'No, no, I wouldn't dream of it. We're grateful you chose to stay with us for so long. With your permission, I suggest we offer a free drink on arrival - prosecco, perhaps? - and then a paying bar.' He winked. 'I'm sure we'll get our costs back that way, do you think?'

She decided she was in love with Mr Matthew - sorry, Simon.

They fixed the date for two weeks away and she sat in his office as he tapped out some wording for a flyer. He swivelled the computer monitor round to show her:

An Exhibition of Sketches and Watercolours
By Lindsay Ferris
6 for 6.30pm, Friday October 16th,
at the South View Hotel

She asked for a copy, gave him a hug and could still smell the mothballs as she sang along to Adele in her car. She pulled into a loading area opposite Sam's hut, and ran down the steps to the beach, bursting to tell him her news.

'Sam! Sam! Come out of there this minute!'

She banged on the door. No answer.

'Sam?'

The Recorder billboards shouted out in thick black felt tip: 'Bay Artist Invasion!'

But they were too late with the news. Mouthy Stan at the station got on the phone to Billy Whistle as soon as he saw them piling off the train. 'I've never seen so many beards and easels,' he said.

Billy didn't waste time. His first priority was to spread the word, but then he set to work painting a new sign a garish shade of yellow, explaining to anyone who'd listen that it was *in honour of that bloke who painted the sunflower*.

It wasn't making much difference to his turnover just yet, but the omens were good: Marine Parade was busy soon after 11 most days.

The immediate concern was that so many of the new visitors were younger than the usual crowd, and, more significantly, had money. Pubs had doubled their turnover in a week; the South

51

View didn't have a spare room; the caravan park was booked out; and it was nigh impossible to park on the esplanade.

But the question was, what could the shops do to get a share of this bonanza?

If it was great news for Whistle Bay, it wasn't making any difference to Sam. If anything, it had got worse. The newbies didn't need deckchairs. Most of them carried a bag over one shoulder and a camping chair over the other.

They set themselves up on the esplanade, gazing artistically out to sea, or towards the hill that Lindsay loved so much.

He told Lindsay he was finding it tough. She was nice about it, but what could she do? She told him she was having an exhibition in a couple of weeks, and she was selling paintings as quick as she could finish them.

Sam sighed: 'I've always been ok on my own, but I can't see how I can make the money I need to keep going. Everybody thinks I'm young, so I'll be the one coming up with ideas, but I haven't got one. I'm seriously thinking of packing it in.'

He shared his frustration with Aaron later: 'I thought I was wasting my time drawing, so I knuckled down like Dad always said; got here bright and early to set things up; and look - they've brought their own chairs!'

Aaron poured him a Vimto. 'I don't know what to say, Sammy lad. I'm rushed off my feet. They all want food and drink, don't they, if they're out all day, drawing or whatever? You'll just have to -' He looked over Sam's shoulder and switched on a smile. 'Yes, my lovely. What can I get you?'

Sam carried his Vimto back to the hut and stared across the beach. Even Gary had abandoned him, probably seeking out left over fish and chips.

He'd tried to think what Dad would do, but that train of thought just annoyed him: he should be able to come up with something on his own, surely?

The sun was low in the sky, and he hadn't had a single customer. Sam walked out onto the beach. The sea was lapping gently, that slow rhythmic splosh that always soothed him. He stood on the wet sand, closed his eyes and relaxed his shoulders, feeling the tension ebb away.

Somewhere in the sighing of the sea, he could swear he heard Dad's voice. He used to stand here, at his side, talking about how lucky they were to be here: 'It's our time Sammy. We spend six months looking after them; well now, we can look after ourselves. It's our turn.'

Sam opened his eyes and felt a kick of adrenaline. There *was* something he could do.

'Thanks Dad,' he whispered.

Chapter 8

Next morning, Sam put a new A board by the steps on the esplanade, then tacked on a poster. The letters were in different colours:

Original Art
by The Chair Man

Aaron, Jim and Billy were his first visitors. He was expecting the usual banter, but Jim just said: 'They're alright Sammy', sniffed and stood outside smoking.

Sam told Lindsay he'd been nervous about putting his pictures on show.

She said she remembered that feeling. 'But you'll forget all about it when they start buying.'

She was right. He punched the air like a footballer when he sold his first one for £25. It was an acrylic painting of a red and yellow chair deckchair against a sky-blue background. The woman who bought it was from Cheltenham.

She said she'd come to Whistle Bay for a weekend to paint landscapes after hearing about Lindsay. 'I always like to go back with a souvenir, something that will remind me where I was. I've been in all the shops and couldn't find a single thing.'

He was painting all day now, and sometimes at night, and it wasn't long before his cash box was full. He was first in the paying-in queue at the bank on Thursday, too.

Walking back afterwards, he saw Lindsay, holding hands with Grace. They were coming out of the greengrocers; the one Lindsay had laughed about because it had the most imaginative shop name: *Fruit and Veg.*

He covered his awkwardness by talking too much. He told them he was spending all his time drawing and painting: 'It's out of season, so I've got time to do stuff. Don't know why it took me so long to work it out.'

He remembered Grace from school. She was the one everyone fancied, and he would have been tempted too if Sally hadn't come along.

He promised he'd go to Lindsay's exhibition and headed off towards the hut.

He'd only taken a few steps when Lindsay ran up and grabbed his arm: 'Hey! I just had a thought. Why don't you do some more of your pictures, and I'll put some on display for you at the exhibition?'

He said yes without thinking, but she was horrified when he told her how much he was charging. 'Double it!' she said. 'And sign every one of them!'

He ordered business cards, and stickers for the back of his pictures, and did a deal with Shirley Sugar (so called because she was always eating sweets) to be his picture framer. They met at her place - The Photo Shop - and decided the frames needed to be bright to match the deckchairs.

He made Aaron laugh later: 'I gave her a bag of wine gums - as a sweetener…' That was a lie, but he was pleased with the joke.

By the middle of the month, he was getting a dozen customers a day, and he reckoned half of them bought a picture. Even so, he was running out of hanging space.

Lindsay sighed: 'You're hard work sometimes. Think about it… Keep changing them around. Keep stock at home and swap them now and again, so it always looks like you've got new stuff.'

He was used to her bossiness now: 'Yeah, I will. And I was thinking about doing like, you know, online sales? Take photos and put them on a website? Trouble is, I don't know how. And then I'd have to wrap them and post them, so…'

She seemed to like the idea, but she just reminded him to save his best ones for the exhibition, and he thought no more about it until he got a call two hours later…

'Sam? It's Grace. Lindsay says you need a hand with a new website. Come round to my office tomorrow and we'll see what we can do. 10 o'clock?'

He rang up for a takeaway delivery that night. It felt like luxury. He could afford it for once.

He gave the delivery girl a tip and ate every scrap: chicken in black bean sauce, egg fried rice, and vegetable spring rolls. He washed the containers out and put them on the worktop, so he didn't forget to put them in the recycling.

He yawned and looked at his Dad's old watch: a Seiko automatic, a present from Mum thirty years ago.

Soon be time for the cup match on tv. It had been a while since he'd enjoyed a game, so he decided to take a night off from being an artist and spread out on the couch to watch. If there'd been beer in the fridge, he would have had one, but a mug of tea would have to do.

There was a knock on the door just as he switched the kettle on. He sighed. Probably her next door, needing a job doing.

He switched the outside light on and opened the door. It wasn't the woman next door.

It was a woman in shorts and running vest, with tattoos on her arms and legs.

'Hi. Sam? I'm Karen. Mikey's friend.'

She had a nice smile, but Sam couldn't take his eyes off the dragon tattoo on her shoulder. 'Oh, yeah. Hi. Come in. Erm, do you want tea? I'm making one.'

'Oh yeah. Just a small one, please. I've got to run home after.'

She sat in the living room, surprised by how clean it was. He did live alone, didn't he? She smiled briefly, no wonder Mikey preferred her messiness.

People had told her how different the brothers were, but the contrast was amazing. Sam was only about ten years younger, but he looked like a teenager, with his jumbled fair hair and his awkward manner. He was good looking, with blue eyes, long legs in tight denims, broad chest.

She suddenly felt awkward and undressed. Weird. It had never bothered her before. She told herself not to be so pathetic, and twisted to look round, noticing large cards leaning against the wall by the window.

'Those are my pictures.' Sam held out a cup and saucer and she nodded her thanks. He switched the tv off and sat on the couch opposite her. She took a deep breath. There was no easy way to say it and it was better to do it now.

56

She felt his eyes taking her in, but then he jumped up and took some of the cards from the pile. 'I thought you'd like to see these.'

'Oh they're lovely. Did you paint them?'

'Yeah. A friend helped to get me started. I was looking for something to do in the off season, you know. Do you like them?'

'I love them, they're so bright and cheerful.'

He seemed grateful and shy at the same time. He was going to take this hard, but she couldn't put it off. She'd been rehearsing how to say it.

'Sam?'

He looked up. 'Yeah?'

'I'm here about Mikey.'

He shook his head and sat down. 'Oh okay. What's he done now? Is he in trouble?'

'He is.' Her mouth felt dry but she couldn't stop now. 'It's bad, I'm afraid…. I'm sorry to have to tell you this, but he's got cancer.'

Sam didn't move; he didn't even blink. He stared over her shoulder. She decided to keep talking.

'It's in his liver, and the doctors say it's spreading quickly. It came as a shock, but he's being brave about it. I'm so sorry, Sam, but -'

Sam slowly ran a hand through his hair. 'He's going to die, isn't he?'

'They think he has another couple of months, at best.'

There was anger in his voice: 'I kept telling him to stop drinking! He wouldn't listen to me. I'm just the little brother…' He looked up and Karen saw tears in his eyes. 'Why didn't he tell me?'

She moved to sit beside him. 'He's frightened, Sam. Doesn't want anyone to know. Doesn't want to see anyone. I told him if he wouldn't tell you, I would.' She put her hand on his shoulder. 'He told me about Sean. How much you loved him. He didn't want you to be hurt anymore.'

'There's only him and me left.'

She put her arm round him and he leaned into her. She felt his warmth on her neck and his hand on her back.

57

He sat up. 'Sorry. I didn't mean to -'

Instinctively, she kissed his cheek and whispered: 'Don't be sorry. It's okay.'

He became conscious of her soft skin, her legs pressed against his, his hand on her thigh. He lifted his face and her lips parted. Her breath smelled so sweet.

'Sam... no, Sam.'

He moved his hand up her thigh and over her lycra shorts and under her tight vest and he felt her shudder and he was breathing hard, and she was tugging at his t shirt and unzipped him and moaned as he pushed into her as she lay on the floor and forgot everything in a blind breathless burst that seemed to build up forever until they cried out together.

He stroked her arm as she lay beside him, her leg across his thighs, her face pushed into his neck.

'Karen, I -'

'Shhhh, it's okay.'

'But -'

'- but nothing. It just, happened.'

'Wow, it was good.'

She giggled. 'Where am I? Why am I lying on your carpet?'

'Oh God... I should be feeling bad, but -'

'Don't. You don't need to worry about Mikey's feelings. We're friends; good friends; but that's all. So neither of us are cheating on him.'

'Oh right, so you're not...?'

'You sound like my dad. You can say the word. No, we're not having sex.' She reached up to the couch and grabbed her vest and shorts. 'Come on, I've got to find the energy to run home.'

Sam yawned and stretched. 'Yeah, right.' He sat on the arm of the couch and tugged his pants on. 'Hey, do you want me to come with you?'

She smiled. 'Really? You're a runner? Well, if you fancy it, and you've still got the energy, yeah, come on!'

'I feel like I could run a marathon after that.'

'Slowly...'

'Very slowly, yeah. Right, I'll get my gear on. Help yourself to water, or there's juice in the fridge.' He stopped at the door. 'Do you think I should come in with you and see Mikey?'

'No, leave it for another day. He'll be in a bit of a mood when he finds out I've told you, but he'll calm down. Give me your number and I'll call you when he's over it.'

'Ok, and Karen …'

She pulled the vest over her head. 'Yeah?'

'Well, that was amazing, you know…'

'But it was a one off, right?'

'Was it?'

'It was just a moment. It happens, so don't beat yourself up. We both needed it. So let's be friends, and you never know…' She winked.

Sam looked suddenly serious. 'I'm not beating myself up, but I feel guilty about Mikey.'

She took his hand. 'Don't. I know he's your brother, but this doesn't change anything. You still care about him and so do I. So let's just be happy and make his last few weeks as good as they can be. We'll be his team; help him, and each other. I'm scared too. He's been a good friend. Right?'

'Right.'

His legs felt weak at first, and he had to work hard to keep up as they ran through the back streets to her flat. She noticed him slow down when they saw Mikey's boat under the harbour lights.

They hugged in the darkness outside the flat and she blew a kiss as she closed the door.

He ran back slowly the long way, along the esplanade, past the hut, up Marine Parade and onto the bright lights of the ring road where the late night shoppers were tuning into the supermarket car park.

The house was dark and empty but his thoughts seemed to fill the space… Sean and mum and dad; and now Mikey; and the guilt, always the guilt.

The silence pressed in on him. It felt like everything he knew was being taken away, and the fear he'd tried to bury for so long resurfaced. If everyone in my family is dying early, how long before it's my turn?

59

Grace King Property occupied the ground floor of what had been a semi-detached house on a street running parallel to the esplanade.

The window was made up of A5 display cards, bearing colour pictures of houses and flats, and Sam noticed a lot of them were *SOLD STC*.

'Oh, don't worry about that! We're getting new ones coming in all the time. Anyway, we've got to sell yours first - if that's what you want?'

She looked immaculate in her black leather chair behind the white desk, in a dark trouser suit and white blouse. It made him feel like a beach bum. But she was friendly and his mind was made up: 'Yeah, it's the right time. Time to move on.'

'Good for you. Oh! Tea and biscuits, Sam? Lindsay told me you're a tea addict.'

He thanked her for her help with the website and told her he'd made a few online sales already. They chatted about school and the old days as she tapped on her keyboard, stopping occasionally to sip tea and turn the screen round for him to see. Her desk phone trilled a few times but she switched on the answer machine.

'House rule. Never answer the phone when you've got someone sitting in front of you.' She smiled and turned to lift a piece of A4 off the printer. 'That's the sort of price we'd expect to get for your property, Sam.'

'What, really?'

'Yep. We're seeing a big increase in demand. Quite a few people coming in from the cities, and, speaking to the other agents, there's definitely been an upsurge. People with money, some of them looking for second homes.'

Sam nodded. He was struggling with the concept of the house he grew up in being worth more than a quarter of a million pounds.

Grace smiled. 'It's a lot of money, Sam. is it just you? No family?'

'No. Just me. I've got a brother, but he's moved out and he's really ill.'

He was hoping they could just talk about the house and how quickly she could sell it, but she looked so concerned and he knew from when Dad died he'd have to get used to people being sorry and wanting to talk: 'Oh, I'm so sorry. Is he in hospital?'

'Not yet, but he will be soon. Cancer.'

'Oh Sam! Are you ok? Can Lindsay and I do anything? Please, please ask us if you need any help, or just someone to talk to.'

Sam smiled and said thanks but he was used to coping on his own.

'Of course, yes, sorry. I didn't mean to -'

'No, it's fine. I never see much of him. I found out from a friend, but it's still a shock.'

'Gosh, yes, it must have been. Well, we're both here for you... Anyway, let me explain how we work and what our costs are. And don't worry, we'll be doing mates' rates for you.'

He went through the sums as he walked back to the hut, stopping off to collect his sandwiches from Loud Louise.

He'd expected to sell for a lot less than Grace was suggesting and be no better off because he'd spend it all on a one bedroom flat. But Grace told him it would make more sense to rent somewhere, so he'd have more chance of a quick sale.

She said she'd only charge him £500 and she knew a solicitor who'd do the conveyance for a bargain price, too.

He worked out he could have close to £300,000 in the bank. But by the time he got to the hut, he'd convinced himself Grace was having a laugh. No-one would pay that much. It was nowhere near the sea and who'd want to move in over the winter anyway?

He pulled the tarp off the chairs. There were still a few people strolling around looking interested in anything that moved, so he laid out a dozen of the red and yellow chairs in three rows.

Karen was standing by the hut steps when he turned round. She looked tired. 'Sam, I think it's time you came round to see Mikey.'

He was wishing he hadn't let Lindsay persuade him to get new clothes.

He followed her round the shops in Hightown like a sulky teenager.

She seemed oblivious: 'You need to make an impression at the exhibition. If you look too scruffy, they'll discount you. You need to look like you're earning a decent income, without looking like something out of a Gucci shop window.'

He did as he was told and here he was, clean shaven for the first time in weeks, smelling of a free cologne sample, and feeling imprisoned in a navy blue jacket with cream buttons, a red polo shirt, khaki chinos, and Nike trainers, gulping orange juice and hoping to avoid getting into conversation.

He'd never been inside the South View Hotel before, and he felt totally out of place. Everyone was talking and he wondered how they could possibly hear what the person next to them was saying. Or maybe they just preferred the sound of their own voices.

Someone tapped a glass and the chatter switched off. Lindsay was on a raised stage, in a multi coloured frock that went right down to her ankles; her hair tied back.

He could see Grace, too, and a bloke with a dark suit and shiny black hair. He looked like he was at a funeral. He held up a microphone, but she shook her head. Sam smiled. Lindsay with a microphone?

'Good evening, everyone, and thank you SO much for being here! I am SO excited you wouldn't believe it! As you already know, I've fallen in love with Whistle Bay. I came here to paint, find a new vibe, rediscover my art, and, of course, to paddle and eat chips.'

Sam joined in the laughter.

'Tonight, is my opportunity to show you what I've been doing, and hopefully for you to go *WOW! I must have that on my wall!*

'I'm happy to see so many familiar faces, good friends, and thanks for all the lovely feedback and support you've already given me. Oh, yes, and thanks to this lovely hotel for hosting the event.

'But now, the good news is the bar is open, and you can stay as long as you like - just as long as you are admiring the pictures and buying drinks. And, while you're doing that, take note of some amazing pictures by a new artist, and a lovely man. He's standing right at the back and I know he doesn't want a fuss, so I'm not going to embarrass you … Sam.'

He kept his eyes fixed on Lindsay and managed to nod and smile as heads turned his way.

'Sam is a dear friend, who has recently discovered art, but his gorgeous pictures are already selling, and he is definitely one to watch. I think he has created little masterpieces. Sam is the deckchair man at Whistle Bay, so guess what he's painted… He's already sold a load, and if I were you, I'd grab a few tonight - after you've bought all mine, naturally!'

Lindsay disappeared and the noise levels went back up. Sam moved to the window and looked out. There was a faint pink glow on the horizon. He felt a touch on his elbow.

Grace smiled: 'It's all a bit much, isn't it? Do you want to get some fresh air?'

It felt good out on the terrace. The chatter inside was drowned by the steady slap of sea on sand. Sam looked at his watch. The second high tide was on its way and the wind was picking up.

Grace swiped her hair off her face. 'Did you know you'd already sold half your pictures?'

'What? No way!'

She laughed. 'I thought that might cheer you up. I know these events are tough. I should enjoy them but I'm no good at idle chit chat; never have been.'

Sam thought that was odd for an estate agent, but nodded and undid the top button of his shirt. 'I don't know what to say. I just nod and smile and go to the buffet table.'

'Good tactics. Anyway, Lindsay wanted you to know that it's going well and she's so happy you came. We both know how much you were dreading it…'

'Yeah. It's just me. I'm not used to all this.'

'To be honest, most of us aren't. You just learn to go with it, smile a lot and join in the buzz, and then crash out, glad it's over. I bet you most people in there feel the same, they just play the game, you know?'

'Well… maybe I could have a go then.'

'Come on then. Let's stick together, see how we get on.'

63

Sam had given Lindsay 25 pictures to put on sale. As he walked round the long table where they were propped up on plastic supports, he counted 19 with red dots on them. Grace linked his arm and steered him to the end of the table and showed him the list of buyers.

'Look at that!'

Sam was busy trying to do the maths: 19 times 50... He'd made 950 quid in an hour and a half.

A man with a scarf round his neck and a whisky in his hand slapped him on the back. 'You're Sam, right? Love your pictures! Absolutely bloody marvellous! So naive. Genius!'

Grace squeezed Sam's arm in encouragement, and he smiled: 'Thank you. Yes. I'm pleased but I'm still learning, so - '

'We all are. Never stop.' He drained his glass. 'Well, must dash. Well done sir!'

Grace chuckled. 'There, that wasn't so difficult, was it?'

Sam stayed for half an hour, kissed Grace on the cheek and checked his list on the way out. Only one picture unsold.

He walked back along the esplanade, the wind in his face - an easterly carrying in drifts of sea spray that beaded on his jacket and made his lips salty. He lifted his face and breathed it in.

The weather was turning.

Chapter 9

An hour later, the wind had picked up to Force 7 and Karen was jogging towards him. He'd changed into a hoodie and jeans at the hut, but her only concession to the weather was a pair of yellow knee-high socks.

He dreamed about her last night. She was lying on her stomach while he traced his finger along a snake tattoo that was twisting and coiling round her spine. Then she turned over and smiled and hissed and bared her fangs. He'd woken up, turned on and terrified.

He'd slept badly after that, feeling guilty, imagining how Mikey would react if he knew; and how it would be, meeting him again. He knew he should be grieving, but they'd been strangers for a lifetime.

Karen stood close, running on the spot, puffing her cheeks. 'Almost wish I'd put my hoodie on too.'

'You can borrow mine.'

'Don't be daft.' She turned away quickly. 'Thanks though. Ready for this?'

He followed her up the steps to her flat above the greengrocer.

Mikey raised a hand as they walked in. He'd lost so much weight he looked like someone else. His face was thin, his hands were boney, and his eyes looked black and lifeless.

Sam tried to keep his voice steady. 'Hi Mikey.'

His voice seemed higher, weaker: 'Come in and sit down, nipper.'

Karen pulled out what looked like a school chair, and he sat close to Mikey. He smelled like he needed a wash, and he was losing his hair.

Karen had warned him it was bad, but this…

Mikey squeezed Karen's hand as she handed him half a glass of water and steadied him so he could sip.

He turned his head slightly. 'Well, at least I've stopped drinking, Sammy, eh?'

'Yeah? About time an' all.'

Mikey wheezed out a laugh. 'Thanks for coming. I'm a mess and I'm sorry I didn't tell you myself, but I wanted to tell you now.'

'Tell me what?' Sam looked at Karen, but she avoided his glance.

He sounded so matter of fact he could have been talking about the weather. 'They told me at the hospital they want me to go into the hospice: make me comfortable. The pain's getting worse and it's not going away. So, that's it, really.'

'The hospice? What, already? I mean, you've only just found out -'

Karen put a hand on Mikey's shoulder. 'It's spread everywhere. There's nothing they can do, apparently.'

Sam stood and walked to the window. 'There must be s-something.' He paused. 'I've got some money. Sold a few pictures; done all right last month. We could pay for treatment. Go s-somewhere else!'

Mikey shook his head. 'Don't waste your money, Sammy. I'm okay. I just want you to know I'm sorry for being such a useless brother. I was a bit jealous, the way you and Sean were like best mates. I was just the fat fisherman. You were the young 'uns - mum and dad's favourites.'

He coughed and winced, and Karen put a couple of drops of something in his water.

'I'm on the hard stuff now, Sammy. Morphine. Works wonders. Much better than a pint of best.'

Sam sat down again. 'Me and Sean - it wasn't like that, Mikey. We were just younger, that's all. We must have been like idiots to you, running around, playing football, racing. Just different ages...'

Mikey sighed and his eyes drooped a little. 'Yeah, whatever. I'm sorry, that's all. I just don't want you to worry. I've got used to the idea. Anyway, they'll look after me...'

His head rolled back. Karen pulled a blanket over his chest and gestured to Sam to follow her.

She poured them glasses of water and leaned back against the sink, still in her running gear. Sam shook his head and spoke in a whisper. 'There must be s-something I can do.'

She drank the water and poured another. 'There isn't. He knows it's over and he's ready to face it. Don't make it harder for him.'

'No, no, I didn't mean -'

'I'm sorry Sam, but you have to face up to it, too. That's the best thing we can do. He's accepted what's happened. He wants to go with it; go peacefully.'

'Yeah, I can s-see that. But he was always the one to kick up a fuss about the slightest thing. I thought he'd be more... angry.'

She nodded. 'Yeah. You learn something new every day.' She sipped water and turned away to top it up again. 'I lost my dad a few years ago. Cancer. He had chemo, tried a million different diets that he swore would give him the edge, took supplements, cold showers, anything he could find.'

Sam saw the anger in her eyes.

'He kept telling us: *if I keep going for long enough, they might come up with something.* It was like that for over a year, and it wore mum out. She was a wreck. And so was he. It almost killed her, watching him fight but turning into a skeleton. After all that, he died drugged up in a hospice. He was like an alien plugged into a machine. Didn't even know we were there. Scattered his ashes on his allotment. We told ourselves that at least he wasn't suffering anymore.'

She put a hand over her eyes. 'Let him go, Sam. He wants you to have a life. I know he's an awkward bugger, but he does care about you. So don't fight it. Let's do what we said: just be there for him; try to make his last days happy.'

'Okay.' The first drops of rain gently tapped on the window. 'Getting angry is like a way of getting through it. I used to get myself psyched up for a game. I was a lot smaller than most of them, but I couldn't let them see I was s-scared. So I got angry.'

'The main thing is to be strong, for Mikey.'

'Yeah. I'll visit him every day and maybe we'll end up liking each other; what do you reckon?'

'I reckon it'll mean the world to him.'

She reached out a hand and he fought off the urge to pull her towards him.

'I'd better go,' he said. 'I'll come back tomorrow if that's okay.'

#WhistleBay was trending on Twitter.

The town councillors didn't mind. Their homes increasing in value and they were the centre of attention, debating a new vision, which would in the words of their newly appointed Head of Marketing and Tourism, *maximise the benefits of the Bay's national profile by communicating its core attributes.*

Away from the Victorian edifice of the Town Hall, traders were unimpressed by the jargon, special meetings, sub committees, and working parties. But they weren't complaining about the upsurge in business.

Billy Whistle found time to share his disdain at length to anyone foolish enough to linger too long.

'Head of Marketing? Twenty-five grand for two and a half days a week! I wish they'd spend that on smartening the place up. Have you seen the state of the station? What kind of marketing is that!'

Jim at the arcade puffed on his cigarette and declared his intention to 'spruce his place up a bit more'. Then, to universal amazement, Aaron announced he was going to invest some of his extra income in re-fitting his kiosk. Jim's reaction made Sam laugh: 'Blimey, he only bought it twenty years ago.'

All across the town, shops were being re-painted, re-shelved, re-designed, and sometimes re-invented.

But the biggest surprise was when Aaron turned up in new clothes: a plain white T shirt and jeans.

Billy was obviously shocked because he told Sam he was worried about being left behind. He went quiet for a few days, then told everyone in confidence about his grand plan. The white vans arrived while Sam was having a flat white, but he resisted all attempts to get him to reveal the full story.

'Wait a couple of weeks,' he said. 'I might even invite you to the opening do.'

Sam picked up the local paper on his way home. The headline filled the front page: *'New lease of life for the Bay!'*

He turned to page two to read more:

New marketing boss Kelly King said she was delighted to see local traders responding to the council's Build a Better Bay strategy. 'We're putting Whistle Bay on the map and every business sector is reporting an uplift from increased visitor numbers. The key is to make the Bay a go-to destination at any time of the year, and we're well on the way to doing that. But we don't just want to be a mecca for artists, we want to get the word out that everyone's welcome. We want to get the world Whistling!'

Grace came round later, and he showed her the article. 'That's typical. Traders do all the hard work and spend their own money, while they come up with slogans and hold meetings. Still, at least something's happening.'

He made tea while she measured up the house. He heard her talking into her phone. Sam felt edgy, imagining how mum and dad would feel about someone else living here, but Karen and Lindsay said the same thing: it was time he moved on.

Grace sat at the kitchen table while he opened the new tin of biscuits he'd bought at M and S. She smiled: 'Sam! Belgian chocolate biscuits…lush! There goes my diet.'

He looked over her shoulder as she flicked through the photos she'd taken on her phone. He nodded: 'Yeah, it looks ok. Erm… I'm just thinking…'

'Yes Sam?'

'Well, you know Mikey's really ill?'

'Yeah.'

'Well, Karen - his friend - reckons he'll be going into the hospice in the next couple of weeks, and I was wondering… I thought I might see if he'd like to come and stay here for a few days before he goes in.'

'Oh Sam, what a lovely idea. I'm sure he'd like to. Why are you asking me? Are you worried about it?'

'I'm not sure, but we've never really got on and I'm worried he might do it for my sake, and…'

'…not because he really wants to.'

Sam nodded. 'Yeah.' He sipped his tea and looked out of the window. The rain was tapping hard against the glass.

Grace shivered slightly and reminded herself to tell Sam to put the heating on to make sure it worked. 'I'd make the offer. Even if he says no, you can say that you tried.'

Sam sighed. 'I know, but I don't want him to worry. He might just say yes because he feels guilty, and then hate it. I can't do that to him when he hasn't got much time left. We said that we'd do our best to make him happy.'

'Yes, but what a lovely thing to do for a brother you've never connected with... If you don't, you'll probably regret it. And just imagine how it would make you both feel to be together, finally.'

She finished her notes, checked the heating, and packed her things.

She turned at the front door. 'Invite him, Sam. I'm sure its the right thing to do. But put the heating on; it's cold in here!'

Grace told Lindsay later that she was falling a bit in love: 'He's been on his own for ages and it can't have been easy, but he just gets on with life, and tries to do the right thing. He's our age but I always thought of him as younger, you know? But he seems to have grown up a lot lately.'

She was used to seeing Lindsay's wistful look when Sam was mentioned, and she could understand it now. They'd both made their choices long ago after traumatic relationships with men. But Sam was different.

Lindsay stood at the window, looking out to the beach. She could see the roof of Sam's hut in the distance. 'I guess he's older and wiser.'

'But still just as gorgeous. It's hard to believe he's not met anyone yet, isn't it?'

'I know. Stop it now, or you'll make me want to marry him.'

Grace walked up behind her, put her arms round her waist and kissed her neck. Lindsay swivelled round and kissed her eagerly. And Sam was forgotten for a while.

October still had a few days to run its course.

Storm Bronwen moved North, leaving behind fallen branches, upturned patio chairs, a handful of insurance claims

70

for broken windows and roof tiles, and a disproportionate number of newspaper headlines.

The prediction now was for a spell of milder, more settled weather, so Sam opened all the windows, hired a skip and got down to some serious cleaning, ahead of Mikey's arrival at the weekend.

Old newspapers, lager cans, and cigarette packets went out through the bedroom window. Most of it ended up on the back lawn, despite Sam's attempts to throw them straight into the skip.

Bay Homestyle turned up next day to deliver a new bed, a high back armchair, a flat screen tv, and a new carpet and curtains. The store was run by Dave - also known as Dave The Deal, a nickname that had stuck since his schooldays when he used to carry a bag full of sweets to sell at break time. No-one knew where he got them, and at his prices, no-one cared.

Karen came round the night before Mikey was due. 'Wow Sam! It's like a little palace. He won't be able to cope with somewhere as tidy as this.'

He laughed: 'He'll have to. I'm not scruffing it up again.'

She looked good in tight jeans and a puffa jacket.

Sam spent another restless night thinking about her.

He was watching from the kitchen window as Karen helped Mikey out of the cab next morning.

She looked like an athlete in her shorts and vest; Mikey could hardly walk.

Sam leaned on the sink, fighting down an emotion that should have been grief but felt more like self-pity.

The doorbell rang out like a church bell on speed. He ran his hands over his face and smiled as he opened the door.

'Hi Mikey. Erm, welcome home!'

He helped him up the step and felt the coldness of his brother's hand as it clutched his wrist like a claw. It was the hand of a man who'd fished at sea, arm wrestled and fought outside pubs, shoved Sam through the back door in an argument, lifted pints and saluted goals; and who now leaned on his brother because he couldn't make it to the living room on his own.

'I've put the fire on for you, so you should be ok.'

He spoke in short bursts. 'Bloody hell Sam. Fire on, during the day? Mum'd kill you for wasting gas.'

Sam laughed and held on till he'd sat down.

Karen sat on the arm of the chair, her hand on Mikey's shoulder. 'Are you two going to behave, then?'

Mikey chuckled softly and looked at Sam. They said it together: 'Not if we can help it.'

They went into the kitchen while Mikey napped, and Karen handed him a paper bag: 'His medicine. He just needs to take these two in the morning…this one at night. And be careful with this; just a few drops in water if the pain gets too much. You'll have to ask him if he's in pain because he's so stubborn he doesn't like to admit it.' She pointed to the bag. 'I've written the hospital and the hospice numbers on there, just in case. And that's my mobile and the shop number, so just call any time, all right?'

Sam nodded. 'I think we'll be okay, and I'll only call if I have to. I bet you need a break.'

'Yeah.' She turned to go, then stopped and put a hand on his arm. 'Thanks. He's so chuffed about this.'

'That's okay. I'm glad he said yes. Anyway, go on, enjoy your run and don't worry.'

'Take care of him.' She walked down the hall to the front door. 'See you in a few days. I'll call tonight.'

He watched her bending and stretching at the front of the house, and he grinned as he imagined the stories the woman next door would come up with.

Karen pressed a button on her watch, then turned and waved and ran quickly away. She seemed to glide over the road.

He opened the living room door. Mikey was snoring softly. He propped the door open and went back into the kitchen to get his sketch book.

He'd bought a new easel and paintbox at Shirley's newly repainted - Photo And Paint Shop; renamed without regard to the schoolboy giggles she was generating. She'd even painted each first letter in a different colour.

He set himself up by the window so he could keep an eye on Mikey.

He'd been thinking about how to give the paintings a new look, but he didn't want to move too far away from the style that everyone liked. He'd tried sketching his new subject separately and it came out ok, but he'd been putting off incorporating it until he found the right paint shades.

It was surprisingly difficult to get the right colour. Not only did he have loads of colours, but loads of shades, too. As if that wasn't confusing enough, Lindsay told him to try mixing them together to get even more colours. His new paint box was already two thirds full.

He'd spent forever looking online, and finally went for Titanium White, Cool White, Portland Grey Medium, and Cadmium Yellow Medium.

He was ready. He sat down in front of the easel and began to paint.

'What do you think Mikey?'

He slowly pushed himself out of the chair and stood for a moment to steady himself. He moved behind Sam's chair. 'Yeah, that's good, matey. Karen said you were into it. Yeah, good, good.'

'Fancy a look round?'

'Yeah, go on. Live a little, eh?'

Sam went ahead, making sure there were no trip hazards, and waited in the kitchen. He could hear his brother's shuffling steps, the tapping of his stick, and his laboured breathing and wondered if he really could get up the stairs.

Mikey paused for breath, leaning against the door frame and pointed. 'Dad's table.'

'Yeah. Newspaper, mug of tea.' Sam smiled. 'Remember him, counting his money? Doing the books.' Sam picked up the account book he'd brought home. 'Here it is.'

'Hell's teeth. Is that it?'

Sam helped him sit in Dad's place and opened the book for him. 'I still use it.'

Mikey mumbled to himself as he turned the pages, and Sam could see his eyes widen when he saw the latest entries.

'You were right about the money. How come?'

Sam told him about Lindsay, about his paintings, and the exhibition and how he was selling them for fifty quid a time. But it wasn't long before he could see his interest fading. He seemed to stiffen in the chair and zone out.

Sam remembered what Karen had said and put three drops of morphine in a glass of water.

He drank it and looked at Sam. His eyes were clearing, and he seemed brighter again. 'Thanks, Sam, for... you know.'

'Well let's be honest, it is the least I could do.'

'Yeah, I suppose. What's the most you could do?'

'Good question. Depends on you. What do you want the most? - Ah, no, don't tell me. Not the pub?'

'No mate. I'm over all that. Should have given it up years ago. Too late now. No, you know what I'd like the most?'

Sam shook his head.

'I'd like to go down to the hut.'

'Really?'

'Yeah, I've not been there since you took it on. Karen said you'd been working hard.'

'How about tomorrow, then?'

'If you insist.'

'Cup of tea now?'

'Go on then.'

Sam opened the drawer where the family photos were stuffed in envelopes, and they sat together to look through them, laughing at how they looked when they were kids.

Mikey picked another out of an envelope and went quiet.

'What've you found Mikey?'

He put it down. 'It's you and me Sammy.' He sniffed. 'I've never seen a picture of us, together. Must be the only one.'

Sam looked closely. Mikey looked so big next to him. He must have been in his teens, which would make Sam about six or seven.

'Blimey. I've never seen this before. Wonder where we were?'

'Blackpool. It was the last time I went on holiday with mum and dad. I hated it. But you and me played football on the beach every day, and I started enjoying myself. We got back to the B and B and we were knackered. Every single day. That was the

74

last time I can remember when I was like a proper brother. I just left you to it after that. Even when mum died, and then dad.'

His shoulders shook, and Sam scraped his chair closer and put an arm round him.

Mikey shook his head like a wet dog. It was a gesture Sam remembered from when Dad used to have a go at him for not helping round the house. It was his way of moving on. He patted Sam's hand. 'Feeling sorry for myself. Okay now.' He tried to stand, and Sam put a hand on his back to steady him. 'Ta, nipper. Time for some shut eye, I reckon.'

Sam helped him back into his chair in mum's room and closed the door, just as the doorbell rang.

Lindsay shrugged off her padded jacket and draped it over the banister at the bottom of the stairs.

She was wearing her new sleeveless top and purple leggings. Sam said it without thinking: 'Wow! You look so hot.'

She froze for a moment, making him wait just long enough to realise he should have kept his mouth shut, then laughed and kissed his cheek and demanded a cup of tea.

He whispered: 'Sorry, I wasn't thinking.' Then pointed towards the living room door down the hall and put his fingers to his lips.

She mouthed the word: 'Mikey?'

He nodded and she followed him into the kitchen.

She was even more full of it than usual. 'I'm prepared to forgive you for the stereotypical assumption that I dressed like this to make you fancy me. But that's only because I am a nice person and it was actually a compliment, I suppose. And anyway, I had the most amazing idea last night. Sam, you will LOVE it! You and me, working together.'

He decided against asking what perfume she was wearing and stopped mid-pour. 'What do you mean?'

'Well pour my tea, Mister Stereotype, and I might tell you. Tea first, you should know that. You make the best tea in Whistle Bay, if not the continent of Europe.'

Sam shook his head, smiling, as he stirred and pressed the tea bag until he achieved the perfect shade. 'There you are madam - Raw Sienna.'

'Ah, merci, mon brave. Nice colour, that.' She slurped noisily.

Sam sat down with a bemused expression that made her laugh more. 'Come on, what's this great idea?'

'I'll tell you in a minute. I want to see your new picture first. Hurry along, I haven't got all day.' She winked: 'I've on my way to a hot date with Grace.'

All the emphasis was on the word hot, and Sam cursed himself as he retrieved the picture from the cupboard under the stairs.

He came back and held up the picture anxiously.

'Oh, Sam... that is bee-you-tee-full! Is it meant to be your Gary? Let me have a closer look.'

She laid it flat on the table and stood over it, leaning in occasionally, holding her hair back with one hand. 'Only one comment Sam. Just one improvement I think you could make. Is it alright if I say?'

He sat down with a nod.

'Composition. Think about where you place things. Look at it again. Now, where is the seagull in relation to everything else?'

'Erm... in the middle?'

'Yep. That's the thing. You've got it perched right in the middle of the back of the deckchair, which is right in the middle of the picture.'

'Why is that wrong?'

Lindsay sat down next to him. 'Oh Sam, it's not wrong! I'm just trying to help you get even better. Don't worry, I do this to myself all the time. Never stop learning, ok? What happens when you do that is that it's hard for me - the viewer - to see beyond it. There's no depth to it, you see? And you've abandoned those lovely backgrounds you were doing. So, think... what's the star of the show and what do you want your picture to say?'

She stopped, and her eyes widened. 'Hey! Why not really break the mould and do a larger painting?'

Sam frowned. 'Larger?'

'Yes! How amazing would that look? A landscape of chairs: maybe a line of chairs, and a gull perched on one a bit further back. Imagine all the colours you'd get in, and the gull would look amazing in that gorgeous whitey grey you've used. And so much easier to compose.'

Sam stood up to look again, and nodded slowly, then looked at her. 'How much bigger?'

She laughed. 'Think spectacular! Show everyone what you can do! I know art lovers in London who would pay a fortune to have a picture like that on the wall of their dockside apartment. Why not aim for one the same size as the side of your hut?'

Sam stepped back. 'What?'

She looked at him and he saw the light in her eyes and felt it burning into him, giving him confidence, just like it had from the first day he met her.

He didn't hesitate. 'Okay. I'll try.'

She clapped her hands as she sat down, and he poured more tea and she told him about her new idea.

Chapter 10

Builder Bob was in his eighties. He'd had the yard next to the Wanderers ground for longer than anyone could remember. He still wore the sandy coloured toupee, jeans with turn ups and a donkey jacket. Some of the locals said he was past it, but Sam always pointed out that he was still doing 12 hour days, unloading deliveries and stacking shelves.

The bell on the stiff old door rang out when Sam shouldered his way in. Bob came out of the back office and pretended to be busy. Then he looked up, and his eyes disappeared in a maze of wrinkles as he smiled: 'Sammy! Good lord! Come in, young fella!'

Shelves that had once towered over the schoolboy version of Sam were head height now, and still stacked with paints and varnishes. The brushes and rollers were in their usual place in a bin nearest the counter; then, off to the right, racks of new tools that Sam remembered pestering Dad about... *what does that one do?*

Sawn timber was neatly racked on the back wall. Sam caught the sweet sharp scent of it as he walked past.

Bob grabbed his arm: 'Fancy a brew?'

It was the first time he'd been invited into the office, and his desk was as neat as Sam expected.

Bob wheeled his desk chair next to Sam, inspecting the project drawing he'd made with Lindsay. He nodded. 'Looks okay, but that little lot's going to set you back a bit, nipper.'

'Oh it's all right, I've budgeted for it.'

'Have you now? That's what I like to hear. Good lad. Let's have a proper look at yer list then....'

He scanned it quickly. He was still full of enthusiasm after what must be 60 years running the same business. Sam had always loved Bob, looked up to him. He used to think of him as a perfect granddad.

Bob scraped his chair back, thought for a moment and tapped his nose. 'Now keep this to yerself, but I reckon I can save you a bit. Come round the back and feast yer eyes on this.'

He said he'd put in the winning bid for a factory demolition in Hightown and hadn't priced it all up yet. He made Sam feel like he'd won the lottery, and he happily signed up for first pickings which cost half the amount he'd allowed for. Bob even got one of his lads to load up a truck and deliver it free. It was just as Dad used to say: 'Bob knows how to look after his customers.'

Sam felt his strength as they shook hands. Behind them, the delivery lorry engine rattled into life, and they watched it bounce through the potholes and out onto the main road.

'Dad was talking about you right up to the end, you know.'

Bob nodded and smiled, and started to say something, but someone shouted his name. He put a hand on Sam's shoulder. 'I still miss the chats we used to have; me and yer dad. I know he was always proud of you. You ever need anything, you know where I am, alright son?'

Sam drove off in Dad's old Fiesta, stopping off at the supermarket to buy protein bars and bananas, and got to the hut just before Bob's lorry.

He helped unload and worked until dusk, fixing plexiglass roofing sheets to the cross beams and assembling a storage cupboard.

He knew Dad would have been proud, not just because it looked good, but because he'd got his materials from Bob.

He and Mikey had talked about Bob on his visit to the hut. Sam told him the yard still looked the same, but smaller somehow. Mikey sat in the armchair, interested at first, but said he was tired after the climb up the steps, and seemed to enter a kind of trance. But then he'd smiled, still with his eyes closed, and said, as if to himself: 'You can almost smell the family history.'

They sipped tea and reminisced until the light faded.

It was fading now as Sam stepped back to look at his hut extension. He felt his back twinge. Concreting in 12-inch square support posts last week had been the hard part. He told Lindsay it had felt like he was digging down to the earth's core to find solid ground, but she looked bored and asked why they needed to be in so deep.

He'd given her a look. 'Have you ever been down here in a south westerly gale?'

'No.'

'Well you'd best leave me to get on with it then. Anyway, it's my money paying for this.'

She just laughed. 'Oooh, sorry I spoke!'

Aaron was a regular visitor, drawn in by the sound of sawing and hammering, and he wasn't the only one of the gossips desperate to know what was going on. Sam enjoyed being cagey, though he didn't have a choice. Lindsay insisted it had to be a secret until it was done.

He felt bad about not being able to tell Mikey though. Karen phoned and said the doctor wanted him to stay at home as long as possible: 'Mikey knows the days are ticking by, but he really enjoyed staying with you. It gave him such a lift.'

'Well, you'll both be getting an invitation from me and Lindsay soon, so tell him he's got to come.'

'Yeah, what are you up to down there? Turning it into a hotel?'

Sam laughed. 'I wish! I can't tell you yet. But I'm excited.'

Karen's tone of voice changed. 'Are you and Lindsay a thing?'

'What? No way!'

'Oh, right. It's none of my business, but you seem to spend a lot of time together, that's all. Always talking about her. I just thought -'

Sam hesitated. 'Well, she helped me a lot when she first came here; got me into art, brought new customers, too. She's a good friend, but she's not…'

'Not what?'

He hesitated. 'Well, you know. She's a friend and that's it, if you know what I mean.'

He went for a slow run that night to try to loosen up, clear his head of thoughts that confused him.

He drank a glass of milk and soaked in the bath, but he couldn't relax. If he wasn't thinking about the new project, he was worrying about Mikey; and if it wasn't Mikey, he'd be wondering about the three women who had suddenly invaded his life: Lindsay, Grace, and Karen.

They were all beautiful and nice to be with. His mates would think he'd got it made, and he imagined how it would be to have one of them as a permanent girlfriend. But which one would he choose?

If it was just on looks alone, Grace would win every time. Lindsay made him feel happy - she was just so funny and bright. But Karen ... he couldn't forget how good it felt when they - Oh, but what's the point? Grace had moved in with Lindsay, Karen's with Mikey, and he was still alone: daydreaming like a schoolboy.

He was too wired to sleep, so he got down to the beach early to set up the chairs, hammer in the windbreaks and test the new patio heaters.

Lindsay turned up later in yellow trousers and a bright green jacket and pulled him close so she could take a selfie, with the hut extension in the background. 'It looks so gorgeous, don't you think?'

She'd had the brightly striped windbreaks specially made and she added a few lengths of the same material to the hut wall, hung a couple of her pictures, and arranged more fabric and driftwood on the esplanade wall.

He flinched when she showed him the photo. She laughed: 'You are allowed to smile, Sam. Come on, try again.'

He tried to copy her, but baring his teeth made him look like he was snarling, so she held up a mirror from her shoulder bag and forced him to practice... 'That's it! Just do that. Right, this time!'

She gave him a high five, so he tried to hang onto the same expression as the first customers arrived.

Forty people turned up for the 9.30am start, having booked through the Facebook page Lindsay had set up.

They held out their phones, patiently waiting while Sam used old technology - aka, a pen - to tick off names on a list he'd printed out.

He decided not to bother putting any deckchairs out. It was pretty fresh, even for November, and he was on refreshment duty later, carrying trays of drinks in re-usable cups, and cupcakes that Grace had made.

81

He took his chance to look at their work during a break, while they gathered around Lindsay in an adoring huddle.

The class finished at one, and Lindsay helped him fold the tables and stack them up.

'What did you think Sam?'

'My jaw's aching from smiling, but I thought it was amazing. Great turn out, and you're a good teacher.'

'You think so? Really?'

Sam couldn't work out if she was just pretending to be surprised. He locked the tables in the cupboard, and they started gathering up paper for recycling. 'Yeah, I mean it. But some of the pictures were a bit…'

'A bit, what?'

'Well, it made me think I'm not doing s-so bad.'

'Sammy, you need to be more confident. You're right, you're not doing bad at all.'

He stopped. Aaron, Jim, Billy, and the guy who ran the Chamber of Commerce, were walking towards the hut.

Sam called out, laughing: 'Hello. You're a bit late for the art class!'

None of them were laughing. By the look on their faces, this wasn't a social call.

Billy looked at the others, then stepped forward, arms folded across his chest.

'Can we have a word?'

Lindsay took Sam's arm and whispered. 'I'll wait in the hut.'

Sam had met the Chamber guy at a breakfast event a few months ago and wondered if he was a rugby player. He was certainly built like one, plus, he shaved his head, and obviously liked a bit of macho stubble on his chin.

But the high-pitched voice didn't match the look: 'We're here on behalf of the Chamber of Commerce, of which you are a member, Sam.'

'What's the problem?'

'We've had complaints about activities at these premises. The problem is that you're holding events which take people away from town centre businesses, most of which are members, too. Not only that, you did this without any consultation, and

82

you have also begun providing catering services in direct competition with existing traders, who are struggling as it is.'

He paused. The others nodded, apart from Aaron, who had his head down. Sam clenched his fists. So they'd been watching, like spies. Where were they? Billy's bedroom window, with binoculars? He was concentrating hard, determined not to be intimidated - trying to think like a grown up when he really wanted to lash out like a child.

The silence lasted and he could see they were growing fidgety, waiting for his reaction. It made him feel more in control. He took a few calming breaths and decided to let them stew a bit longer.

The Chamber guy - Philip Potts, he remembered - looked particularly uncomfortable. Sam wondered if they'd expected him to hit back, lose his temper, and now they weren't so sure of themselves.

Potts put on a bad attempt at a smile. 'So, Sam, you know that Whistle Bay traders have always stuck together. We're just asking you to stop holding the art classes here and to stop providing refreshments to people who visit your hut -' He smiled. '- sorry, art gallery.'

Sam remembered what Dad used to call him: Chamber Potts. He struggled to keep a straight face.

Billy clearly misunderstood the smile. He stepped forward, acting like Mister Reasonable: 'What do you say, Sam? You could have your classes at my place, no problem. I'd do the teas and coffees. I'd only charge mates rates for the hire.'

Jim chipped in, cigarette glued to his lips as usual. 'We reckon you had 50 people here this morning, fella. They could have been spending money in town. We just want you to think about Billy's offer. They'd come out of Billy's and be right next to the shops. When they come here, they just get on the esplanade and bugger off back to their b and b's.'

They all turned as the steps creaked. Lindsay walked down and stood next to Sam and Billy's smile turned into a sneer. 'Oh hello, here's his London lass coming down the stairs to blind us with posh talk.'

Lindsay laughed in astonishment. Aaron shuffled his feet in the sand and cleared his throat: 'Now, come on Billy, that's not fair. Let's hear what Sam's got to say.'

Chamber Potts nodded and folded his arms: 'What do you say, Sam?' He looked so smug that Sam wanted to punch him in the face.

Lindsay must have sensed it. 'Come on Sam. Don't let them get to you. Shall we have a chat first?'

He shook his head, trying to get his thoughts in order. He'd been brought up to believe that traders stuck together, and yet this is the reaction when all he's trying to do is make a future for himself; make the most of an opportunity instead of sitting back and moaning.

He took a breath and felt the tension release. The words began to spill out: 'I can't believe you're doing this. My Dad and I have run this place for, what, thirty years? I took over this year and I've worked hard to keep it going. It's been tough but I still found time to help people like you with repair jobs. Remember? Just like Dad used to do?

'But I'm only young, as you all keep telling me; and stupid as well, because I believed it when Dad told me we were a team: that we stick together. But it's bollocks, isn't it? Because now I'm doing something new, for new people coming to the town, and you're trying to stop me! It's a joke.'

His voice was getting louder, but he couldn't stop now.

'I'm just trying to make a living, like you. I don't complain when you do new stuff do I? Should I go running to the Chamber to complain that you're pulling people away from me when you have a sale or a new shop window? Does my business not count because it's not in the bloody town centre? Is that what you're saying?'

No response. He took another breath, gathering his thoughts, calmer now.

'The council keeps talking about a new image for the Bay and how new people are coming. Why do they come here? It's not for Marine Parade! It's not for the Chamber of Commerce either, is it? They come for the sea and the beach and the views and the fresh air. That's why Lindsay came, and she's done more for this town in two months than any of you.

'You were all telling me a few weeks ago how great it was with all these new people around. Oh, sorry, did you forget about that?'

Sam looked up at the sky, and lowered his voice: 'You know what? I don't care what you think! This is my business, my life, and you'd be better off working out what you can do to get more customers yourself, instead of slagging me off, alright?

'Oh and before you go, you might like to know this: I got all my supplies for my pictures - the frames, the paints, everything - at a local shop. Bob supplied all the materials I needed for this extension, too. Dad and I must have spent a bloody fortune in your shops over the years. Never thought of that, did you?

'I thought you were my mates. If you really want to know what I'm doing, I'll tell you: I'm trying to make Mum and Dad, and Sean and Mikey, proud...'

Sam felt his lip begin to tremble, and he turned away, breathing heavily.

Lindsay stared at Potts. 'I think you've got your answer, don't you? It's up to you what you do next, but I'd think very carefully if I were you. Any more harassment and I'll start talking, too - to the media. *Traders At War:* now that's not a headline you want to read just when the Bay is beginning to take off as a visitor destination, is it? How would that sell at the Chamber? The Chamber tries to shut down an art class just when Whistle Bay is getting known as a destination for artists? How would that sell at the Town Hall? Now, if you'll excuse us...'

They looked at each other and shrugged, but just as they turned to leave, Sam walked up to Potts.

'Oh by the way, just so you know, I'm cancelling my subscription.'

He shook his head. 'Don't, Sam. You're making a big mistake. I can see you're upset. I understand why. Please, just try to calm down and think it through, ok?'

Sam stepped closer and smiled into his face even though he felt his body shaking. 'You're the one making the mistake. Now get off my property.'

They watched them walk back towards Marine Parade. Lindsay shut the hut door behind them as Sam sank into the old armchair. 'Wow, Sam; impressive!'

'I don't know about that. What have I done? They'll never speak to me again. The word'll get round and I'll be on my own. Dad would be bloody furious.'

She sat on the arm of the chair. 'No, Sam, come on! You were spot on. Times have changed and I bet if your dad could hear you, he'd be so proud of you. And did you notice - you didn't stutter once? What does that tell you?'

'I don't know.'

Sam looked up and she gently ruffled his hair. 'It's because you spoke from your heart. That was the real you, not the version you put on display for people. You know as well as I do, this town needs shaking up. I bet you anything that lots of people will be on your side. And if they're not … well, so what? You're doing well enough without their so-called help, aren't you?'

Sam leaned his head back and sighed. 'Yeah, I suppose. But I promised Dad I'd look after things.'

'But you are! And you're doing it your own way, too. You're making more money than he ever did. You're so young but look at this place now! It's like a little palace with your pictures, the new extension - and outdoor heaters, for God's sake!'

Sam smiled. 'Dad would go ape about them.' He mimicked grumpy Dad: 'Throwing good money after bad.' He sighed. 'I can't believe I said all those things.'

'You said them because they were inside, waiting to come out. You've been like a slave to your family, and it's time you broke free.'

'What do you mean?'

Lindsay leaned back on the high stool, her elbows on the window shelf, looking down at him. She remembered when she met him that first time, how innocent he was; like a child. She needed to choose her words carefully.

'You've done an amazing job, Sam, taking over the business at your age. But you've never seen what else there is out there. There's more to life than Whistle Bay. I left home after sixth

86

form, went to uni, made a career for myself.' She put big emphasis on 'myself' and Sam looked up.

He leaned forward, elbows resting on his knees, looking at the floor. 'Yeah, I know. But I promised him, Lindsay.'

'Sam! You are doing what you promised! The business is doing so well. But you're not your dad, are you? What do you think he would have done when those jerks turned up?'

Sam hesitated. 'I think he would have apologised.'

She nodded. 'There you go. He would have wanted to keep the peace, even though they should have been apologising to him. And I bet you anything that, after, he would have been ashamed that he'd not stood up for himself. It's always easier to keep things as they are. It's safer to spend your life not changing anything, not upsetting anyone, going with the crowd. But if nothing ever changes, nothing ever gets better.'

Sam stood and gazed over her shoulder. The sea and the sky were the same shade of grey. 'I haven't even put the house up for sale yet. I told myself it was because of Mikey.'

'Oh Sam... do you really think it would affect him that much?'

She was right in front of him, inches away, and he felt her warmth, her brightness, filling the hut, filling him. Just her being there made everything feel better, somehow. Like it was when he was with Sean.

She was telling him he could change his life, and in one instant he could be. He just had to make the move; kiss her, hold her, feel her body pushing against his.

And yet, something held him back.

It was as if she knew. She held his hand in both hers and looked up at him and spoke so softly it was like torture: 'Oh Sam. I do love you, you know that, but not in the same way. You're like the brother I never had but always wanted. Please, don't spoil it. Can't we settle on being friends: friends for life?'

Sam couldn't find any words.

He just nodded and tried to smile and leaned into her; and she wrapped her arms round him and squeezed.

Her warm breath was in his ear. 'I've got a framed picture on my wall. It says: today is the first day of the rest of your life.'

She heard him splutter and pushed him away. 'What's wrong, are you ok?

He was wiping his eyes and grinning at the same time.

'Lindsay: that's so cheesy. Fancy a quick pint?'

They linked arms as they walked towards the pub. Sam turned round. The hut looked like a piece of Toblerone against the chalk hills in the distance.

Lindsay squeezed his arm: 'What are you thinking?'

'About what you were saying. That place has been my whole life. It looks so small, too. It feels weird.'

'Life is weird. Get over it. Come on, pub.'

Sam couldn't remember the last time he'd tasted Bay Bitter. The Crown was quiet, just as he always remembered it: a big guy in a high vis jacket hogging the bar, a scruffy bloke with a glass of cider and a sad looking greyhound, and a couple of old boys in the corner.

Not surprisingly, the landlord seemed pleased to have the custom. 'Sam! Not seen you for ages.' He winked at Lindsay. 'But I know you very well.'

She grinned: 'One of your best customers, aren't I, Gerry? Anyway, Sam, it's your round…'

Lindsay sat at the table by the window, its dark wood gleaming in the weak sunlight.

Sam drank half his pint and smiled, remembering. 'I had my first beer in here. Down in one. Dad couldn't believe it.'

Lindsay sipped a white wine spritzer: 'Nothing new there, then. Thirsty, are we?'

Sam pointedly took a delicate sip. 'Yeah, I am a bit. I'd forgotten how good it tastes, to be honest.'

'I keep telling you: you need to get out more.' She smiled as Sam shook his head. 'Gerry seems friendly enough, doesn't he? See? No need to worry about your reputation.'

'Yeah, but wait till he hears about me losing it earlier.'

'Don't be daft. I bet he already has. I'm telling you, most people will be on your side. But, come on, let's change the subject. How's your brother?' She winced. 'Sorry, not a great choice of topic.'

'It's ok. I don't mind talking about it. But it's hard to say. He never did give much away, and he hasn't changed. Karen reckons he's going to be ok for a bit longer, though.'

'Before they take him in, you mean?'

'Yeah, to the hospice. She's taking it well, and he's acting like he's accepted it. I'm dreading it. Another member of the family, dying young.'

'Well thank God you're all right. Not sure how I'd cope.'

'I thought I'd be ok, but it's starting to get to me now. I was never close to him before, but…'

'You were just getting to know each other, as well, weren't you?'

He sighed, staring into his empty glass. 'Yeah.'

She leaned forward, playing with a beer mat. 'Karen's nice.'

Sam looked up suddenly, surprised. 'Do you know her?'

Lindsay sat back; her eyes fixed on him. 'It's allowed, isn't it? If you must know, she did a tattoo for me a couple of weeks ago.'

'Oh, right.'

'What does that mean? Don't you approve? God, you're such an old man sometimes! Anyway, it's in a private place, and I'm not going to show you.' She laughed as Sam fidgeted with his phone. 'Anyway, come on, your reaction is a dead giveaway… what's going on with you and Karen?'

He'd thought about telling her before, but he couldn't. Not yet. 'I really like her, that's all.'

'Oh I see. You like Grace, too, don't you?'

'Yeah, I do. What's wrong with that?'

'Now, now. Mister Touchy.' She winked. 'Have you and Karen… you know…?'

'Don't be daft.' He put his phone on the table. It looked like an antique next to hers. Karen gave him a knowing look but he ignored her. 'Fancy one more?'

'No, you have one. I'm ok with this.'

He made his decision in the time it took for Gerry to pull his pint. He wouldn't tell her about Karen. She'd tell Grace, and it would soon be all over town. He could imagine the gossip: *Can you imagine? He's shagging his dying brother's girlfriend!*

89

He leaned back against the bar. Lindsay was looking at her tablet. Her dark hair was tinted gold by shafts of sunlight. She was concentrating on something so maybe she'd lost interest in Karen. He leaned in to get a better view. She was looking at photos she'd taken at the art class.

She turned to look at him, flicking her hair behind one ear. 'They're good, aren't they? I'll be putting them on the Insta page later.' She checked her watch. 'Actually, I need to get back. Things to do. And the wifi's better there.'

She stood, drained her glass and kissed him on the cheek.

'Sorry, got to go. See you soon, little bro.'

Sam smiled. 'Yeah, sure, sis. When?'

'Tomorrow probably? We've got arty things to talk about.' She smiled and waggled her fingers in farewell. 'Bye. Love you.'

Gerry called out: 'Bye love' .

She laughed. 'Not you! See you soon, landlord.'

Sam watched the door swung shut behind her

Alone again.

But it wasn't for long.

He didn't need to look up; the high-pitched voice was instantly recognisable: 'Mind if I join you?'

Chapter 11

Philip Potts grunted as he squeezed into the chair. He placed his wine glass precisely on a beer mat and held it there. The glass looked small in his hand.

'Sure I can't get you a drink?'

Sam pretended to be interested in a beer mat. 'No thanks.'

Potts sighed: 'Look, I know I made the wrong call, and I can imagine how you feel. We've been losing membership lately, and I was keen to be seen to back them up. I feel bad about it. You handled it really well. I was impressed by what you said.'

Still staring at the beer mat. 'What are you telling me this for?'

'I just want you to understand.' He sipped his red wine. 'We're a club, and our members sometimes want different things. It puts pressure on us. You pay your subs and you rightly expect our support. But people like Billy and Jim are members too, and we have to represent them.'

Sam looked up; the anger itching inside. 'Hold on. You weren't representing me. You were threatening me.'

Potts held up his hands in surrender. 'I know, I know, and I'm sorry. I thought you'd think it wasn't such a big deal. I'm on your side - no, not quite true, the Chamber of Commerce is on your side.'

Sam rolled his eyes. 'What?'

'I know how it looks, but, listen, can we start again? And call me Phil, please, ok?'

Sam watched the foam on the side of the glass gently disintegrate. 'I don't get it. What do you want? And how did you know I was here anyway?'

'I was having a conversation with Aaron when you and your friend left the hut. He wanted me to make peace with you. He wanted my thoughts on how we could make things right.'

'Well, that's something.'

'I told him I felt the same. I promised I'd try, so I followed you; saw you'd gone into this pub, and thought I'd come and join you. But my phone rang, so I sat on a bench sorting a couple of things out. After that, I was hoping to catch you and your friend.'

Sam glared: 'Her name is Lindsay, and she's gone. I still don't know what you're saying. What's going on?'

He shuffled his chair to keep the sun out of his eyes. 'The thing is, Sam, you're doing a fantastic job at the hut and - I don't know if you realise this - it's becoming quite an attraction. Visitor numbers for the Bay have gone up by a quarter since the word got round about Lindsay Ferris and your art at the hut. Most of our members report significant increases in turnover in the last two months. You two are having an impact.'

Sam couldn't resist a sarcastic dig. 'So, right... now you want me to carry on doing what we're doing?'

Potts smiled: 'Fair point. A bit more than that, Sam. That phone call I took was from the council's new marketing boss. You heard about them doing these campaigns to keep the visitor numbers up all year round?'

'Yeah. I read that they're having lots of meetings about it.'

It was his turn to roll his eyes. 'Yeah, I know, tell me about it. But they're serious and we've promised the backing of the Chamber. The point is, they want you and Lindsay to front the campaign.' He smiled at Sam's shocked expression. 'Posters, interviews, videos... two good looking young people; it's just the image we want. They want to make you an offer, too. And we're talking serious amounts of money.'

'Money? For me? To do what?'

'I hope you don't mind, but I've told Michelle, their head of marketing, that you'd go and see her tomorrow so she can tell you herself. Take Lindsay with you, if she's free, or I'll come if you like. But I'll tell you this: it's a massive opportunity, for you and for Whistle Bay.'

Not for the first time lately, Sam couldn't find any words. He tried to imagine what the big plan might be. 'Billy and Jim will love that, won't they? Me and Lindsay on posters.'

Potts smiled. 'Don't worry about them. They'll benefit big time. What went on today will be the last thing on their minds.'

'I don't get it. One minute you're ganging up on me. Now you're on my side.'

'I know. I'm sorry. It's a lot to take in.'

'It's happening too fast.' He looked into his glass intently. 'If the council want to give me money, there must be some sort of catch.'

Potts laughed: 'You sound just like your dad. You've got your head screwed on, just like he did.'

Sam looked up. 'Did you know him?'

'I met him a few times. Could never persuade him to join. He wouldn't do anything he didn't want to. But he was always friendly. We all liked him; respected him.'

He finished his wine in one gulp and held out his phone. 'Please call that number when you've got over the shock, and book in to see Michelle. You won't regret it. All you have to do is listen. You don't have to say yes.' He smiled. 'I know you won't unless you're one hundred per cent sure.'

He kept talking as Sam keyed the number into Dad's old Nokia.

'I hope you can forgive me, Sam. I told Michelle what happened and how great you were, the way you handled it. I think that clinched it for her. So, 11 o clock tomorrow ok for you?'

'Can we make it half twelve? The hut's usually busy at 11.'

Potts grinned and nodded. 'Your gallery, you mean. Sure. Business first. I like that. Consider it done.' He held out his hand. 'Forgive me?'

Sam held out his hand: 'Yeah, erm…thanks.'

Michelle Brogan took pride in the fact that her ex-colleagues thought she was crazy to leave Birmingham. The usual question was: why would anyone want to work in that prehistoric tumbleweed town, and for less money?

Michelle loved proving people wrong. She wrote on her application that she wanted the job because: 'I achieved everything I set out to do in Birmingham and this would be a completely fresh and exciting challenge.'

And it was working out as planned. The best bit, apart from being able to see the sea from her office window - if she stood on tiptoe in exactly the right place - was that she felt valued. Her opinion counted here, and everyone from the chief exec down took her as she was.

One or two of the male councillors couldn't help patronizing her at her welcome buffet, but they were pussycats compared to the chauvinists in Birmingham.

She gave a speech while they drank sparkling wine, and she kept the notes in her little black book as a reminder of why she'd come here: *Whistle Bay is on the cusp of a new era. With careful planning, fresh thinking, and canny seed funding, the council can steer the town into a very bright and prosperous future. I feel we're all in the right place at the right time.*

Michelle wasn't just talking about Whistle Bay, either. She'd needed to get away to re-build her life after Adrian's passing.

She'd got a reputation in Birmingham for always finding the right words to say in meetings, but lots of local government officers had the same skill. She hoped that what set her apart was that she wanted action, too. And all the signs were that Whistle Bay was ready for it.

Now, two weeks into the job, she was looking across her desk at a good-looking tousle haired lad whose idea of dressing up for a business meeting that could change his life was to wear a shirt and tie under a hoodie. If the rumours were true, he was not to be underestimated, though, and she was impressed by the firm handshake and the eye contact.

He seemed nervous, but in control. She liked that.

She saw something else in his eyes, too: signs that she'd come to recognise in herself since Adrian died. It spoke of a certain vulnerability. She'd read a line in a poem that captured it for her: '*like the dim light of loneliness.*'

Sam looked across the desk, into the eyes of a woman who was about half his size standing up, but seemed to be looking down on him now. Her hair was streaked with silver but her face was young, and he couldn't work out how old she was.

Walking to the town hall, he'd wondered if it had been a mistake to come alone. Lindsay had offered, to join him, but had seemed distant when he was telling her what Potts had said; as if she had something else on her mind. He told her he'd face it himself, and she looked relieved. He still couldn't work out what that was about.

Michelle looked up from her notes and seemed to make her mind up about something. She stood: 'Come on, Sam, let's get comfortable, shall we? This is supposed to be a chat, not a job interview.'

They walked over to leather armchairs in the corner of her office. Her head was on a level with his chest; her office was twice the size of his hut.

She sat opposite, immaculate in a dark grey trouser suit and white shirt, with a Remembrance Poppy badge on her jacket lapel. Sam made a mental note to buy one this week.

She crossed her legs and put a black notebook on the arm of the chair.

'So, Sam, you look like someone who can't quite believe what's happening, is a bit suspicious, and would just like to get on with it. Am I right?'

He nodded. 'Yeah. Things seem to be happening fast after being quiet for so long.'

She nodded. 'That's exactly right. It's a good summary of the whole situation here. The pace of change causes problems for some people, as well as bringing opportunities. It can be hard to cope with. What really counts is the attitude you take. Everything I've heard about you tells me you are an extremely capable, hardworking, dedicated person, who doesn't recognise his own abilities. Do you think that's fair?'

Looking back on it later, it felt like that was the point at which he began to believe in himself. If people were really saying that, he must be doing okay.

But now, he just smiled, nodded and shrugged his shoulders. 'Yeah, that sounds like me.'

She winked at him as she opened her notebook. 'Sorry. It's my age, I have to write everything down.' She flicked to the page she wanted and looked into his eyes again. Sam liked it when people did that, and he was happy to look back.

She cleared her throat. 'Let me read you from notes I made earlier about Whistle Bay. Visitors from August Bank Holiday to current date, up 28 per cent over last year; visitor spend in the same period, up 39 per cent; length of stay up from an average of two nights to 3.5; retail and hospitality turnover up by 20 per cent.' She looked up. 'Does anything in particular strike you, Sam?'

He picked up on it straight away. 'Visitor spend is up by a lot more than retail turnover?'

She nodded. 'Brilliant! Exactly. And do you know why that is?' He shook his head. 'It means a high proportion of visitors are spending their time and money on other things, particularly arts and culture.'

'So they're not going shopping and stuff?'

'That's right. The GBS Theatre has had a great time lately, packing them in. You and Lindsay have done well, too, with your picture sales and the art classes. Oh, and can I say how much I love your pictures?'

Sam smiled: 'You should come to the hut and have a proper look.'

She grinned: 'Thank you, I'd love to, but, sorry to be a bore, back to business... Let's be honest, Lindsay is a massive boost to the town. Her reputation is sky high in the art world: even I've heard of her. And so many people come here simply because she's in town.

'The knock-on effects are clear to see. You said earlier how much better your deck chair rentals have gone. The library has been busier, too, and books in the arts section are the most popular. I could go on... Even the cinema has been selling out seats when normally they only get a few men in raincoats on a wet Wednesday night.'

Sam laughed, and she joined in. 'Sorry, my sense of humour is always getting me into trouble. Forget I said it. The real point is, it doesn't take a genius to see that Whistle Bay has an opportunity to put itself on the map by widening its appeal so that all businesses benefit, and we attract new ones. Come with me, will you, Sam?'

They walked down a corridor of oak doors and big framed paintings of important looking people. Sam wondered if Dad had ever been here. Michelle leaned against one of the heavy doors and he followed her in. It was a big room, intimidating, with wood paneling, tall leaded windows and giant radiators.

There was a long table with padded chairs arranged around it, and a large sheet of paper dazzling against the dark wood.

Michelle invited Sam to stand next to her.

She laughed: 'I couldn't believe this either. I was amazed that a little town like Whistle Bay could find the money to spend making the town hall look like a stately home! Perhaps we shouldn't be too surprised: maybe it just goes to show what a prosperous place it used to be.

'But don't let all this intimidate you. I don't. This room is where we have committee and planning meetings. I wanted to bring you in here to convince you that we have a very serious proposition to put to you. A few of us - including the leader of the council - were here last night, discussing... this.' She slid the sheet to their side of the table, and they leaned in.

Sam could see the outline of a building in blue. He frowned as he tried to make sense of the typewritten notes dotted around, and the boxes of text and arrows that were pointing in all directions.

Michelle turned to lean back against the table. Sam sensed she was building up to something and he felt his heart thudding.

'This is our big idea, Sam. You see, we don't just want you and Lindsay to be the faces of our new marketing campaign. That's important if we are going to provide wider business opportunities, but we'll talk about that another time, with both of you.

'At this stage, we want you to say yes to this... the redevelopment of your hut to create a brand-new arts and cultural centre for Whistle Bay.' She held up a hand. 'I know it's a surprise but bear with me. It would be a home for theatre, exhibitions, art courses, talks, and a whole lot of other stuff. It wouldn't just be a visitor attraction, it would be a benefit to local people, encouraging them to get into arts of any kind, learn and maybe start a new career. It would also include a shop and we'd want to encourage local craftspeople and suppliers to help us stock it up...'

She stopped and looked apologetic. 'You'll have to forgive me. I'm rabbiting on because I'm so excited. So, come on, just tell me, between us, what's your first reaction?'

Sam looked at the drawing again. 'You mean, you want to build this where my hut is now, right on the beach?'

She nodded and pointed to the drawing. 'It would be two floors, and the main entrance would be on the esplanade level. See? People would enter here, then there would be a lift and stairs down to the lower ground floor – beach level, if you like - which would be fronted by decking and a wall to keep the sand out, hopefully. It will look fantastic. I know it's a lot to take in but tell me what you're thinking. First instinct is so important.'

Sam stared at the drawing. 'Well, yeah. It does look amazing.'

She smiled and gestured towards one of the chairs. 'Good. Now let's talk it through.' She pressed a button on the wall and sat next to him, one hand resting lightly on the architect drawing.

'Do you want me to carry on talking, or do you want to ask questions?'

'Erm, I just wondered what happens if I say no?'

She nodded: 'Good question. Well, it turns out that the freehold of this bit of the beach was granted to your family back in the day. I thought you'd just be the leaseholders... But if you didn't want to sell, we would have the option of a compulsory purchase order, which would mean we effectively force you to let us buy it; or we could of course find another site and build it there.

'But we want to do it here. It's an iconic location and it's got that connection with the past through your family business, which is priceless. It's just a perfect symbol of Whistle Bay's regeneration. We think it would be unique in Britain. Built and heated sustainably. Maximum impact. A massive draw. Next question.'

'What about my deckchairs; my business?'

'We could offer you a different location on the beach, or you can take the considerable amount of money we will be offering you, and do what I've done, and do something new.'

'How much money?'

'That's to be negotiated, and not by me; but I can tell you we are looking at a significant sum, which would be the market rate for any property in that position, plus a bit on top as compensation. You must keep that to yourself for the time being, ok?' Sam nodded. 'I think it would make sense for the new centre to retain the deck chairs, as part of the beachside, heritage vibe we want to generate. So we'd be happy to buy your stock as part of the package.'

Sam twisted round as the door creaked open. A grey man in black trousers and white shirt pushed in a trolley and put cups and saucers, a teapot, and a plate of biscuits, on a side table.

Michelle smiled as he pushed the rattling trolley towards the door: 'Thanks Keith.' Sam saw him struggle to get out without bashing the door, so he held the door open, earning himself a grateful smile: 'Thank you sir.'

Michelle nodded. 'Let's take a breather. Would you like some stewed tea and an out of date digestive?'

Sam laughed. 'Yes please!'

She poured the tea. 'Sorry to throw all this at you at once, but there's no other way, really. And please don't be overwhelmed. It's early days. You don't have to say yes to anything. We very much hope you do, but…'

Sam accepted the cup with a nod of thanks. 'Dad told me it doesn't matter how long we think things through, we always know what the right thing is.'

'I'm sure he's right.' She dunked her biscuit. 'You took over the business from him last year, didn't you?'

'Yeah, I promised him just before he died that I'd look after everything for him.'

Michelle nodded. 'I lost my husband last year. The people you love; they never leave you, really, do they?'

'I'm sorry. What happened? Was he -?'

'He died on duty, in Syria. It was just a routine patrol. They hit a landmine. He wouldn't have known anything about it.'

'Oh, that's…'

'Yeah… he was a good man. Had to be to put up with me. We both knew the risks. He told me he faced danger every day, and he always said that if anything happened to him that I should do what I think is right. Like your dad, I suppose. I think he meant that he would understand if I met someone else; that he trusted me… Not that I have met anyone.' She put her cup and saucer on the table. 'Tell me about your dad. What was he like?'

Sam smiled. 'Tough as old boots; well, that's what he always used to say. But everybody liked him. He got dementia in his 60s.'

'What about mum?'

'She died a few years back. She never got over Sean - the youngest.'

'You lost him too? Oh God, I'm so sorry. You've been through so much.'

Sam decided not to tell her about Mikey. 'Yeah, well, so have you. Just got to get on with it. The business was everything to Dad. It was his life, you know?'

She nodded. 'You must have a lot of conflicting feelings. But you're right, we have to get on with it. I'm not trying to be clever, but that's exactly how I feel about Whistle Bay. It's been at rock bottom for too long, and it would be so easy to just sit in a corner and feel depressed. If people like us don't do something, the place will just fall into a state of decay.'

She checked herself, smiling. 'Sorry, I'm off again. Come on, we need more tea. And at least two more digestives.'

Sam stayed for another half an hour, listening mainly as she went through the architect drawings. She stopped to check her watch and he told her he shared her excitement about the project.

She walked with him to the entrance hall and shook his hand. 'I'm so pleased to meet you, Sam. And, don't worry, we'll get back to you very soon with an offer.' She winked: 'One you won't be able to refuse.'

Sam walked along the esplanade, feeling light headed. It felt so familiar: the pastel colours of the three storey hotels facing the sea; the smell of fish and chips; the sound of the sea and the scream of argumentative gulls; the cold salty air.

This was all he'd ever known, and it was all about to change.

In the distance, the hut looked like a squat dark arrow pointing straight up into the cloudy sky.

Chapter 12

Next day, Sam jogged towards Marine Parade.

The rain was bouncing off the pavement and he was just thinking he'd never seen the place so busy, when an umbrella snapped open right in his face.

'Oi!'

The umbrella lifted to reveal Lindsay and Grace, who managed to look apologetic and amused at the same time.

Lindsay held the umbrella over Sam's head, giggling: 'Oh gosh Sam, sorry! Where are you off to in such a hurry?'

'To get coffee, somewhere dry.'

Grace linked his arm. 'Don't be grumpy. Come under here with us. We'll buy you a coffee, won't we Lindsay?'

Sam smiled: 'Okay, you're on. I was on my way to Billy's place.'

Lindsay gave him a look: 'What? In there? The enemy? He'll kick us out straight away, won't he?'

Sam shrugged: 'Let's find out.'

They walked up the crazy paved path through Billy's gaudy collection of garden gnomes.

Billy was in the back, whistling a tune none of them recognised, or wanted to. They were the only customers and Sam pointed to the table nearest the counter. The display was filled with high rise sponge cakes, and plate size scones and teacakes. He watched as they took in the rack of rude seaside postcards, and the 'bathing belle' cuckoo clock.

Grace wasn't impressed: 'These are gross.'

'It's only a bit of fun. Anyway, don't walk out; I want to show him there's no hard feelings.'

'There will be if his coffee's as crap as the decor. No wonder the place is empty. Anyway, what's in the carrier bag?'

'Oh, just a little present.'

The whistling stopped and Billy emerged, wiping his hands on a cloth, and stood behind the counter. 'Good morning, all. What can I get you?'

Sam raised a hand in greeting. 'Morning Billy. All right?'

'Yeah, yeah. Absolutely great. Fine. You?'

'Yep. Thought I'd bring you a couple of new customers. This is Lindsay, who you've already met, and Grace, who you probably already know.'

'Yeah, the estate agent lady.'

Grace smiled patiently. 'The estate agent, yes.'

Billy avoided Lindsay's gaze and came out from behind the sanctuary of his counter. 'What can I get you?'

They ordered coffee and cake, and Sam invited Billy to sit with them.

'I've brought you something, Billy. Hope you don't mind.'

He looked suspicious. 'Oh? What, like a present you mean?'

'Yeah, like a present. I went to see Michelle at the council, and she told me about your plans for this place. I wanted to wish you luck. It sounds really good. Good news for the town, you know.'

Lindsay was absorbed in the task of carefully slicing her walnut cake into bite size pieces, but Grace sipped tea and admired the way Sam was handling this. He was making peace, and letting Billy know that he wasn't intimidated by what happened. She thought that casually mentioning that he was on first name terms with senior people at the council was a stroke of genius, too.

Sam reached for his carrier bag. 'Yeah, we'll come and support you, and put the word round. So, anyway, I brought you this.'

He handed over one of his framed pictures, showing a line of deckchairs in front of the hut.

'Oh, thanks. That's nice of you. I'll definitely... Yeah. Erm...' He stood up quickly, scraping his chair back. 'Just wondering, like... would you like to have a look, when you've finished?'

Lindsay was still chewing on cake, as they followed Billy through a makeshift hardboard door at the back.

The storage rooms and the brick shed had been knocked out to create a large space that was fitted out like a ship, with marine artefacts on the wall, and a teak floor.

Billy kept up his enthusiastic and high-speed patter. 'I'm going to call it Whistle Wine Bar. I'll do wine and tapas. I've

102

got the licence sorted, so I reckon I'll open soon: didn't want to do anything too near Remembrance Day, you know.'

Sam nodded. 'What will you do with the cafe, Billy?'

'Oh, I'll keep that going, just get rid of the old fixtures and fittings so it looks more like this. Spruce the old place up a bit.'

Billy was all smiles when they left, and they promised they'd be there on opening night, if invited. 'Invited? Oh, yes, definitely! Two pretty girls - oh, and you Sam!' He laughed uproariously.

The rain had stopped. Lindsay and Grace linked arms with Sam as they walked to the hut. He told them they made him feel like he'd won the Lottery.

Lindsay squeezed his arm: 'Well, you have, haven't you?' She did a good impression of Billy's booming voice: 'Two pretty girls on your arm.'

'I know he's not PC but give him a break. At least we're talking again. Anyway, are you ok to have a chat?'

Sam opened up the hut, made tea and told them he was going to sell up to make way for a new arts centre; and that he was sure Dad would have said yes, too.

He looked out across the beach, blinking against quick flashes of sunlight. 'The money will set me up. But I'm worried. I'm doing ok now. But I keep wondering, what will I do when I haven't got the hut and the deckchairs?' He turned to Grace. 'I was going to put the house up for sale, too, so I'll have money, but it won't be enough to live off. The way it's going, I'll end up with no work and no home.'

Grace crossed her legs and leaned back in the chair. 'You don't have to sell the house straight away. You could change your mind any time. Keep it, spend some money on it; anything you like. There's no need to worry about that. You haven't committed to the sale, but it's on our books, ready when you are.'

Lindsay nodded. 'That's the thing, Sam. There's no need to rush into anything. You know what councils are like. It'll be months before they get cracking, so just take your time.' She paused, glancing at Grace. 'But if you want my opinion...'

Sam leaned forward. 'Yeah, course I do!'

'I think you should use it as a chance to get away from here, even if it's just for a while.' She paused, putting her mug on the floor. 'I mean, look at me, for example. I love it here, but I won't be here forever.'

Sam looked down at his tea, his hands wrapped round the mug. 'Does that mean you're leaving? Both of you?'

'No Sam, not both of us. Grace is staying. She's got a great business here and loads of friends.'

'But I thought -'

Grace smiled. 'We love each other, Sam, course we do. And we'll keep in touch. But we're trying to let you know it's not the end of the world when things change. We'll still see each other. London is only an afternoon away on the train, and we'll be together for holidays and weekends; and talk every day on the phone – for hours.'

Lindsay smiled: 'You should think about it, Sam. Maybe this is your opportunity. You could go anywhere: London; why not? A guy with your talent, and good looks. You'd have a fantastic time, sell a lot of pictures, have girls panting at your front door…'

Sam spoke quietly. 'Doubt it. So, when are you going?'

'I don't know yet. Not for a while. I've committed to be here while we do that marketing thing for the council, remember? It would look bad if I buggered off back to London straight after telling everyone how gorgeous it is here.'

'Yeah. So, what, a few more months?'

'Yeah, maybe a couple. I'm hoping Michelle will let me give out messages from London after that. But I can be back here in a few hours if I'm needed.'

She looked into his eyes, and he remembered how he felt the first time she did that. He looked away.

Lindsay leaned closer, her voice softened: 'I'm going back, Sam, but I'm not doing the same things. Like you, I'm not sure what I'll do, but we're young, right? We should take chances, see what turns up. It's exciting! I'll still be telling everyone to come and study art here. And I absolutely have to be here when that gorgeous new arts centre opens. Someone told me the uni at Hightown is starting up a new arts degree course next year as well. Isn't that fab?'

Sam glanced at Grace. Was she really okay about Lindsay going? He'd wanted to talk to them to help clear his mind. But he was even more muddled now.

Then his phone rang - Karen.

He answered as he walked down the steps onto the beach. The sand was still pockmarked from the rain and the dark grey clouds were swelling on the horizon.

'Hi Karen.'

'Hey Sam. Just checking in. Nothing to worry about. We wondered if you'd like to come round tonight. Have a bite with us?'

'I'd love to, thanks. Be a chance to give you some good news, too.'

'Right, brilliant. About half six then - give me time to get home and shower and stick the oven chips on.'

Sam laughed. 'Oven chips! I was expecting gourmet dinner.'

'Rude! Takes a lot of skill, heating up ready meals.'

'Yeah, I know. Anyway, thanks, and see you later, Karen.'

He turned to find Lindsay and Grace coming down the steps, giving each other the eye.

'*See you later, Karen.* What do you think, Grace?'

Sam shook his head, but he was laughing. 'Give it a rest.'

He looked at them, standing on the bottom step: Lindsay, slim with her long legs squeezed into tartan leggings; and Grace, in a short skirt and close-fitting red jacket. And he had zero chance of dating either of them. Maybe Lindsay was right: he might have a chance of meeting someone if he moved on.

Karen had laid out the table with a green cloth, knives and forks, and blue Whistle Bay salt and pepper pots.

Mikey had a glass of water with his morphine dropper next to it. He winked. 'Welcome to Karen's caff.'

'Don't let her hear you. Where is she?'

He was having to catch his breath with every few words. 'Having a shower. Still can't believe … she runs there and back … every day.'

'Me neither. Was she always a runner?'

'No idea. Think so. Got medals at school.' He sipped water slowly, his hand shaking as he lifted the glass. 'Got news?'

'Yeah. Shall I tell you both, or…?'

'Yeah, wait… for the boss.'

They heard her footsteps just before she rushed in. She looked at the clock. 'Oh God, I hope this isn't burned!'

Sam turned to look. 'What is it?'

'Chicken kiev and chips. It's been in there five minutes too long.'

'Anything I can do?'

'Yeah. Get the plates out. Cupboard behind you.'

She dished up, and when she sat down Sam caught the fresh smell of her hair.

She got up twice to cut Mikey's food into smaller portions and swapped his fork for a teaspoon.

Sam felt uncomfortable but Mikey seemed oblivious. He patted his lips on a paper towel. 'That was good, chef.'

'Nice to have a happy customer. You okay with it, Sam?'

'Yeah, really nice. Homemade too.'

'Made it last night and kept it in the fridge.'

'You made a lot. Did you know I was coming?'

'I knew you wouldn't say no. Chance for an hour or two with Mikey.'

'And with you, love.'

'What? Sam's here to see you, aren't you?'

Sam nodded. 'Can I tell you my news then?'

'Let's get cleared up first. Help Mikey into his chair in the other room while I shift this lot.'

Sam went back into the kitchen after he'd got Mikey settled. 'Thanks for dinner. Can I do anything?'

'Good timing. I've just done the washing up.' She smiled as she saw his guilty look. 'Is he still awake?'

'He said he wanted a nap, so…'

'He naps most of the time now. The carer says he can hardly get a word out of him.'

'He seemed all right at the table.'

'Yeah, but that's his big effort because you're here. He's trying to make you think he's ok.'

'I can see the change since I last saw him.'

She nodded towards the table and sat with him, screwing up the dishcloth and throwing it into the sink. Sam saw her eyes misting over and reached out, but she backed away: 'Sorry, it's just… the carer called today and told me he's going to have to go in. I've been putting off saying anything. He doesn't know yet. God, I feel awful.'

'I thought he was going to be ok for a while longer?'

'He's taking so much morphine, and they can manage it better if he's in there. I hate myself for saying it, but to be honest, it's the best thing for him. He doesn't do anything; can't even concentrate on the telly. Neither of us are sleeping much, and -'

'Could he come and stay with me for a bit? Give you both a break?'

'No, it's no good, Sam. I'm sorry. I don't want him to suffer any more, so I said yes.'

Sam leaned back in his chair. 'When?'

'Tomorrow.'

He stared. 'Tomorrow? Is that why you -?'

She nodded. 'I didn't want to tell you on the phone. I just thought it would be for the best if you came round to see him, have a little bit of time, before -'

Sam shook his head. 'It's okay, yeah, I understand. I feel so bad about it. I've been thinking about myself all day. Full of it, I was.' He stopped. Karen was controlling her breathing, regaining control, wiping the wetness from under her eyes. 'What happens? Do they come and get him, or do we take him?'

'They're coming at about ten, they said. I've shut the shop for the day. I'll go with him, stay for a while.'

'I'll come and visit later then. Do you want me to stay tonight?'

She shook her head. 'Let's just sit with him, give him your good news, then you can help me get him comfortable, ok?'

'Yeah, course I will, whatever you want.'

She tore off a paper towel and blew her nose. 'What's that look for?'

'I don't know. I've got so much going on in my head. It's like my whole life is changing; something new every day. My job, my house, people in town slagging me off…'

'And then Mikey.'

'Yeah. But what have I got to moan about?' He held her hand briefly. It felt so warm, so soft, so strong.

He smiled, and stood, and pulled her up with him. 'Let's go and have a chat with Mikey.'

He stayed for an hour, doing his best to be upbeat. Mikey listened intently when he told them about the plans for the arts centre, and laughed when Sam told him he might be on a poster advertising the Bay.

Karen sat on a dining chair, watching and listening, as Sam described meeting Michelle at the town hall, and Billy's face when he handed over one of his pictures.

Eventually, Mikey's attention began to wander, and he helped Karen get him into bed.

She followed him down to the door and kissed his cheek. 'Thanks Sam. You cheered him up.'

'I just wish there was something I could do.'

Her voice was flat. 'Just get through it. Like he is. That's what it's all about, isn't it?'

He walked home through a mist of rain that looked ghostly in the glow of the esplanade streetlamps.

Everything he'd been so excited about felt like it was happening to someone else, somewhere else.

The lamps were still out of action in his street, and the house was a dark silhouette against the outline of trees beyond.

He could still hear Karen's voice as he turned the key and pushed through into the hall: 'Just get through it.'

He leaned back against the front door until it clicked shut, then went upstairs and fell onto the bed.

Sam drove round the hospice car park twice before he found a space.

Karen messaged him with the room number, and Mikey was grinning when Sam walked in, feeling like he was bouncing on the cushioned flooring.

Mikey pulled the buds out of his ear: 'You found me then?'

'Blimey. You look better than me. Have they got any spare beds in this hotel?'

'I'll put a word in. It's alright here. Especially the nurses…'

'Behave or they'll chuck you out.'

Mikey chuckled as Sam walked to the sliding glass door. He whistled: 'You've even got your own decking. Is there a bar an' all?'

'There might be, but I'm on the waggon, so change the subject, will you?'

Sam smiled and threw him a copy of the Bay Times. 'Read that instead. There's a good story on page 3.'

He sat on a new looking armchair and stretched out his legs, waiting for Mikey's reaction. He didn't have to wait long.

'Oh look at you, nipper... I like the headline. You should frame that, matey.'

He held it up: *Council picks dream team for town campaign.*

Sam rolled his eyes. 'I won't be able to show my face in town.'

Mikey laughed. 'You won't have to. Your ugly mug is all over the paper.'

Sam sighed. 'Yeah, whatever. Anyway, what's going on? You look really well.'

'I feel good. They've put me on these new drugs. It's like they said - their job is to to make me feel comfortable, help me through - what do they call it? - oh yeah, the end of life.'

'Well, you're in good hands. Best place to be. You gave me a surprise, looking so chirpy. Has Karen gone home?'

'No, she's talking to the boss, apparently.'

Sam nodded and Mikey shuffled so he could swing his legs round. 'Give me a hand to that armchair, Sammy.'

Sam pointed to the flashing lights on the wall behind his bed. 'Should you be getting up?'

'Yeah, yeah. They only hook me up a couple of times a day; like charging a phone.'

They sat facing each other, gently warmed by weak sunlight that looked like spilled milk in the greyness of the sky. Sam watched as a blackbird hopped on the decking and cocked its head, watching him.

He was conscious of Mikey gazing at him. 'What's on your mind, Mikey?'

He frowned: 'Ah, it's weird. I feel good, and what a place to be, eh? Little palace. Funny, really, it's the nicest room I've ever been in... The thing is: I'm worried about Karen.'

'She seems all right.'

'I know, but she'll still need help.'

'Don't worry, I'll keep an eye on her.'

Mikey nodded. 'She's been a great mate to me, and, well, I'd like it if you and her could carry on being friends.' He grinned. 'Let's face it, you need friends, even though you're a celebrity. Hey, can I have your autograph?'

'Bugger off!'

They laughed, just as the door opened.

A nurse came in. 'That's music to my ears - Oh sorry, didn't know you had company.'

Mikey just nodded and winked at Sam.

She was wearing a bright blue uniform and her brown hair was tied back into a pigtail. She was carrying a plastic tray with a bottle and some containers which she put on the table next to the bed. 'There. That's your stuff sorted for later. I'll see you soon.'

Sam was impressed. She was so calm, unhurried. She smoothed the bed sheets and plumped up the pillows, and smiled as she left, the door closing softly behind her.

Mikey winked: 'Told you.'

'Yeah, she seemed nice.'

'Blimey, you sound like Dad.'

'What?'

'Well, you do. You need to get out there; find a woman. Nipper like you, there must be someone who'd have you.'

Sam pretended to be interested in a plant pot on the terrace. 'Can we talk about something else?'

'The weather?'

'You are feeling better, aren't you?'

Karen came in, carrying flowers. She patted Mikey on the shoulder, sat on the bed, and read out the card from the bouquet: 'With love and best wishes. We're thinking of you. Lindsay and Grace.'

She carried on talking, but he was only half listening. She raised her voice: 'Sam, are you alright?'

'Oh, sorry, yeah. Just thinking, you know.'

'Bad idea.'

'Yeah. Sorry, what were you saying?'

'They've got a spare bedroom here for family, in case one of us needs to stay over.'

'Okay. What are you going to do? Go home tonight?'

'Yeah, I'll go for a run, and get some tea. Soon be time for us to go anyway. The boss'll be round to check up on you, Mikey.'

'I hope it's that fit one.'

Karen laughed. 'Whatever they're giving you, I want some. Anyway…' She put an arm round his shoulder. 'See you tomorrow. Sure you're alright?'

He nodded and patted her cheek.

Sam gave Mikey the thumbs up on his way out, and walked to the car park with Karen, along pea gravel paths through neat flower beds.

She looked up at the building. 'I can't believe this place.'

'It's amazing. I'm glad he's looking so well.'

'Yeah. He's livelier than I've seen him for ages. Weird, isn't it? He's not got long to live and he's happier than both of us put together.' She looked at Sam for a moment.

'What is it?'

'The nurse said we mustn't build our hopes up. He's dosed up; she says he's nearly on the maximum already and there's not much more they can do. She said to think of it as giving him a few days off.'

Sam sighed. 'Right.'

She shook her head. 'It might be a few days before they have to knock him out, so he doesn't feel any pain. They're very nice but they tell it like it is. His whole body is shutting down, Sam.'

She turned and kicked the front wheel.

Sam put an arm round her shoulder. 'I know it's a crap thing to say, but I'm glad he's here and he's not going to suffer. We've just got to hold on, like we said.'

'Yeah, you're right.'

'Mikey asked me to look after you.'

'Oh, did he now? Well, thanks, but I can look after myself.'

'I do know that.' They laughed and Sam spoke without thinking. 'Can I see you later? Maybe go out for a meal? We need a break.'

She opened the car door, took off her leather jacket and looked at him for what seemed like forever. Then she smiled: 'I'd like that. I might even dress up, so you'd better pick somewhere nice. Oh yeah, and since you've got to look after me, you're paying.'

Chapter 13

Michelle's wolf whistle echoed round the town hall foyer as Sam and Lindsay pushed in through the revolving doors. 'Look at you two! Shall we go before I'm thrown out for inappropriate behaviour? The car's waiting.'

Sam had tried to resist buying a new suit, but Lindsay won. At least he felt comfortable in the one Lindsay chose for him: a charcoal Paul Smith three piece. She also persuaded him to buy black leather brogues, a non-iron shirt and a blue patterned tie.

He checked his reflection in the glossy paintwork of the limousine that was waiting on the cobbled forecourt. Lindsay came up beside him in her red skirt and jacket: 'Don't worry, darling, you look gorgeous.'

'Shut up!'

Michelle sat in the front and half turned. 'Travelling in style today; better get used to it. You both ok?'

Sam nodded. He'd gone over it with Lindsay: 'Just be yourself; don't try to be clever; don't add anything; just answer the question and remember the key points; and keep your head still when you're talking.'

Michelle checked her notes: 'We've got a good turnout today. Regional TV, the Beeb and the commercials; radio; and a few papers. There's a rumour the Guardian is interested too.'

Lindsay was checking her lipstick in a tiny mirror. 'That doesn't surprise me. This has got art and cool and retro written all over it.'

Michelle laughed and pointed at the three of them: 'Which is which?'

Sam just came out with it: 'I'm definitely retro.'

Lindsay snorted: 'Stop it Sam. You'll make me smudge my lippy.'

Michelle reminded them of the running order as the car turned past the harbour and onto the esplanade, slowing to a crawl over each speed bump, before pulling into a space that was being cleared of cones by a woman in a high vis jacket.

A handful of police officers stood in front of a crowd of onlookers.

Lindsay squeezed Sam's hand and whispered: 'We've got an audience. We'll be a great team.'

Michelle said the Mayor would be hosting the event. 'Try and stop him,' she'd laughed. He used to own a sweet shop, and Sam remembered buying Sally a box of Maltesers from him, asking him to wrap it in brown paper and write her name on it. The shop shut down a few years later and re-opened as a kebab takeaway.

And there he was: a roly poly man, now Councillor Chivers, who liked to be called Your Worship, but was forever known to Sam's generation as Choccy.

He showed no signs of recognition as they walked up to join him on the platform. The redness of his face toned nicely with his Mayoral robes. 'How'do. Big day; proud day. Are you ready.'

Then he cleared his throat, and glanced at Michelle, who was ushering the onlookers into a semi-circle. She gave him a thumbs-up, then stepped onto the platform with them.

Sam wished he had her confidence: 'Good morning and welcome everyone. Thanks for being with us at the launch of what we all intend to be a new era. We're going to put the Bay well and truly on the map. And this is just the beginning. Now, can I introduce our Mayor, Councillor Chivers… Mr Mayor.'

Sam managed to look interested through his speech, then, after polite applause, the Mayor led the way to a trailer covered by a blue tarpaulin.

His Worship beamed as he pulled the rope to reveal the poster, which showed Lindsay and Sam waving against a backdrop of a framed picture of the sea and the hills that she had painted, with giant letters: WHISTLE BAY - IT'S PICTURE PERFECT!

Sam joined in the applause, then followed Michelle and Lindsay to one side. He had his notes in his pocket, but it was too late now. He muttered to himself; keep smiling, don't stutter.

Most of the attention was on Lindsay, and she laughed and chatted as if she was meeting friends. Then a guy turned round wielding a microphone and with a recorder hanging off his shoulder: 'Hi, Sam, isn't it?'

'Yes, Sam Taverner, that's right.'

'I'm Josh, Independent Radio. So, Sam, tell us how it feels to be on a poster that's going to be plastered all over the country.'

Sam clicked into right gear straight away: 'Well, it's an honour, simple as that. My family has been in business here for a long time. They were always proud to be in Whistle Bay and now I'm proud to be helping to tell everyone about what a great place it is.'

He could see some of the others edging nearer, a few taking notes. Michelle and Lindsay smiled encouragement as he glanced across.

The radio reporter pressed buttons on his recorder and looked up again, moving the microphone slightly further away from Sam's face. 'Great, thanks, Sam. So what would you say is the big attraction of this place? I mean, let's be honest, it hasn't exactly been top of the visitor charts lately, has it? And you must be one of the youngest here.'

'Maybe, but it's changing, helped by people like Lindsay who rediscovered Whistle Bay after coming here as a child. I think she's shown that there's a lot of natural beauty here, and it's thanks to her that so many people are coming here to do art. But there's lots for everyone here, including young people - like Lindsay and me - and it's fantastic that the council and local businesses are investing for the future.'

'You're an artist, too, I gather?'

'Oh, well, trying to be, yes. Lindsay encouraged me to take it up and I'm learning every day.'

'Final question: we all want to know. You look like a really happy couple on that poster. So, tell us, we're all dying to know: are you two an item?'

Sam laughed. 'No. Lindsay is a great friend and a brilliant artist; that's all, honest!'

Michelle stepped in:. 'Okay, shall we leave it there for now? You're all invited to come back with us to the town hall for a bite to eat, and something to drink, obviously. You can chat some more with Lindsay and Sam, too; or even me, if you like.'

Sam glanced across at Jivin Jim's upmarket new sign: 'Traditional arcade games for discerning people'. It looked good against the new red and cream paintwork, too. He wondered briefly if he'd modernized the music he played, too.

Michelle linked his arm and spoke softly: 'That was perfect, Sam. Thank you so much. Can you survive another hour?'

'Yeah, that's okay. Don't tell anyone, but I've enjoyed it.'

Lindsay appeared from nowhere. 'I knew it! You were born to this. You've been hiding in that hut too long. He's a star, isn't he?'

Michelle nodded and steered them back to the car. 'I've been in this game a long time, Sam, and I've never seen anyone seem so natural. Young, and handsome, too. Where have you been all my life?'

Lindsay laughed: 'He didn't even blush when you said that.'

The noise in the committee room reminded him of Lindsay's art exhibition. But this time, he felt part of it. He moved round the room, fielding questions, flicking through phone pictures of his hut and some of his paintings, and didn't stutter once.

Michelle introduced him to a lifestyle magazine reporter called Shelley, who said she was fascinated by the beach hut and his paintings and could she come round to do an interview sometime.

'We could go now, if you like.'

'Really?' She checked her watch, almost spilling her wine in the process. 'Oops! Well, yes, I'm up for that.'

Sam told Michelle and she nodded her approval.

An hour later, Shelley was closing her notebook, promising him a double page spread and waving goodbye. Sam felt good. He changed into jeans and a flannel shirt, and sat on the highchair; elbows - and a mug of tea - on the shelf, watching the gulls glide and swoop. The sea was choppy, and the sky was threatening.

The door creaked, reminding Sam the hinges needed replacing. But then he wondered whether there was there any point; it was all going to be knocked down soon.

The sounds evoked a memory of Dad in the armchair, frowning over a word search. He'd be shaking his head at the sight of Sam in a suit, giving interviews: 'What are you doing, all poshed up?'

Sam smiled and whispered: 'It's time to move on, Dad.'

He relaxed that night by painting a new deckchair picture.

When he took it to Shirley Sugar in the morning, she gave him a wine gum and said it simply had to have a sandy coloured frame.

As he stepped out onto the street, it struck him that Shirley had a reputation for being stand-offish, but he'd always found her very friendly. A bit flirty at times, too, but he didn't object to that.

Her shop door jangled like a wind chime as he closed it. He wondered if Shirley's life had also changed, thanks to the new visitors and the interest in the arts. Business was obviously picking up because she'd already got new display units and a new card reader.

It was a short walk to Grace King Property Services, so he took the chance to look at the other shops on the way.

He'd always thought it must be harder, being tucked away on the back streets, away from the esplanade. Most visitors headed for the beach, naturally enough.

But there were signs that they were doing better here, too: some fresh paintwork at Doris's DIY Shop; a smart metal bistro table with flowers in pots outside the florist; and a new A board outside Phils Phones.

Sam smiled: he still hadn't got round to putting the apostrophe in. He was known as a penny pincher, and the joke was that he did it to save himself on printing costs. Aaron claimed credit for his nickname - Foolish Phil.

Grace came out from the back office. Sam liked the way she'd tied her hair back and wanted to say so but thought better of it. She offered him coffee, but he said he wasn't stopping: 'I just came to say that I'm not going to put the house on sale yet, if that's ok.'

'Of course, it is, Sam. There's no rush. What decided it for you, just out of interest?'

117

'There's too much happening all at once. It's not just the hut, you know, and the paintings, and the bloody poster.'

Grace smiled. 'You both look great. I'm so jealous.'

'Yeah, right. You can take my place if you like... You and Lindsay would be a much better look.' He felt himself blushing. 'Anyway, it's mainly because of Mikey.'

'Oh yes, of course. How is he?'

'He seems fine. Really bright. But we have to make the most of it because he's in a really bad way. They don't think he'll hold out much longer.'

Grace shook her head. 'So sad.'

They talked about house prices, and she asked him what would happen to Mikey's place. 'Karen, isn't it? Do you think she'll stay there?'

'Yeah, I think she will.'

Grace topped up her coffee from the machine and told him she and Lindsay were going to Billy Whistle's opening night. He showed her his invitation: 'I'll see you there. I'm a VIP guest.'

Grace laughed. 'Yeah, Lindsay got one of those. Wonder what special privileges we'll get?'

'Toasted teacake and a mug of tea, if we're lucky.'

But the Grand Opening of the Whistle Wine and Tapas Bar exceeded everyone's expectations.

Billy looked chipper in a dinner jacket and red bow tie. His newly recruited staff - allegedly poached from Poundland - wore blue jackets with WW badges on the lapel and worked the crowd with their trays of wine - 'white or red, sir, madam?'

Sam stuck to orange juice and chatted with Aaron, who looked like something out of Strictly Come Dancing, in a glittery jacket and pink shirt.

'Hope we're forgiven, Sammy?'

'Course you are. I was narked at the time, but I can see now why you might be annoyed. It's been a tough year. We were all a bit down, I reckon.'

'Anyway, you're a good lad, and - oh, hey up, here comes trouble.'

Michelle smiled and nodded at them both. She was clutching a large glass of red and it looked like it wasn't her first. She squeezed Sam's arm as she stepped in between them, so close he could smell her perfume.

'Can I have a word, Sam?' She smiled sweetly at Aaron. 'Can I just borrow him for a second? You don't mind, do you?'

Aaron gave her a toothy grin. 'Help yourself, love.'

She giggled. 'Don't mind if I do.'

They found a corner near the door that led out onto the new terrace. 'Things are moving quickly, Sam. We're getting a great reaction to the posters; quite a few callers say they've seen it and it made them want to know more.'

Sam nodded: 'That's good.'

'So; how would you feel if I said the Leader wants to fast track the arts centre scheme?'

'I dunno. What does that mean?'

Michelle drained her glass and picked a new one from a passing waiter. Sam wondered briefly how he managed to keep the tray balanced when one was taken off, but Michelle was still talking.

'He wants the new arts centre up and running in time for the new holiday season, which means we have about three months to get it done.' She paused. 'Which means we need to finalise the deal, Sam.'

He looked round. 'Now?'

She laughed a little too loudly and Sam saw a few heads turning their way. No sign of Lindsay and Grace, though. 'Well not right now, no. How about tomorrow morning, my office, ten o'clock.'

It wasn't a question. He nodded: 'Yeah, that's fine.'

She smiled, then looked over his shoulder. 'Right, good. See you then. Must move on. Mix and mingle, that's me.'

Just when he needed a drink there wasn't a tray to be seen. He smiled and nodded at people he didn't know as he pushed through into the other room.

He heard them above the noise before he saw them. Lindsay and Grace waved from the bar and pointed at something between them.

Lindsay looked cross. 'Where have you been? We've been saving this stool for you for absolutely ages.'

Grace grinned. 'Well about ten minutes, since Lindsay blagged a couple of blokes into giving their seats up for us.'

'Shut up, Grace.'

Sam sat between them, and Lindsay announced cheerfully that it was his round and it was the least he could do to make it double G and Ts. 'Well, you can afford it, can't you darling?'

Sam caught Grace's eye and winked. 'So, you don't want to share a bottle of champagne then?'

Lindsay kissed his cheek: 'Sam, I've always loved you, you do know that don't you?'

He felt slightly dizzy when the fizz kicked in, but Lindsay solemnly advised him to stick at it. 'Practice, Sam; I keep telling you – practice, and plenty of salted peanuts.'

The rest of the night passed by in a haze of laughter and perfume, and shouted conversations with strangers. But by the time he'd walked home through a curtain of fine rain, he couldn't recall a single thing anyone had said.

The call came just after 8 next morning.

He was sitting at the table in his boxers, rehydrating with his second mug of tea, and trying to be interested in radio news reports about politics and the value of sterling.

He switched it off when the phone rang.

'Sam. It's Karen. The hospice has been on. Mikey's worse. They think we should go and see him today.'

'Oh God. I thought he'd have longer…' The phone crackled, then he heard other voices. 'Hello?'

'Sorry, had to go out to get a better signal. They want to stop the pain, but that'll mean sedating him.'

'When are you going in?'

'I'm going to shut the shop at lunchtime. So, about two.'

'Right. See you there then, or shall I leave it a bit later?'

'Get there about half two if you can. Are you alright? You sound a bit hoarse?'

'Yeah, I'm fine.'

'See you later, Sam.'

120

'I wish I could take Mikey out to the pub one last time. He'd love that.'

He could hear the smile in her voice. 'Let's smuggle a barrel in with us; see if they notice.'

His denim jacket was hanging on the back of the kitchen door. He put his phone and wallet in the inside pocket, then whisked three eggs in a bowl, melted butter in the smallest pan and put bread in the toaster.

He could hear kids outside shouting and laughing, on their way to school. He'd seen a few girls in the park when he opened the bedroom curtains, having a smoke behind a tree.

School... where everything was mapped out for you and your parents told you to work hard because it was the best way to set yourself up for the rest of your life. But no-one knew how long that would be. Sean didn't have long. Now it was Mikey's turn. Was there something in the family genes?

He thought about that as he ate. The more he went over it, the more it felt like he needed to make the most of his time.

Things had changed for the better, financially, at least. He should be buzzing, but sadness and guilt always seemed to be lurking.

When he'd met Karen at Valentine's a few nights ago, she said it made her angry the way parents put pressure on their kids. She thought he'd been caught in a trap by his promise to look after things when Dad died.

'What does that mean anyway? Look after things? It's unfair to put that on someone. You need to tell yourself you've done your best, then take your chances when they come. Stop looking back. It's your life.'

Her words had fired him up at the time, and they did again now.

He couldn't do anything about the past, or Mikey, but maybe it was his chance to change his life.

He put the dishes in the washing up bowl to soak, grabbed his denim jacket and changed his mind. He threw it into the wardrobe and twenty minutes later, he was walking into town to meet Michelle; wearing his Paul Smith suit.

He sat in the Town Hall foyer, feigning interest in an out of date edition of The Economist. He'd felt confident on his way in, but he wasn't so sure of himself now.

There was something intimidating about the marble floor, the wood panels, the people looking important with their folders and briefcases.

He gave up on the magazine and tried to concentrate on the notes he'd made. When he looked up again, Michelle was walking towards him. They shook hands and she asked him if he was ready, and he smiled and said he wasn't but let's do it.

He followed her to the room with the big table where she'd shown him the architect drawings. The suit was meant to give him confidence, show everyone he was moving up, but he was wondering if he'd have the guts to negotiate if she made a low offer.

Then he saw three other people gathered by the window, and his stomach lurched.

Michelle called them over and Sam flicked on the smile he'd used for the poster launch. He shook hands with the leader of the council; a guy in a v neck sweater from the planning department; and a stern woman with felt tip eyebrows who introduced herself in a surprisingly deep voice as Julie, head of finance.

Michelle pulled out a chair for Sam and sat next to him, His shirt collar felt tight and he longed to loosen his tie. Michelle poured him a glass of water.

The council leader seemed a long way away, on the other side of the table. He looked like his face had been polished, and Sam reckoned he'd had his teeth whitened. But he sounded matey enough.

'Good morning, everyone, and a special welcome to Sam. I'm not staying for the meeting, Sam, but I wanted you to know how impressed I am with the way you are representing our town. I'm seriously wondering whether to embarrass you even more by nominating you as our ambassador.'

Sam saw Michelle nodding. 'I also want to say how excited we all are about the opportunities that lie ahead, and to promise that you will be happy with the offer we make to you today.'

He looked at the others. 'The officers know my stance on this. We want to make the arts centre happen, but we don't want to do that in a way that makes you feel resentful or dissatisfied. You and your friend Lindsay have done a lot for the Bay already, and we value that. So, if you have any concerns about what these people put to you now, you must let me know, ok?'

Sam nodded and cleared his throat: 'I will, sir, thank you. I'm sure it'll be fine.'

He nodded and smiled, then glanced at Michelle. 'I think that's a subtle hint. It will be fine, won't it, Michelle?'

'I'm sure it will, Leader. Do you want me to get started?'

He patted Sam on the shoulder as he walked out. Michelle slid a sheet of paper across.

'I know this must be a bit intimidating, Sam, so let's just get on with it. That's our offer, and we're all praying you're happy with it.'

Sam didn't trust himself to speak, his mouth felt so dry. He hunched over the proposal as if it was the start of an exam. and scanned the column of figures. The room was so quiet he could hear her breathing.

He looked through it again, like Grace had said, just to make sure.

He looked up and managed to keep the excitement out of his voice.

'That looks fine, thank you.'

'350 thousand quid? Sam! That's amazing... No, it's not. It's a realistic price, so fair play to the council.' Grace gave him the thumbs-up. 'And you didn't even have to haggle?'

'I just said I'd take the agreement away so I could check it all over, and I'd sign it and give it back tomorrow.'

'Sam, you're doing all the right things. Your mum and dad wouldn't believe it, would they?'

Sam shook his head. 'I can't believe it either. It's bonkers. I reckon it must be happening to someone else.'

'Well, it is, isn't it?' She smiled as Sam frowned. 'No, I mean you're a different person now. You've changed, even from when I first met you.'

She pointed to the sofa against the wall by the window. 'Why don't you sit down, let me make you coffee and we can talk about what you need to do next.'

'Next?'

She pulled a face. 'Yeah, next. Like for instance, what are you going to do with that money? Stick it in your back pocket? You've got to have a plan.'

'Well I was just going to put it in the bank for a bit.'

'That's not a bad start, but it's a lot of money to just leave there, gathering dust for you, but earning interest for them. Plus, you need a solicitor to help you with the sale of the hut. And you need to make sure that the offer covers everything.'

'Like what?'

'Like compensation for your lack of earnings from the business. You are giving up a company that's making money, remember.'

Sam sniggered. 'Yeah, right. Just about.'

'Come on. You've done well lately and it's the latest figures that count, so you need advice.'

She talked and he sipped coffee and ate shortbread biscuits and listened.

He promised to read the stuff she printed out for him. She gave him a folder to keep it in and he shook his head: 'I'll do without the folder, thanks.'

Everyone in the queue turned as Loud Linda wolf whistled. Sam just looked at the cakes.

By the time it was his turn at the counter, he'd made a big decision. 'Got a spare table, Linda?'

She gave an over-the-top show of surprise then grabbed a menu with an elaborate flourish and bustled off into the back room: 'Clear the way! Celebrity incoming.'

Sam followed, shaking his head in rueful apology at the few faces he recognised, and sat by the window that overlooked the back of Billy Whistle's new terrace.

Linda was obviously determined to make the most of it. 'And what would sir prefer for his luncheon?'

'How about a big mug of tea and a bacon buttie?'

124

'Would sir require the brown or red sauce with his sandwich?'

At least now she wasn't talking loudly enough for the whole place to hear. He laughed. 'Brown, Linda. Cut it out, will you?'

'Sorry, love. Only teasing. We all love ya, you know that don't you?'

'Yeah, course I do. How's business anyway?'

'Good, darling, yeah... A lot better thanks to you and that gorgeous girl of yours.'

'What; Lindsay? She's not my girl!'

'Oh, so you're not taken then. Right, just wait till I tell the staff.' She stopped and smiled. 'Won't be long with your grub, love. Take no notice of me.'

He realised as he waited that he'd got over the excitement of the council's offer. He kept telling himself it wouldn't change his life; it wasn't like winning the Lottery, it would just mean he didn't have to worry about money - if he was careful.

The doorstep sandwich was up to Linda's usual standards. He sat back and dabbed the grease off his lips, then sliced off a few strips of the rind and wrapped them in a serviette.

Half an hour later, he was sitting on the hut steps, trying to tempt Gary, who was keeping his distance today.

'What's up Guv'nor? Is it my suit?'

Gary angled his head so he could keep an eye on a rival on the hut roof.

Sam loved watching Gary. It was difficult to believe that something that was just white and grey with dots of yellow could be so beautiful and so aggressive: and then so gentle when he took food from his hand.

He'd tried to paint him, but none of the pictures looked right and he hadn't been able to work out why. But now, he wondered... maybe he was forgetting Lindsay's first instructions at the art class, to draw what you see, not what you think is there.

Gary was different. Special. He had his own character.

Sam sat for a moment, lost in thought, the sting of sand on his face. He just had to find a way to capture that character.

The wind was picking up and Gary mewled softly. Sam sensed he knew it was time to move on. He took a couple of paces and flew up to face into the wind. He adjusted his wings to steady himself, then turned and let the invisible force carry him away.

Sam watched until he was just a speck of light against the charcoal sky.

Mikey was sitting on the terrace, wrapped in a green blanket.

Karen was with him, and they talked about the weather, mainly to keep a conversation going for Mikey's benefit. He just raised a bony hand when Sam appeared and looked into the distance.

'Brought you some flowers, Mikey.'

Karen took them off him and put the bouquet on his lap. 'Look at those, aren't they lovely?'

Mikey nodded once.

'I'll put them in your room. Come and help, Sam.'

She talked as she arranged the flowers. 'He's out of it. I spoke to the nurse, and she said the cancer is so aggressive it's surprised them.' She sighed. 'Sorry, Sam, but we're going to have to face up to it. He's not going to last much longer.'

'I don't know what to say to him.'

'I know. I managed a little chat on the phone, before the drugs kicked in. They said to try and be as normal as possible now. He can hear and he understands. He's just so full of medication.'

Sam punched his fist into his hand. 'I just wish there was something we could do. Can't we just take him somewhere?'

'Come on Sam….'

'Look, why not? We can push him in the wheelchair, can't we? Take him to the beach, or something.'

'Sam, stop… It wouldn't do him any good. Let him be. He told me again that he's ready.' She sat on the bed. 'He told me last week he reckoned dying would be like going out to sea on his own.'

Sam felt the lump in his throat and sat with her and held her hand. 'I'll go and get us a brew and we'll sit with him for a while. We don't even have to talk, do we? Just be with him.'

They sat with him for an hour, then a nurse came. "Hi Mikey. We need to get you back inside now, get you comfortable.'

She asked Sam and Karen to wait for her in the corridor as she got him settled in. They sat in silence, until they heard the regular beep of the machines as the heavy door opened and closed with a sigh.

The nurse's name badge said Machiko and she told them she came to England from Japan ten years ago. 'Mikey is very weak now, but I wonder how are you both? This is difficult time and we can help if you want to talk any time.'

Karen nodded. 'Thank you, but I think we will be okay.'

Machiko looked at Sam. She was so small and thin, and he guessed she was younger than him, but she seemed so strong. 'And you, sir? Sam, isn't it?'

'Yeah. Same, thanks. How long, before …?'

She pointed to the waiting area, made up of blue upholstered armchairs, and a coffee table with today's newspapers. Sam was about to say it looked like a smart living room, but then he thought that hospices wouldn't have living rooms, for obvious reasons.

Machiko gestured gracefully: 'Please, let's move over here for a moment.'

She sat on the edge of her chair, knees pressed together, hands clasped in her lap, eyes fixed on them.

She spoke so quietly, gently, and firmly: 'Remember that everything you are feeling is normal. We all react differently. Sometimes, it can be a relief and people feel guilty for that. Maybe it helps to remember that Mikey is suffering a lot, and soon he will not be suffering any more. Also, please know that we are here for you as well as for him, so you must talk to us anytime.'

They thanked her and walked slowly to the car park.

'How do you feel now, Karen?'

'A bit better. She made it seem like, I dunno, natural.'

'Yeah, that's how I felt. It is, I suppose.' Their steps crunched on the gravel. The only other sound was the distant drone of traffic. 'Were you tempted to see the chaplain, like she offered?'

127

'No. I'm not into that. When it's over, it's over.'

'My mum used to believe in it. Made us all go to Sunday School, learn the Lord's Prayer. I can still remember it.'

'Do you ever say it?'

'No.'

'There you are then.' She turned to him. 'Call me if it starts getting to you, ok?'

'I'll be okay. I've got it in my head that he was right.'

'What do you mean?'

'I can deal with it if I think he's going out in his boat and he's not coming back.'

She opened the car door. 'See you soon, Sam.'

He waved as she drove away; her car shrinking to nothing down the long straight driveway.

Chapter 14

November was shivering towards its conclusion while Sam was adding names to the art class waiting list and trying to find new ways to capture the elusive essence of a seagull called Gary.

There wasn't much point doing maintenance at the hut, so he put the heater on and experimented with colours and techniques. When he had created eight versions of Gary, he gave in and asked Lindsay for help.

She stared at them, turned and smiled: 'They're top, Sam.'

They warmed their hands on mugs of tea as she passed on some tips. 'Work on bleeding the colours; try the splatter technique to add more texture; and think about the focal point.'

She picked up his most recent attempt and studied it again: 'This is the one, Sam. Look at that expression. That is Gary!'

Sam nodded. Lindsay moved to sit at the window, chin resting on her hands. 'I'm leaving in a couple of weeks.'

'I thought you were s-staying till next year.'

'I thought I was too. I've been dreading telling you. But they've offered me a big exhibition, and a residency at the V and A -'

'What's that?'

'The V and A? It's a big -'

'I know what that is, I meant the residency thing.'

She turned and put a hand on his arm. 'Sorry. Treating you like a village idiot. The residency means I get my own space to work on new ideas, new art, and get other people excited and involved. It's a big thing Sam. I can't say no.'

Sam watched a gull glide effortlessly out to sea. 'What about the art classes?'

'I know. I'm sorry. I'm such a pain. That's why I wanted to tell you now. Either we find someone else, or we just have to cancel for a bit, till the new arts centre opens.'

'Yeah, but that'll be months.'

'Could you do it?' He looked incredulous. 'Come on, it's not a bad idea.'

'I've only just learned. I can't teach anyone.' He nodded at the Gary paintings. 'You're still teaching me. Anyway, I stutter.'

'No, you don't! Hardly ever... Look, I could give you all my notes. It's all written out - every lesson. Why not? Look ... we could offer for a reduced price. We could say we can carry on with the lessons using my notes; tell them we won't be able to offer any personal tuition, but they can still come and practice and meet other artists. I bet lots would jump at it. And the women would just love having you as their tutor.'

Sam frowned. He knew he was sounding sulky, but he couldn't stop himself. 'Well, maybe... I'm going to need to keep busy during the winter, what with you going, and Mikey ...'

'Oh Sam. I'm sorry.'

He stood with his back to the window. She moved into his arms, and her voice was muffled. 'I can hear you thinking.'

He closed his eyes as if that would somehow preserve the moment. 'Yeah, I do think sometimes. What am I thinking?'

'You're feeling a teeny bit sorry for yourself.' She looked up. 'I can't blame you. It's awful about Mikey. I feel sorry for myself, too: I'm going to miss you loads.' She pushed away. 'But you're going to come and see me, and promise me you won't tell anyone, but I'm going to invite you to come and spend a week with me at the V and A. We could work on something together. Imagine that! Michelle would wet herself at all the publicity we'd get, plus you'd get your name known in little old London. And we'd be together for absolutely ages... What do you think?'

'Are you serious? You're not just saying it to make me feel better?' She shook her head, and he could tell by the smile on her face that she knew she'd won him over.

'Well, yes! So, tell me when you're going, and I'll come and wave you off.'

'Hang on. I haven't gone yet! Anyway, you can only come if you promise to stand on the station platform and cry a lot as I dab my eyes with an embroidered handkerchief and blow you a kiss from the train.'

'I'm not promising that -' He stopped. 'Wait a minute…I'm being dumb. I've just agreed to sell the hut to the council, and they want to start work in a few weeks. So where am I going to do the art class?'

Lindsay smiled annoyingly. 'Ah, well, you see my dear, I have a cunning plan.'

He had to admit it was a master stroke.

During the day, Billy's new extension was more like a large conservatory, so there was plenty of natural light. It was big so they'd be able to increase class numbers, so the extra income would compensate for Billy's fee. And Billy would think his little protest at the hut with Chamber Potts had been a victory.

Billy said yes straight away and offered to provide free tea and coffee.

They shook hands on the deal and Sam walked back to the hut to work out the numbers and try to imagine life without Lindsay.

He was washing the dishes after lasagna and oven chips when Karen called. He left the pots in the sink and told her he'd meet her at the hospice reception area.

He drove fast; the mixture of sadness, self-pity, panic and grief growing inside. As he turned into the car park, he remembered Mikey's words: 'Don't worry about me. Just be there for Karen.'

It felt so familiar, making promises to everyone in his family just before they left him. But this time, he realised it helped him bury his feelings, take his mind off what was really happening.

He repeated it under his breath as he walked along empty grey corridors to Mikey's room: *just be there for Karen; just be there for Karen.*

She was in black jog pants and a red hoodie, her face white. She took a step towards him, twisting her hands together. He put his arms round her and they pulled apart when they heard a voice.

Machiko spoke gently: 'Karen. Sam. Mikey's in his room if you'd like to see him.'

Sam felt Karen flinch, but her voice was strong: 'Is he still…?'

She nodded. 'Please, go in; have all the time you need. He's peaceful, very comfortable and I'm sure he will feel your presence. Would you like me to bring you anything… tea?'

Sam shook his head. 'Thank you. We'll be fine. Can I ask, erm..?'

Machiko had answers to all the unspoken questions. She nodded. 'You must understand that he may pass away at any time now.' She smiled gently and opened the door of his room. 'Please; he may not speak or acknowledge, but he will know you are there.' She let them in. 'Just open the door and call my name if you need me. I'll hear you. Or pull the red cord next to the bed.'

They stood at the end of the bed. Karen whispered: 'He looks so peaceful. I don't know what to do. Should we sit down? Talk to him?'

'Shall we just say goodbye? Do you want to be on your own with him for a bit?'

'No, no… stay.' She looked up at him. 'I don't know what to say.'

'He always said he wanted us to carry on, didn't he? Let's just talk about our day.'

They sat on the sofa by the window and Sam told her about the art class and Lindsay leaving, and how the council had said all the legal bits of the hut sale were straightforward, and how nervous he was about it all.

He kept going, though Karen was only half listening and he felt like he was talking for the sake of it. They looked at Mikey. His eyes were closed, and it was impossible to know if he was even still breathing. Sam suddenly realised why it was so quiet: they'd turned the machines off.

Karen walked over to the bed. 'I think we ought to say goodbye. It's just feels wrong sitting here talking to each other. He can't hear us. He doesn't know we're here. I know he'd just tell us to bugger off and let him get it over with. Let's leave him in peace, yeah?'

Sam's voice was trembling. 'Yeah. You're right. We should go.'

They stood facing each other across the bed, their heads bowed. Sam saw Karen's lips moving but couldn't hear the words. He waited till she stopped, then bent to put his hand on Mikey's chest.

The physical contact jolted him, and he struggled to get the words out: 'Bye Mikey… G- God Bless.'

Karen leaned over to kiss the top of his head, and sobbed as she walked quickly out of the room.

Sam stopped at the foot of the bed, taking deep breaths, finding composure: 'I'll look after her. Cross my heart, Mikey.'

The Griffin was noisy, but they found a table in the corner furthest from the bar: so far away it looked like the cleaners hadn't found it yet. Sam carried the empty glasses to another table and used a sodden beer mat to scrape crisp shards onto the threadbare carpet.

Karen looked round. 'Mikey used to love this dump.'

Sam shook his head: 'Yeah. He always said they know how to serve a pint.'

'And he knew how to drink one.' She laughed harshly. 'Stupid sod.'

'Surprised he didn't catch a disease. It needs fumigating.'

She smiled and Sam noticed how tired she looked. She put her hand on his. 'How do you feel?'

The piped music and the chatter seemed to be coming from somewhere else. Sam sighed.: 'I don't know. We knew it was going to happen. I should feel sad, but Mikey was so laid back about it. And seeing him there, it was like he just fell asleep. I think I'm ok now. S-Sad, you know; thinking I'm the only one left, wishing I could have done something, but…'

Karen looked into her empty glass: 'Resigned to it, accepting it.'

'Yeah, that's it.'

Sam put his hand on hers and she smiled and put hers on top: 'It's like one of those kid's games.'

'Yeah, I remember playing that with Sean. I take mine away from the bottom and put it on top, and we just keep doing that. Stupid. Don't even know what it was called.'

133

'Or what the point was.' They laughed, and Sam got another round in.

He shuffled his chair closer to the table. 'Mum and Dad used to have a real go at Mikey about his drinking. He'd come home after school sometimes, and I could smell it on him even then.' He raised his glass. 'Still, he's right. It does taste good.'

Karen poured more tonic into her gin. 'We're going to have to give him a good send off.'

'Is that what you call it?'

'Yeah. Why, what do you call it?'

Sam scratched his head. 'Well, it was always just a funeral, you know. But send off is better.'

'He wasn't religious, and he ordered us not to fuss, so… what do we do? Any ideas?'

Sam nodded. 'I talked to him about it when he came to stay.'

'Really? He never said.'

'Yeah, well… He was okay about it; nothing too heavy. He said we should just have a party.'

'Sounds like Mikey. Plenty of booze, by any chance?'

Sam smiled. 'Not really. What we thought was - well, this bit was my idea - we could get everyone down on the beach round the hut, light a fire, get someone to do the catering.'

Karen nodded. 'At this time of year, we'd need the fire…Yeah, that sounds good.. I think he'd approve.'

Sam hesitated. 'You know he wanted to be cremated…' She nodded. 'Well, he said he'd really love it if we could make a little boat and float his ashes out to sea. He liked that idea: sailing away. Remember?'

She wiped her eyes quickly with the back of her hand. 'Dying is like sailing out to sea on your own; yeah.'

'Yeah. We didn't talk about it again, so I'm thinking that's what we should do. What do you think?'

She gulped her drink and nodded. 'Yeah, let's go for it.'

'One more?'

'Go on then.'

'Mikey would be pleased. He said we should celebrate.' He paused. 'It's weird. I'm sorry he's gone, but glad for him, you know? I feel guilty that I'm not crying.'

'Yeah, don't beat yourself up. You did a lot for him, at the end. Made him happy. You know what he said to me?' Sam shook his head. 'He said we should both get on with our lives. Don't look back. Don't feel bad.' She reached into her shoulder bag and pulled out a notebook. 'Look, I wrote it down.'

Sam mouthed the words as if that would help him absorb them. 'Don't look back. Don't feel bad.'

They walked to her flat. The night was quiet and still and cold after the noise and heat of the pub. They stopped at the harbour, watching the boats sway gently. Their breath gusted like steam, glowing white in the lights.

Karen turned to him. 'So, what next?'

'What do you mean?'

'Are you going to do all the horrible stuff, like registering the death?'

'Oh, yeah, I guess.'

'Shall we work on the funeral together?'

'The send off? Yeah, please.' He turned to her. 'Karen…'

'What?'

'I ... I don't know how you feel. I don't want to mess things up.'

The look on her face said she understood. 'You won't mess up. Let's just do what we must do for Mikey, and then see where we are.'

'He wants me to make sure you're alright. Look after you.'

'Story of your life, eh?' She smiled and put her arm through his. 'Maybe you're the one who needs looking after. Come on. Walk me home.'

He saw her hesitate when they got to her front door.

'See you, Karen. Are you okay?'

She turned the key and the door swung open. She stepped inside, then turned. 'Will you stay with me tonight?'

'Erm… well, yeah. Course I will, if you're sure.'

'I need company tonight. But I'm putting a pillow down the middle of the bed, okay?'

Sam opened an eye. He opened the other and remembered where he was.

The white clock on the bedside table flicked to 0627. He turned over and the pillow barrier was there, but Karen wasn't.

He lay on his back, enjoying the Sunday morning feeling that follows a rare, good night's sleep: one he hadn't expected. Sunlight glowed briefly through the thin red curtains, then was gone.

He sat up when he heard a door open, then close. But then, silence. He got up anyway.

She'd left a note propped against the teapot: 'Gone for a run. Thanks for staying and not snoring. Have a brew. Won't be long x'

He drank a glass of water; still muzzy after more beer than he was used to.

Everything looked different in daylight. He looked round, taking in the old enamel sink with its big taps; the shiny yellow and green flowery vinyl top that was beginning to peel off the table edges; the fridge door with its brightly coloured magnet messages like 'Never give up', and 'Life is a gift'.

They'd sat up till after midnight; talking about Mikey, their families, sharing stories; her shop, his art, what the future might bring.

Sam told her he was enjoying doing the art classes on his own, then started yawning, and she told him to go to bed first. He stripped off and felt a shiver of excitement at the thought of her taking her clothes off and climbing in next to him. But she'd already put the pillow in the middle, and she kept her t shirt and knickers on.

It was the first time he'd spent the night with anyone, and she just squeezed his hand and whispered goodnight. He lay there for ages, his frustration gradually soothed by the rhythm of her gentle breathing.

But now, more conflicting feelings. She'd lived here with Mikey, but although they didn't sleep together, his brother's clothes were probably still in the wardrobe and he'd sat at this table, poured tea from that pot, drunk water from this glass; stayed up late with her, talking.

Was he fooling himself? What seemed natural last night suddenly felt so wrong.

He'd told Mikey he'd look out for Karen, but that didn't mean he had to be with her all the time. Or bloody well sleep with her. What the hell was he doing here? He had no idea what she really thought of him: did she fancy him, or was she yet another woman who just wanted to be a 'good friend' Was he just an idiot who said yes to anyone with a pretty face and a nice body? And how long would she stick around now Mikey had gone?

He drank another glass of water and looked out over the slate roofs towards the distant grey line of the sea.

He found a pen in the cutlery drawer and propped his note on top of hers: 'Thanks for a great night. Couldn't wait, sorry. Got things to do. See you soon. Call me. Sam x'

He walked home through the quiet Sunday streets.

The town hadn't woken up, but it was looking good. So many shops had new paintwork and signage; there were new waste bins on every corner; new planters everywhere, and no graffiti.

He walked under the banner that flapped noisily across Marine Parade: 'WE LOVE WHISTLE'.

Sam turned right towards the hut, drawn by the noisy squabbling of gulls and the channel of cold sea air that always seemed to blow this way.

He stood next to the bollards where Aaron parked his kiosk and closed his eyes, savouring the thud and hiss of the waves that had become the soundtrack of his life.

Over to his left, the beach hut was partially screened by green painted hoardings with architect drawings and long complicated sentences about the new arts centre.

He walked onto the beach and sat on the hut steps. Michelle had told him it would be demolished in a couple of weeks. He decided he'd tell her about the plans for Mikey's send off, and ask if she could hold off till it was done.

Sam walked up to the tide line. His were the only footprints.

The train stood silent on platform four.

Sam hated goodbyes, but he'd promised.

Lindsay looked elegant in a dark trouser suit, her hair tied back, a splash of red from the scarf tied loosely round her neck.

They walked towards the front of the train because, she said: 'I'll have to run like a rabbit to make my connection at Birmingham.'

She stopped and pressed the button and the door hissed open.

'Well, Sam, good luck with the classes. They all love you; you know.'

'Really?'

'Don't look so doubtful. Would I lie? Okay, don't answer that. I've had a lot of messages about it, so just do what you're doing. And listen, I meant what I said. I'm going to invite you down for a week first chance I get, and don't you dare say you're too busy.'

Sam smiled and stepped aside as a silver haired lady climbed in.

Lindsay checked her watch. 'I bet she'll be on her mobile phone the entire journey.' She looked up at the platform clock. 'Gosh, two minutes! I'd better get in.' She dropped her handbag and put her arms round Sam's neck. 'Oh God! I'm going to miss you so much. Promise me you'll call me. Promise you won't forget all about me the minute I'm gone.'

Sam hugged her hard and tried to keep his voice steady. 'What was your name again?'

She pushed him away and laughed, then her face crumpled, and she buried her face in his chest.

He wanted to stroke her hair and kiss her, but he broke away. 'Will you text me when you get home?'

She reached into her bag for a tissue and dabbed her eyes. 'Course I will, you numpty.'

She climbed in and blew him a kiss and told him to look after Grace.

He shouted, 'I will!' and waved as the door beeped and slid shut and the guard waved a green flag and the station master blew a whistle and the train gathered speed as it slid away in a whine of electricity.

Chapter 15

"It's never too late to become who you want to be. I hope you live a life that you're proud of, and if you find that you're not, I hope you have the strength to start over."
— F. Scott Fitzgerald

The crem was on the hill, and the long approach road was lined with cars.

It was a cold grey morning, but Sam was warm in his charcoal suit.

He sat with Karen on the front row. He leaned in and whispered: 'I can't believe how many people have turned up.'

'I'm not surprised. He's been thrown out of every pub in town. Maybe they just want to make sure he's really gone.'

Sam suppressed a smile as the celebrant stepped out from a side door and signalled to someone at the back. She had short blond hair and was wearing a dark red trouser suit and a white blouse.

Sam told Lindsay he chose Helen Taylor to officiate because: 'It was like meeting my favourite auntie, and I knew Mikey would like her.'

She gave them an encouraging smile: 'I apologise to the front row, but I'm going to have to use all my lung power today so you at the back can hear me. And as my kids will tell you, I can shout all day.'

She turned to face the coffin as the laughter faded away. Karen had placed a bunch of white roses on top, and they shone under the spotlight.

Helen clasped her hands. 'We're here today to remember Michael Taverner – Mikey. To be thankful that we knew him; and to wish him well on the next step of his journey. He would be so delighted that he's attracted such a big crowd today. But then, from what I hear, he always loved having an audience.'

The laughter felt like a release. Sam had shed tears for Sean, Mum and Dad, but this was different. He knew Mikey would approve.

Even so, he felt nervous as he waited for Helen's invitation to 'say a few words.' He'd got much better at controlling the stutter lately, but would the stress get to him? Helen said he should keep the S words to a minimum if they were the ones that tripped him up.

She'd asked for some notes about Mikey, and she was using them in her introduction now, summing up his life in two minutes and sounding like she'd known him for ages.

Sam had written out his speech, wrestling with the impossible job of summing up the life of a brother he scarcely knew. He pulled the notes out of his jacket pocket and tried to relax. It didn't work: Helen turned to him: 'Mikey's brother, Sam, will now say a few words.'

He cleared his throat and fixed his eyes on the back wall. Helen had told him to force himself to smile: 'It may feel odd, but it will give you confidence.'

He glanced at his notes. 'I've never been asked to say a few words before. Normally, I can't get a word in.' He heard subdued laughter and felt better. 'Mikey preferred it that way.' More laughter. 'He was my big brother and we'd never been that close, to be honest; but that changed when he found out he had cancer. It brought us together. We talked more than we'd ever done, and I found out how tough he was, how brave.'

He felt his bottom lip begin to tremble, so he bought time by scanning his notes - another of Helen's tips.

Taking a deep breath, he looked up again. 'I was glad we had time to talk, and I know he was, too. He wasn't s-scared. He was trying to make me feel better, most of the time. He kept telling me not to worry; that he was okay about it.

'Mikey was daft, and he drank too much. By the way, that's not me - that's what he said to me a couple of weeks ago.' More laughter, louder this time.

Sam risked looking at some faces. He could see Aaron sitting next to Loud Linda, Billy and Jim, and Michelle was at the back, with Lindsay and Grace. 'He was half right. He wasn't daft.' More laughter.

'He was brave. He managed to make losing him bearable somehow. He said he thought it would be like sailing away on his own and that's a good way of looking at it.' He could see Helen nodding. 'If he could be brave and take it as it comes, so could Karen and me. Easier said than done, but we're getting there.'

He caught Karen's eye. She was smiling and nodding too. Sam puffed out his cheeks, looking up to the ceiling, fighting against tears that felt like they were pooling behind his eyes. Telling himself: *Just get through this next bit. Nearly there.*

'My family has been in Whistle Bay a long time and I know Mum and Dad will be looking down on us now. They'd want to thank you for turning out to s-say goodbye to their son and my big brother. There's lots of people here I'd like to thank too, for the way you've looked out for me since Dad died. I've lost my family, but I know you're there for me and that means a lot.

'You all knew Mikey. He was everyone's friend, but especially Karen's. She meant the world to him, I know.'

He stopped and put his notes in his pocket. 'He'd be telling me to get on with it now. He didn't want a big fuss, so I just want to s-say thanks for being my big brother, Mikey, and if there's any justice, you'll be having a pint in heaven right now.'

He looked up again and saw Lindsay dabbing her eyes with a tissue.

He felt his throat go dry and stopped to sip water.

'We're not asking for a collection today, but if you do want to donate, it will go straight to the hospice, who looked after Mikey so well. We'll never forget their kindness. Thanks again for coming, and you're all invited down to the hut after. Thank you.'

He nodded briefly, embarrassed by the applause, and sat down. Karen squeezed his hand.

Helen stepped up: 'Thank you, Sam. That was beautiful. Now let's take a moment to think about your memories of Mikey, what he meant to you, and to say a prayer or simply to say thank you that he was part of your life, however briefly that may have been. So please, let's bow our heads and give thanks in our own way.'

141

The rest of the ceremony went by in a blur of wiped away tears and lumps in the throat.

Sam kept his head bowed as the coffin carried Mikey slowly through the dark blue curtains to the sound of his favourite song... 'You can go your own way; go your own way...'

Later, the rain clouds blew away to the north, the sun started its slow slide to the horizon, and the temperature dropped still further.

Sam lit the heaters, and everyone bunched together in the circles of warmth: everyone except Lindsay and Grace, who left after the service on their way to Heathrow for a long weekend somewhere warm, and Michelle, who was needed at work.

Billy Whistle had provided sandwiches, beer and wine, and told Sam he wouldn't accept any payment. Jivin Jim's wife made cakes, and Shirley helped Sam to copy photos of Mikey which she pinned on a corkboard by the drinks table.

Sam made conversation and shook hands and kept an eye on the time so he caught the tide.

He'd made a raft out of driftwood and bound it with rope from the deckchair store; a mast made from a cut down windbreak pole; and a sail Karen made out of a red pillowcase from Mikey's bedroom.

The hospice had given them his watch and a leather bracelet. Karen asked Sam to fasten the bracelet to the mast. She offered him the watch, but he wanted her to have it, and she was wearing it today.

Sam had stored the raft under the tarpaulin, with the deckchairs. He carried it down to the sea's edge while Karen distracted everyone by offering to top up their drinks.

Sam double checked the tide was favourable and gave her the signal. She called out: 'Can you come and join us as Mikey sails away, please? Bring your glasses, too, so we give him a proper send off.'

Sam rolled up his trousers as they walked slowly across the sand, watched by a few people on the esplanade. He smiled his thanks to Aaron, who was rolling his trousers up, too, then waded out up to his knees in the freezing water as Aaron pushed the raft towards him.

His fingers were numb, but he held onto the raft long enough to make sure the urn was tied securely.

Karen caught his eye as he swivelled round, and she called out: 'Let's all wish Mikey bon voyage.'

He gave the raft a push and it began to glide away.

Karen shouted: 'Ready? One, two, three… let's say it together…Bon voyage Mikey!'

Sam stepped out of the water onto the sand and raised a hand in farewell.

The red sail stiffened and began to carry Mikey away.

Karen stood beside him: 'I wonder where he'll end up.'

Aaron joined them: 'He'll find a pub, I bet. Catch a few mackerel on the way. That's a nice boat, Sammy. He could be travelling for miles.'

He walked back to the hut, linking arms with Karen, but Sam stayed, watching the raft until it disappeared beyond the headland.

'Bye Mikey,' he whispered.

He jumped as he felt a hand on his shoulder.

'Sam?'

He turned, wiping his eyes on his sleeve. It was a face he felt he knew. 'Erm, hello… Sorry …'

She pulled off her beanie hat: 'Hello Sam. It's me. Sally.'

Chapter 16

'Oh my God! Sally? Sally Ilic?'

She laughed. 'Yes, it's me. I like to be called Sladana now, though. My Serbian name, see?'

'Right, well, Sladana…'

'No … Sla dee ahna. Like that.' She stepped back as if she was viewing a painting. 'So, it's been a long time.'

Sam scratched his nose, his hand shaking with the cold, and struggled to find the words. 'Yeah… S- so, look at you. You haven't changed.'

She laughed again. 'Really? I hope I have.'

Sam could see Karen looking their way. 'Erm, right… well, you know what I mean. Do you want to come and have a drink? It's warmer under there.'

'No, no. I shouldn't be here really. I'm sorry. I just wanted to see you. To say sorry for your loss. And say hello. Like the Terminator, yes? I'm back.' She threw her head back and laughed.

She seemed so natural and he felt so awkward. 'Are you living here now?'

She nodded. 'I finish my nursing degree in Northumberland. Got a job at the hospital here.'

She put a hand on his arm, and it was as if the last ten years had just fast forwarded to now. 'I'm sorry about Mikey. I saw in the paper. I hope you don't mind me coming. I thought better than to knock on your door. I don't even know if you are still there.'

'I am, but not for much longer.' He stepped back, aware that he'd been inching closer. 'Shall we meet up for a coffee sometime?'

'Yes, I would like that. When can you?'

The way she talked, her eyes; it was all still there, drawing him in. 'Anytime, really. Oh, hang on…' He patted his jacket pockets then pulled out one of the business cards Michelle had given him. 'Why don't you call me; let me know when you're free?'

Sladana's eyes widened. 'Ooooh,.. artist, and town ambassador. My God! You are celebrity!'

He grinned. 'Nah. I'll tell you all about it. And you must tell me about you.'

He could see Karen was talking to someone, but her head kept turning towards them. He stretched out an arm to shake hands. Sladana had a strong grip and her hand felt warm and he didn't want to let go. But she did.

'Ow! Your hand is so cold! Go and get warm! Oh yes, and it's a deal. Nice to see you after so long. So, yes… Bye.'

She grabbed her hair with one hand and pulled on the beanie with the other, then walked away quickly on flat feet, trying to avoid getting sand in her shoes. Sam watched her for a few seconds, wondering if anyone had recognised her, then jogged up to Karen's side.

Her expression was deadpan. 'Who's your friend?'

'Oh, just someone who'd seen me in the paper. An old schoolfriend. Wanted to ask about the art, you know. S-Sorry about that.'

'Fame at last, eh?'

'Yeah, you could say that. Anyway, how's it going here?'

'They're starting to drift off now. I guess it's time we did, too.'

'Do you mind if I go into the hut? I'm freezing. I need to get changed.' He ran up the steps without waiting for an answer.

She came in a few minutes later. She sat on the highchair, frowning.

Sam was on the floor by the heater, rubbing his feet with an old towel: 'What's wrong Karen?'

'I feel a bit lost. It was seeing him sail away. I was all right till then.'

'I know. It's easier when you're busy.'

'Yeah. It went well, though. Thanks. Anyway, no point dwelling on it. What are you going to do now?'

'I've got plenty to keep me busy. I've got to clear this place before they knock it down and start building.'

'Oh yeah. Then what?'

'I don't know.' He tied his shoelaces and sat back in the armchair, shaking his head. 'Yeah, I really don't know. What about you? Back to the parlour on Monday?'

'I'll go in tomorrow; tidy the place up, check supplies, and hope I've still got some customers booked in.'

'Well, you could always do one for me.'

'I didn't have you down as a tats man.'

'Tats man... Sounds a bit better than Chair Man. Anyway, I did wonder about it, having something that always reminded me of this place.'

She didn't sound convinced. 'Yeah. Well, let me know if you want to go for it.'

'Are you going to be okay? Shall I call you when I've got the hut sorted?'

She nodded: 'Yeah, whenever.' There was something in her eyes he couldn't understand. She must just be upset, a natural reaction to a tough day.

'Are you sure you're alright?'

She told him not to fuss, turned quickly and closed the door behind her.

The sea was whipped up by a strengthening wind that had swung round to the east. No wonder it was feeling properly cold, as Dad used to say.

Aaron was still in shirt sleeves; the last man standing. He drained his glass. 'You look knackered, matey. Fancy a beer? There's a bit left.'

Sam shook his head. 'No, you have it. I'd better start clearing up. I need to get everything out by tomorrow night.'

Aaron nodded. 'End of an era, Sammy.'

'I'm trying to tell myself it's the start of one. But you haven't got rid of me yet.'

'I know what that means. Want a hand, by any chance?'

'Cheers. I thought you'd never ask.'

They filled the bin bags, folded down the tables, stacked the chairs, and dragged the heaters in. He gave Aaron one of his pictures as a thank you, and got a bear hug in return, then locked the cupboard and fell into the armchair in the hut.

He felt drained but couldn't switch off. It was quite a list: his whole family gone; his promise to look after Karen; her strange behaviour just now; the art classes; his paintings; Lindsay in London; Grace waiting to put his house on the market; Billy Whistle and the others; the money stacking up in his accounts; the end of the hut; the end of the family business; Mikey; and now, Sladana, appearing from nowhere with her sexy voice and her amazing eyes.

He was too wired to relax, so he changed into his running gear, then stopped at the bottom of the steps. Gary was there; his cream and grey feathers ruffling as he braced himself against the wind that was blowing sand in ribbon drifts up onto the esplanade wall.

Sam ran back inside to retrieve the plastic bag and shook some cereal crumbs into his hand. 'Hello Gary. Where've you been, mate? Do you want some? Yeah?' He kept talking, cajoling, his hand outstretched, motionless, waiting, hoping.

Catching his breath at the top of the hill, and leaning into the wind, he could just make out the hut in the dark grey of dusk; looking so small and isolated, squeezed between the sea and the town.

The hut would be gone soon, but he didn't want to stop working, and he didn't want to lose the memories, the connections he'd made over a short lifetime. The wake had made him feel part of a family.

Lindsay was always telling him to go and make some more memories; but how could he walk away, especially now Sladana had come back?

The only thing to do was to keep busy, and hope something cropped up. Hold on…Christmas was coming. Sam suddenly knew exactly how he could keep busy.

Sam helped himself to a few M&Ms from the bowl on the counter as Shirley Sugar checked something in the back room.

She came back, nodding: 'Yeah, Sam, that's ok… I can take on the printing. I reckon we'd sell out.'

'Brilliant, thanks Shirl. I've got to go and sign things at the Town Hall now, but I'll pick some images when I get back home, and drop them in later. 60/40 split, ok?'

'Fab, yeah, thanks partner.' She grinned, and they shook hands. 'We need to think of a brand name. Any thoughts?'

Sam chewed his lip: 'Dunno, really. Whistle Bay Cards, or something?'

'Nah. Too obvious. These are going to be artistic and quirky, so we need something else.' She popped a sweet in her mouth. 'What about The Taverner Collection? That sounds alright.'

Sam was about to say no, then stopped. 'That's good, but it's not just me, is it? We're splitting the profits... '

'Let's keep thinking. I'm sure we could come up with some more.' She winked: 'I guess we'll be seeing a lot more of each other now.'

He met Michelle, and signed what she said was the last bit of paperwork.

She poured him a coffee and he told her about the Christmas cards idea.

'Perfect. I'll order a few hundred straight off. Tell Shirley to call me, will you? We can send them out as part of the promotion campaign.'

He called Shirley to give her the news, then stopped at the harbour on his way to the hut for the final clear out. Mikey's boat was there, and it was so easy to picture him there - in his dirty yellow waders and a beanie hat. He'd wanted Karen to have the boat when he died, but she wasn't interested, though she told him she'd done a deal with one of Mikey's mates to collect the lobster catch.

Sam walked on, frowning. She hadn't wasted any time. He didn't want anything to do with the lobster trade, so she was welcome to the money. The way they were cooked alive made his stomach turn.

It felt strange, packing the dusty old books into cardboard boxes, even though he'd decided to put the shelves up at home so he could keep them there. He'd sold the patio heaters and the spare tables and chairs to Billy, and he knew he could have charged more because Billy hadn't haggled, for the first time in his life.

Sam carried the boxes to his car, then sat on the steps. He'd been dreading this moment for weeks, but now it felt like a release.

He walked over to the deckchairs and lifted a corner of the blue tarpaulin.

He ran a hand gently over the beech frames, wondering how many times he'd put them out on the sand, and how many people had sat on them over the years.

He thought for a moment, then untied the ropes and carried six chairs up to the car.

Chapter 17

Her name badge said June, but her face was as cold as December.

Sam returned her feeble impression of a smile and pointedly poured the coffee she'd spilled back into the cup.

Her voice was as flat as her face: 'Enjoy.'

Sam replied with equal sincerity: 'Have a great day.'

She gave him a puzzled look, and stalked off to make sure another customer never came to Billy's Cafe again.

Sam could hear the man himself whistling from the kitchen. The place was busy, even on a windswept winter Wednesday.

He nodded at a couple he remembered from yesterday's art class. They seemed cheerful enough, but they were still looking at the menu, which meant June hadn't cast her icy spell yet.

He checked his watch and flicked through Twitter. He'd signed up to it so he could follow Lindsay but was bemused to discover that people were now following his page, even though he'd only posted a few pictures of Gary and one or two of his deckchair paintings.

Sladana was already five minutes late, but that was nothing new: she always used to keep him waiting after school.

She'd texted him last night: *See you at 10 tomorrow, Whistle Cafe? x* He spent the rest of the night thinking about her: the ice blue eyes; beautiful mouth; the taste of her, the feel of her warm smooth skin as they lay on the grass in the park; that sexy accent.

His phone beeped just as he was beginning to wonder if she was going to cry off. But it was Karen: *'Come and see me after work. Need to talk.'*

He finished tapping out his reply, just as Sladana walked in, in skinny jeans and a light blue fleece over a white shirt. She kept her hair in a pigtail and her eyes were the same blue.

He stood as she put her orange jacket on the back of the chair. She was at least a foot shorter than him.

She smiled: 'Still a gentleman. Standing for the lady. That's nice.'

150

He sat down and held out the menu.

She put her hand on his: 'That's ok. I'll wait for the waiter.'

They snorted at the inadvertent play on words, and Sam moved his coffee to one side. 'So...' He spoke slowly, remembering the way she'd said it. 'Sladana.'

Her voice was teasing. 'Very good. Yes, Sam-you-ell?'

Sam was too wound up to react. 'It's been about ten years, hasn't it? So, come on, tell me what you've been doing.'

She was still smiling, as if she'd worked him out already. 'Ok, this is serious. Straight into the life story, yes?'

'Yes, you go first. I'll tell you mine after, promise.'

She told him her mother had become ill soon after she left school, and how she cared for her, and how that convinced her she wanted to become a nurse. Eventually, mum got better and Sladana applied to universities. She got a place at Northumberland and came out with a first-class honours.

'Wow. Is your mother still ok?'

'Oh, yes, she is good now. Not so mobile. Still lives in same house. Like you. So, now your turn.'

Her eyes never left his as he told her about Sean, and Dad, and Mikey, and the art, Lindsay, and how he had a big idea for the house. He realised he'd never told anyone the full story before.

Sladana shook her head. 'So difficult for you. But exciting now, maybe, too? So you have no family. Just friends?' She paused. 'Girlfriends?'

'No girlfriends. I have three friends, who are girls, but... you know. I've just been so busy, what with selling the business, art -'

'- and being an ambassador.'

He laughed and took a moment to sip lukewarm coffee. 'What about you? Boyfriends?'

'Like you, friends who are boys. Mainly from work.'

Sam saw Billy serving the young couple and waved to attract his attention. He came over, wiping his hands on his apron.

He winked at Sladana, and Sam cringed. 'Now then, Sammy. Introduce us, please.'

They ordered coffees and slices of salmon and broccoli quiche. Billy wrote it down with a flourish: 'It will be my pleasure to serve you. And this is on the house.'

Sam grinned as he saw Sladana's raised eyebrows. 'He's never done that before. You've obviously made an impression.'

She smiled, and leaned forward, so close he could have kissed her. She spoke softly: 'Have I made an impression on you, Sam?'

He nodded, feeling a certainty he hadn't experienced for a very long time. 'Yeah, you have. How am I doing?'

She put her hand on his, so gently it was like a butterfly landing. He didn't even think about it: just looked down and slowly lifted his hand so he could kiss hers.

She smiled: 'You are doing very well.' She paused. 'And can I say, this? No more stutter? It's gone?'

'I never did stutter when I was with you.'

'That's good. You know something?'

'What?'

'I never went with another boy after you.' She leaned back. 'Yes. I think I will stay in Whistle Bay.'

They held hands after, as they walked to the hut. Workmen were tapping wire fencing into place but the foreman nodded as Sam asked if it was ok to take a look: 'Course you can, mate. It's your place, innit?'

They walked onto the beach and watched the grey waves turn white as they slapped onto the sand. She leaned against him, and they kissed, slowly, gently.

Sam put his arm round her waist. 'I was hoping Gary would come to meet you.'

'Gary?'

'My pet gull.'

'Your pet gull. Okay… I think maybe you are going crazy like the man on the desert island.'

'Robinson Crusoe?'

'Yes, him.'

They walked up to the sea, laughing and leaping backwards to dodge the waves. Sam turned round to look back at the hut.

'It will all be gone in a couple of days.'

'No sadness, right?' She grabbed his arm and pulled him towards the hut. 'Let's sit in a deckchair! Come on!'

Sam pulled back the blue tarpaulin and picked out two chairs. He leaned one against his leg and unfolded the other. 'This is yours, miss.'

'Thank you, mister.'

They sat close together, facing the hill, their backs to the wind. He told Sladana this was the view that Lindsay sketched on her first visit.

'Do you miss her?'

'Only a bit. She came to Mikey's service, but I only got chance to say hello. She wants me to go to London for a week to do some painting with her.'

'London! When will you go?'

Sam turned to her. 'I don't know. You're here now, so…'

'You have to go. Take this opportunity.' She smiled, and Sam remembered it was one reason he'd loved her so much: the smile was never far away. 'Maybe I come with you.'

He opened the hut to show her, but it felt like it belonged to someone else. She picked up on Sam's mood and squeezed his hand as they walked away. 'Sad to say goodbye?'

He nodded. He stopped and hugged her. 'But it's nice to say hello.'

He walked to the bus station with her, and they broke into a run as she pointed: 'The bus!'

They laughed as they ran, and she got there just as the driver started the engine. She turned and waved, breathless: 'See you soon.'

'Call me. Promise?'

'I promise.'

She found a window seat and they pressed their hands to the glass as the bus pulled away in a clatter of diesel.

Grace's newly tanned face was hidden behind a mug of tea.

Lindsay had tweeted a picture of them lying on a beach towel, with the message: 'Be jealous! 25 degrees but the wine is cool!'

153

She sipped the tea, then looked at the biscuits on Sam's side of the table. 'Makes a lot of sense, Sam. The important thing is that you're happy, and you feel it's the right thing.'

Sam nodded and pushed the plate of custard creams back across to her. 'The woman next door told me she wants to sell so she can move in with her daughter. I just said I'd be interested, then she said she'd love it if I took it on. Her son came round last night, and we shook hands on it.'

'Well done! You've got a good deal. Maybe I should offer you a job. If she's been there all her life, you'll probably have to spend a few grand updating it, but it'll be worth it. Do you want me to take it from here, sort out the details?' She winked. 'As a friend.'

Sam leaned forward and she pushed the biscuits back towards him. He made that three each. This one put him 4-3 up. He munched and spoke at the same time. 'Yeah, please. And I was thinking... do you know someone who could come up with some plans for me?'

'An architect?'

'Yeah, or just a good builder; I don't know.'

'Actually, Sam, this would be a fab project. It's not quite as simple as knocking a few walls down: you could totally transform this place.'

The custard creams were forgotten as they talked about how he pictured the house.

Grace took notes on her tablet. 'Are you thinking contemporary, or traditional? Big rooms? Extending into the garden at the back? I mean, you could have amazing glass doors to get that view of the park and the trees...'

Sam scratched his nose. 'Well, I was thinking I'd love to make it feel like stepping out onto the beach. I've kept a few deckchairs. I was just thinking I'd use them for some paintings, but then I thought it would be cool to have them here. Michelle said I could have the wood from the hut if I wanted it, so I said yeah to that.'

Grace was tapping on her tablet. 'I love that! That's the sort of inspiration we want. Let's start with that beachside theme and get some visuals done. Then we can get a few quotes.'

She leaned back in the chair and gazed at him. 'I'm really pleased for you, Sam. People lose their heads when it comes to property. You wouldn't believe some of the things people are prepared to throw money at. It'll be like a new house, but with the memories of your hut built in. As my mum always used to say, you've really got your head screwed on. '

He laughed: 'My mum used to say that as well, but Mikey was always telling me I had a screw loose.'

He heard his phone beeping in the hall, came back and sat down without a word.

'What's wrong, Sam?'

'My first girlfriend is back in town, and she wants to meet me for a coffee again tomorrow.'

'Is that a bad thing?'

'No. I went out with her yesterday. We got on well, but then, you know, I started thinking maybe that would be it.'

'So, it might be serious?' He nodded. 'Do you want it to be?'

'She came to see me at Mikey's ceremony. Hadn't seen or heard from her since school.'

Grace nodded and his face felt warm.

'You're still in love with her, aren't you?'

'I don't see how I can be after not seeing her for, like, ten years.'

'But…?'

'Well…I went to see Karen after, and she told me to be careful. She said everyone in town knows how much money I'm making from the hut, and the paintings and stuff.'

'So, what, she thinks she's a gold digger?'

Sam nodded. 'Apparently, she went to have a tattoo and asked for a discount. Told Karen how poor the family is, and how she has to send money to Serbia every month.'

Grace looked horrified. 'For God's sake, Sam! Don't listen to racist crap like that. It sounds like she's trying to poison things.' She sighed: 'It's what inside you that counts. Trust your own feelings.' She pushed her tablet angrily back into its case. 'God! People!'

'There's so much going on. I don't know what to believe any more.'

'Well, do you trust Karen?'

'Erm…'

'There you are. You've got doubts. Do you trust this girl?'

'Yeah.'

'Right. Enough said. So, listen to your auntie Grace… take her out tomorrow. Talk to her. Be honest: do you love her?'

'Stop looking at me like that… Okay, yeah, as soon as I met her yesterday, I wanted to start seeing her again. We got on well. But I wasn't sure she'd want to.'

'Well, now you know.'

'She does.'

'Yeah.'

'There's so much happening. What am I going to do?'

'You're going to buy the coffees, dunk your custard cream in hers and tell her you love her.'

'Shut up!'

They laughed and Grace stood to leave. She turned at the door. 'Don't worry, Sam. You're a lovely guy, and she's a lucky girl. You don't have to put on a performance, just be yourself. So have a great time together. Tell Karen to go and do one. Oh, and you simply have to promise you'll bring her round to meet me first chance you get, okay?'

'What? Karen?'

'No! The girl you're hopelessly in love with!'

'Right. I will.'

'Great. Just wait till I tell Lindsay! Oh - that reminds me - she asked if you'd be up for going to join her for a few days just before Christmas.'

'What? And be away over Christmas?'

'No, no, she's coming back here for Christmas and New Year. That's why she suggested it. You could come back together. What do you think?'

Sam started analysing, then stopped himself. 'OK, yeah. Let's do it!'

'Fab! And Sam?'

'Yeah?'

'I really would think twice about Karen. I know you got close to her through Mikey, but if she's so keen to set you against - what's her name?'

156

'Sladana.'

'Sladana, right. If she's so against her, ask yourself what her game is. It sounds like a dead giveaway to me.'

'What do you mean?'

'She's the one who raised the issue about money. So what does that tell you?'

Sam stood and shoved his hands into his pockets. 'That she's thinking about the money, not Sladana.'

Grace kissed him on the cheek. 'You've got to face it, Sam. You're a wealthy man now. It's going to bring changes. You'll find out who your real friends are.'

He topped up his tea after she'd gone. Maybe Grace was right: Karen was trouble. She was jealous because she wanted Sam to herself; and if she did, it was probably because he was loaded.

The house felt empty and silent again. He sat by the window in the living room and tried to occupy himself by working on the painting he'd started last night.

He'd painted it so the viewer was looking over the back of two striped deckchairs towards the hills, which were glowing in vivid sunset colours. The chairs were the main feature, although he was playing with different colours, and adding more elements now - buildings, trees, texture, perspective.

But it didn't feel complete.

He heard noises from next door: muffled voices, laughter. He looked out towards the park. There was a gap in the trees and someone with a dog on a lead was being overtaken by a jogger.

He looked again at the painting, and suddenly, he knew exactly what was missing.

Chapter 18

'You're very good at keeping still.'

'It is nice change. Never stop moving at work.'

'You said that without moving your lips.'

They snorted with laughter at the same time. Sam threw his pencil to the floor in mock disgust, and Sladana laughed even more.

'I have to move now. Anyway, you've stopped, so…'

'I suppose you'll have to. I'll never make it as a people painter, will I?'

She stretched and touched her toes, then looked over his shoulder: 'That's very good. I like it. You make me look pretty.'

'You are pretty.' He stopped as she winced. 'What's wrong?'

She rolled up her sleeve. Her upper arm was wrapped in cling film. 'Still sore.'

'How long will it be like that?'

'She said maybe few days.'

'You still haven't told me what it is.'

She smiled. 'You hope it is a heart with an arrow and Sam written there?'

'You mean it isn't?'

'No, it is an oak leaf.'

'A leaf?'

She followed him to the kitchen as he made tea. 'Serbia symbol. Long life and strength.'

'I'd like to go there with you.'

'I would love to go back. But…'

'No money?'

'Yes, and not good to leave mother.'

'We could take her.'

'No, I don't think so. We talked about this, and she said if she went she might never want to come back. Anyway, would cost a lot.'

'I know you're short of money. But I'm not.'

158

She nodded, then turned her face away. 'The tattoo lady says I only want to meet you because you are rich.'

'I told you I don't believe that, so don't worry about her. Anyway, I'm not that rich!'

Sladana held the mug to her lips, then put it down. 'I never forgot how you made me feel at school. People call me foreigner.' She shook her head: 'I have lived here twenty years.'

Sam had to know, but was afraid of the answer: 'What kind of things did Karen say?' She just sipped her tea. 'Come on Sladana, Tell me.'

'She said I was just like the others. You know, people like me taking up space and we should go back to our own country.'

'I can't believe she said that.'

'You think I make it up?'

'No, no, I didn't mean that. It's just that I know Karen, and it's a shock to think she could be like that. I liked her.'

'It's okay. She's your friend, so… Anyway, it happens a lot.' She finished her tea and washed the mug out in the sink. 'So, tell me about this portrait painting. A new thing for you.'

Sam was gripping the mug so hard his knuckles were white. 'What? Oh, yeah. Yeah, when I looked at my paintings the other day, I saw it. There were no people. I just paint objects, things, scenery. I think it's because I've been alone a long time: too long. So, I decided to try painting people.'

She took two quick steps and sat on his lap. She kissed his cheek, then his neck and then his lips, and his tension ebbed away. He felt her body, warm and soft; her thighs pressing against him. She kissed his ear and smiled into his eyes as Sam unfastened the buttons of her blouse.

The grey sky had turned to charcoal.

He kissed the bit of her head that was visible. 'Come on sleepyhead. I'll make you something to eat.'

Her voice was muffled under the sheets. 'You are needing calories after exercise.'

He made toast and poached eggs, and they ate quickly; then walked through the park and talked until the street lamps came on.

She hugged him: 'I have to go.'

159

'I'd love it if you could stay the night.'

'Me too. But…'

'Yeah, I know. Mum. Maybe one day?'

'Yes. One day.'

He stood at the gate and waved until the red taillights of her car disappeared.

Sladana's words were still running through his head that night, as he rehearsed what he'd say to Karen.

They wouldn't leave him alone; following him like a swarm of flies down the stairs into the kitchen when he got weary of lying awake in tangled bed sheets; drowning out Willie Nelson on the cassette player; and refusing to allow him to work on a painting at three in the morning.

When he eventually crashed out on the sofa, he dreamed about Karen smashing her car through the hospital doors, racing along grey corridors, tyres squealing, until her headlamps picked out Sladana, who screamed as the car hurtled towards her…

He woke in a panic and told himself that the only way to get it out of his system was to talk to Karen. He'd left messages, but she wasn't returning his calls.

He didn't want to believe she'd behaved like that, but he'd been stewing all morning, and now it was lunchtime, and he couldn't wait any longer.

He drove to Hightown and found her outside her shop, in her usual black shorts and red top.

Sam watched from across the road as she locked the shop door, then began her stretches.

He jogged across the road, dodging a white van with a clattering engine.

She didn't look pleased to see him. 'What are you doing here? I'm going for a run. Back in an hour.'

'I need to talk to you. Can we go inside?'

It was obvious she knew why he was here. 'Why don't you just say what you've got to say.'

He looked down at his feet and took a deep breath before matching her gaze. A small group of people had gathered a few yards away. He kept his voice low: 'I can't believe you said those things about Sladana. You are bang out of order. And just so you know, she's not after my money -'

She laughed: 'Oh don't be so naive, Sam! Of course she bloody is!'

The laughter stung him. He started shouting. 'What makes you such an expert then? How do you know what's in her head? And what gives you the right to slag her off with that racist crap? I was at school with her. I know her. I don't know what game you're playing but it's not going to work, okay? Abusing her - one of your own bloody customers? - and then bad mouthing her to my friends, too. Christ, Karen! I can't believe it. I'm warning you… just, back off!'

Her voice was cold and flat. 'So, I'm being threatened now, am I? She's got you where she wants, hasn't she? You wanna be more careful. I don't take kindly to being shouted at in the street, especially outside my own shop. I'm pretty sure there's a law against that. And what happened to your promise to Mikey, eh? Is this your way of looking after me?'

He swung round, his face inches away from hers, his fists clenched, and snarled: 'I bet there's a law against racism, too, and don't bring Mikey into this.' He stepped back, with an effort. 'Jesus, Karen! What's the matter with you?'

She stepped back, looking shaken, and Sam knew he'd gone too far.

'There's nothing wrong with me. But you should think twice before you slag people off in public. And threaten them. What are you going to do next? Hit me? Maybe I should report you. You know what, maybe I will. And you an ambassador for Whistle Bay, too. How's that going to look?'

She taunted him with a smile: 'Nice talking to you, Sam. I almost liked you once. Just make sure I don't see you again. But don't worry, you'll be hearing from me.'

Chapter 19

The driver and his mate unloaded what was left of the hut at the side of the house, plank by creosoted plank, leaving Sam to stack them onto pallets.

The sleet was sharp enough to pierce through his hoodie, but the mindless exercise helped him to switch off. And by the time he'd thawed out with a mug of tea, the architect arrived.

He wore blue jeans and a black jacket with a scarf tied in a big knot. He spoke with a Welsh accent and said his name was Richard, 'but my friends call me Rick.'

His glasses looked too big for his face, and he spoke quickly, as if he really ought to be somewhere else and didn't want to be interrupted. Sam didn't mind that: Grace said he charged by the hour.

'I'm thinking a house of two halves, okay? Preserve the frontage as best we can, otherwise the planners will throw a wobbly. But have fun at the back, don't you think? I'm liking New England colonial, if you know what I mean by that.'

He pointed to his sketches, obviously assuming that Sam didn't know: 'Let me show you. Basically, we knock out the whole back wall to give you these amazing sliding glass doors, here, and we use all that wood from the hut to make a verandah - you know, the sort of place they sit in rocking chairs and drink whisky in old movies?'

Sam nodded, pretending he knew exactly what he meant.

Rick turned the sheet over noisily to show Sam the internal layout.

Sam jabbed a finger at one corner of the sketch: 'What's that?'

'I'm calling that your studio.'

Sam looked surprised: 'Right.'

'Grace told me what you do. We like to get to know our clients, and painting is obviously a big part of your life. So, I was thinking of using whatever's left of the wood to line at least one of the walls of the studio, to give it that beach vibe. Happy?'

Rick said he'd come back with the detailed drawings they'd use for the planning application. 'We're busy, but I'm reckoning we can get it done and cleared for you by the first week of the new year. How's that sound?'

Sam said it sounded okay and took a picture of the drawings on his phone.

He showed Sladana later and her eyes widened: 'This is - wow!'

'The studio is the best bit, see there… And this wall, that's going to be glass sliding doors, so we can just walk into the garden, and it would be so light in here.'

'It's incredible, Sam. You must be so excited.'

He put his arms round her and kissed her neck. 'Well, yeah, but the only thing that gets me really excited is you.'

She pushed away and wagged her finger in his face, her eyes teasing him. 'Ah. No, no, not today.'

His voice was pleading. 'But I'm going to London later.'

'Of course, but you'll be back in a few days, and we must finish the painting and I have to go to work. I start shift at 3, remember?'

Sam did his best impression of a sulk. 'Oh, all right. You'd better sit still and keep quiet then.'

She smiled. 'Well, if you finish early, who knows?'

She sat still and he worked quickly: 'What do you think?'

'Sam, it's amazing. You're so clever; make me look like film star.'

'I just need to work a bit more on the background, and it's done.' He looked at his watch pointedly. 'So…?'

She shook her head. 'No. Not romantic, watching the time. I better go and you better pack for London.'

'Aww come on.'

She laughed as she picked up her shoulder bag. 'No. You get ready and have a great time. I'll miss you, though.'

'Kiss me goodbye?'

She moved into his arms, laughing. 'Ok, just little one.'

The kiss lasted, but not long enough. He stood at the kitchen window, watching her drive away. It was only 2.30 but it was misty, and she had the side lights on.

He sat at the kitchen table and checked the online timetable. Services to Birmingham and London were on time. That gave him two hours before the taxi was due to pick him up.

He'd washed and ironed his clothes and laid them out on the bed. He'd thought about buying one of those pull along suitcases, but he chose the bag he used for his football kit instead.

Michelle had looked surprised when he told her he hadn't left Whistle Bay since Dad died. She gave him a few tips. 'London's all right in small doses. Don't bother smiling or making conversation on the train. They'll be reading a paper, doing things on a laptop, or making pointless phone calls. Don't be in a rush when the train gets in, either. Everyone leaps up as if getting off first is the most important part of their day, but you all end up in the same queue when you get down to the tube station. Go at your own pace. Buy yourself a bit of time. It can get crazy down there. They don't call it Piccadilly Circus for nothing.'

His biggest worry was travelling on the Underground. He'd memorised the directions: the Bakerloo line from Westminster; get off seven stations later. He'd remembered Michelle telling him to get a combined train and Underground ticket, so that was okay, too.

Ever since Lindsay had said she'd meet him outside the Tube station, he'd had a fear of descending into the depths of the earth with thousands of strangers, and never finding his way out again.

She'd just laughed: 'Oh what? Sam! All you have to do is ask someone. And anyway, there are maps all over the place. There is absolutely no way you will get lost, trust me.'

He saw her as soon as he left the station, jumping up and down, and waving her arms.

She ran towards him: 'Thank God! Where have you been? I was starting to worry.'

'Sorry. I got lost.'

She didn't seem to notice the sarcasm in his voice. 'For half an hour?'

Sam was swung round violently as a man in a suit barged into his shoulder, then he felt a sharp pain in his leg.'

He pointed at a well-dressed woman walking away with a large carrier bag. 'Hellfire! What's she got in there?'

'Bottles of perfume, judging by the vapour trail she's leaving behind.'

Lindsay steered him across a road jammed with cars and buses that, unlike the woman with the carrier bag, were moving slowly. 'Come on. Let's get out of here. Tube station entrances are not the best places to linger. You need a drink.'

She pulled him through a flood tide of faces and a barrage of noise from diesel engines, car horns, and shouted conversation.

Then suddenly, in an arched doorway, the shock of silence.

Sam looked suspiciously down a flight of red carpeted stairs. Lindsay squeezed his hand and he followed her down.

She pushed the door open, and he was hit by another blast of noise and hot air. She pulled him behind her like a kid who didn't want to go to school. 'Welcome to Vin Rogue,' she shouted.

It was just after 7 and they only got a seat because Lindsay asked if they could join four blokes who were hogging a table for six. A man in a blue suit and white trainers started chatting her up. Sam stared at the drinks menu and tried to shut out the noise.

Red wine was apparently the only option, but there were pages of them to choose from, and looking round the room it seemed that buying a bottle was more popular than a glass.

The slimeball in blue leaned across Lindsay and jabbed a finger on the list. 'That's the one to go for chappy. Take my word for it.'

Lindsay raised a hand and a waiter with tight jeans, bleached hair and a lot of dark eye make up appeared, nodding and tapping on his tablet as she yelled in his ear.

She must have given Boy Blue the brush off because she turned her back on him and shuffled nearer to Sam. 'Keep smiling, darling. They'll be going in a few minutes, promise.' She winked. 'Back to their wives.'

The wine arrived: a red puddle at the bottom of an enormous glass. Sam thought it tasted like puddle, too.

He sipped slowly, distracted by a bearded man in his 60s who was stroking the thigh of a girl in a short black dress who must have been in her teens. Lindsay jabbed his shoulder: 'It's rude to stare.' She leaned in: 'That guy is a film director and I bet she's hoping to get a big part, if you know what I mean.'

She burst out laughing at Sam's puzzled expression, then waved at the waiter and ordered another drink. Sam shook his head: 'No thanks.'

He checked the menu: 'The pinot noir grape has a complex set of flavour characteristics that it imparts to Burgundy wine. It produces a rich and complex red that is not particularly heavy or strong in alcohol.'

Sam wondered why they didn't just say: 'Tastes like vinegar.'

Boy Blue and his mates picked up their smartphones and left in a cloud of cologne, and Lindsay could talk without shouting.

'I'll just finish this off and we'll walk to my place. Sorry, I know this must be overwhelming, but you looked like you needed a drink.'

His ears were still buzzing as they walked through wet streets busy with black cabs and double decker buses. It felt good to be outside in the cool air. But there were so many people about! Noisy smokers standing outside bars, well dressed people with blank stares and carrier bags the size of suitcases coming out of brightly lit shops; and a man huddled in a doorway in a sleeping bag with a piece of card that said: 'No home - be kind.'

Sam gave him a £2 coin.

They turned the corner and Lindsay told him they were on Marylebone High Street. 'So, not far now.'

Sam had never been so far from home. This was Lindsay's world. And as far as he was concerned, she was welcome to it.

He woke to the sound of tapping and pulled the covers up to his chin as Lindsay pushed the bedroom door open: 'Come on. Time to get moving.'

He put on jeans and a check flannel shirt and walked through to the kitchen/diner, where she was sitting at a table laid out with toasted muffins, little white pots of yoghurt, matching bowls of mixed fruit, and a big glass jug of coffee.

'Sleep well?'

Sam yawned and stretched. 'Yeah, thanks. I can't believe how quiet it is here.'

'See? London's not all bad. You need to give it time.'

'Sorry I was such a plonker last night. I was knackered.'

'I must admit, it was chaotic in that bar, and I'm used to the noise. I should have just dragged you back here so you could crash out. Forgive me?'

'Yeah, go on then.' He chewed on the muffin. 'What are we doing today, then?'

'Don't tell me you've forgotten? You're only coming to the V and A with me.'

She started getting ready before he'd finished his muesli, and they were out on the street in less than an hour.

He felt like he was on a school trip, with Lindsay as the teacher. 'We just go down here, to Edgware Road tube station, jump on and get off at South Kensington, then walk to the V and A. Doddle.'

He took a calming breath as they stepped onto the steep moving staircase. At least he wouldn't get lost down there today. He tried to focus on the posters that glided past: perfume, sunglasses, theatres, phones, cars. He was puzzled. It wasn't as if there were any shops down there.

They found seats together on a train that rattled and screamed and bounced, full of more adverts that everyone except Sam seemed to ignore.

He enjoyed the walk at the other end, and before long he was breathing fresh air and looking up to gape at the spectacular museum entrance on Exhibition Road: 'It looks like a cathedral.'

'That's a good way of looking at it. I've always thought of it as a sacred place.'

Lindsay told him Queen Victoria laid the foundation stone in 1899. 'And now, you're here to make a bit of history, Sam. Ready?'

Sam's negativity about London was forgotten. He was blown away by the interior, with its high ceilings and windows, and stared when she showed him the floor plan on a leaflet. 'I'll never see all this if I stay here for the rest of my life.'

Lindsay linked arms and they walked deeper into the museum. 'Don't be overwhelmed. Let's go to the cafe first, shall we?'

She told him more of the history as they walked down a wide staircase. 'Henry Cole founded the South Kensington Museum. He wanted people to come here instead of drinking themselves to death in gin palaces. So, he created the world's first museum restaurant.' She paused for dramatic effect. 'And here it is.'

It looked like a huge hall to Sam, but she pointed to a room on the left. 'Let's go in there.'

Sam found himself staring again. He couldn't believe a cafe could be so beautiful. Lindsay guided him to a table in the corner. 'Henry Cole gave opportunities to new designers, and one of them was called William Morris. He designed this room before he became famous. Sit back and have a gape. See if it inspires you while I get us a tea.'

They talked about the workshop she was running. Her excitement was infectious, as always. He felt self-conscious because the place was busy and she was talking so loudly that people on other tables were looking.

But she didn't notice: 'I'm on a three-month residency, Sam. The idea is that I use some of the collections to inspire new work that I can then share with students and visitors, just like Henry Cole did with people like William Morris.'

'It sounds like a real honour. But what am I doing here?'

She put her hand on his, and all his nervousness dissipated. She smiled and spoke softly. The V and A was huge, but it felt like it belonged to them, just for a moment.

'I want you to be inspired, Sam. Start by walking through the furniture collection to see if anything grabs you. Think about your beach and your deckchairs and the sea and let your mind wander. You're a long way from home, but don't be afraid of it: use it! Imagine a new way of portraying the things you know. That's what my residency is all about. I'm doing the same thing with my landscapes.'

'What do you mean?'

'Landscape isn't just about pretty views. There are industrial landscapes, city landscapes. Think of London, this building is one of many beautiful places. But we are part of it. So many landscapes were made by people, yet you don't see people in landscape paintings, do you?' She stopped. 'Sorry. Talking too much, as per.'

She walked with him to the furniture collections, then hugged him. 'Just message me when you're done and tell me where you are. I'll come and find you.'

'But -'

'Don't over think it, Sam. Just look around. I promise, something will hit you and get you excited. Right. It's that way, mister. Off you go.'

Sam walked slowly through the doorway she pointed at, nodding at a guy in a uniform who looked more like a nightclub bouncer. London had overwhelmed him last night, with its noise. He was alone now and feeling more at home.

He'd only been looking round for ten minutes when he accepted that Lindsay was right: it was inspiring.

He decided to concentrate on the chairs. One of his favourites was dated 1500 to 1560, but he was impressed by some of the more modern designs; particularly one dated 1986: 'Spine Chair' by Andre Dubreuil.

He was under-whelmed by an upright chair made in 1960 from what looked like deckchair fabric stretched onto a metal frame. The variety was amazing. One chair looked like it had been fabricated from a supermarket trolley but was dated 1934.

It took more than an hour, and he was beginning to feel overwhelmed by the range of designs, but he finally found the ones he loved most of all. They were beautifully made using dark wood sections by someone called Charles Rennie Mackintosh in around 1907. The colour reminded him of the beach hut just after it had been creosoted.

Lindsay hugged him when he found his way to her studio. 'I knew you'd find something. Now come with me, and let's see if you can take that idea and come up with something new.'

169

'Then what?'

'Then, my dear Sammy, I will include your creation in the new landscape painting I'm working on. And that very same painting will be hung on the wall in this very same building, and you will be spectacularly proud. So, let's go!'

He said he needed a sandwich, but she wasn't impressed. 'Create first; eat later.'

She showed him to a desk next to a huge stained-glass window. She was right, there was something sacred about this place.

He ignored the rumbling in his stomach and started drawing.

It was day three of what should have been a seven day stay, and he was ready to go home. He thought she'd be annoyed but she just nodded and poured more coffee.

'No, it makes a lot of sense. Go home and start doing new things. Sounds like it's worked, doesn't it?'

Sam nodded: 'It's been amazing. It's just like you said: seeing the museum and listening to you made me see things differently. I just want to get home and get on with it now.'

Lindsay smiled: 'Yeah, and you're missing Sladana, aren't you?'

'Is it that obvious?'

'Yep. 'Fraid so.' She sighed. 'I miss Grace. She's like you, she doesn't much like London.'

'But you'll see her for Christmas?'

'Oh yes, I'm coming back for good old Yuletide. So, make sure you get me a pressie, okay?' She stood and held out her arms, and Sam moved in for a hug. 'It's been so good to see you, Sammy.' She pulled away. 'Oh God, I hate goodbyes! Go on, get off before I start blubbing.'

He didn't get lost this time and relaxed in the quiet carriage as London slid out of sight.

He found himself taking in detail he'd never seen before: grey back yards allowing tall houses to keep their distance from the track; spindly trees like pencil drawings; green fields that weren't green in the dull light of December; and people - people everywhere; in cars, in high vis jackets working on the lines and on the roads, filling up shopping car parks, hanging out washing.

The train hissed and vibrated as it picked up speed, and the view became a blur of indistinct colour.

Sam thought back to his time at the V and A. It felt weird that ancient objects like those chairs could make him see things differently.

He leaned back and closed his eyes and tried to understand.

Chapter 20

Sam stretched out on the sofa and switched over to speaker.

Sladana sounded like she was trapped in a biscuit tin. 'I hope you like her. She can seem little bit fierce. But she will like you. Anyway, it's Mother's Day, so …'

Sam lifted his head off the cushion. 'What? Mother's Day isn't in December.'

'It is in Serbia. Second Sunday before Christmas.' She laughed. 'Tradition is for children to creep into bedroom and tie her feet, so she has to stay in bed, not work.'

'My mum would have killed me.'

'Yes, but we release her if she promises to give us sweets.'

'She'd definitely kill me.'

'We don't do it anymore. Anyway, she is looking forward to seeing you, so no need for worry. Will be nice change for her. She depends on me, sees only me.'

'Okay, I'm nervous, but it will be nice to meet her. You said she never goes out. What does she do all day?'

'She likes reading poetry and watching tv shows about nature and art. She is in love with David Attenborough, I think. And looking out of the window.'

'Okay…sounds all right.'

He was laughing as they said their goodbyes, but the prospect of meeting her mum later made him edgy - if she never saw anyone, what would she make of him?

The water was lukewarm because he'd forgotten to put the immersion heater on, but he showered anyway, then put on black jeans and a fleece jacket he'd bought online, over a blue open neck shirt.

He checked himself in the hall mirror and jogged back upstairs to comb his hair. He tried to remember the last time he'd done that. It was probably for Dad's funeral. He smiled at the thought that, after so long, he could remember where the comb was.

Their house was on a small estate of ex-council houses known as The Barrow. They'd been built around the time he was born on the other side of the ring road, as if the town wanted to keep them as far away as possible.

He scanned the street before getting out of the car. A few of the lads in his football team lived round here, and he didn't want them nosing around. He decided it should be safe: it was cold enough to keep most people indoors, and there was a match on tv.

Sladana opened the door before he'd finished knocking. She smiled. 'You look nice. She's excited to meet you.'

'You look okay too.'

She laughed and pushed him down the hall.

Her mother was sitting by the window. She held out a thin hand but there was strength in her grip. She pronounced her words carefully: 'Hello Sam. I am Marija.'

Sladana had told him she was 49, but at first glance she looked older. Sladana said she'd lost weight since her husband died, and her dark hair was streaked grey. But Sam noticed her eyes shone and her skin was smooth and pale. She wore a grey cardigan and black skirt, and sat very still, like she was posing for a painting.

Her voice was husky: a reminder of how Sladana's voice had first hooked him in.

'Welcome to our home. Please, sit down.' She looked at Sladana. 'Shall we have Slatko now?' She turned to face him and smiled softly. 'Tradition. Little spoon of Slatko for guests.'

Sladana said: 'Guests? Sam is the first we've had, mama.' Marija tutted but gave Sam a half smile.

Sladana came in carrying a tray with a small bowl and three spoons and three shot glasses with a clear liquid in them. They laughed at Sam's expression. 'Don't worry, it's just water, Sam. Try a spoonful, then drink the water.'

Sam took a teaspoonful of the gooey mixture in the bowl and smacked his lips. 'That's lovely. So sweet.'

Marija bowed her head: 'Like jam, yes?'

'Yes, it is. Happy Mother's Day.'

She smiled. 'Thank you. I am lucky mother. Sladana is my angel. Now, please, you must talk to me about your art.'

173

Sam told them about his trip to London and the museum, and how he hated being among so many people, but ended up fixed on the idea that there were no landscapes without people. 'So, I came back and decided I wanted to make my own design of deckchairs, and learn how to paint people in their own landscape, if that makes sense.'

'Yes, I think so. It is our landscape that makes us.'

Sladana sat and listened, smiling occasionally at Sam, as her mother told her story.

She was born and grew up in Leskovac, a city that was almost destroyed by bombs in the Second World War. She said it was tough, but her parents worked hard to make sure she got an education.

She smiled sadly: 'I wanted so much to be an artist. But we needed money, so I had to work from young age. I was married at age 19. Important to work when you could and marry for safety -'

Sladana chipped in. 'Security, mama.'

'Yes, yes. I was lucky. I also marry for love. He was builder. Strong man, hard work. Then troubles came and there was much fighting and killing.'

'When was this?'

She looked at Sladana, who answered. 'Late 80s and 90s. It was a very violent country and mama and papa paid to come to Britain when I was just a baby.' She paused and put a hand on her mother's. 'Papa died soon after. Heart attack.'

Marija took a deep breath, keeping her eyes on Sam. He noticed the faint vertical lines where her eyebrows met, and the slight downturn of her mouth. The more he saw, the more he wanted to paint her. It struck him that she seemed slightly different every time he looked, like the view from the deckchair hut.

All his nervousness was gone as she leaned towards him, talking confidentially, as if this was a secret between the two of them. 'He was a good man. He brought us here and we are safe. That was his wish.'

Sam nodded, uncertain what to say. She reached out a hand and touched his knee and when he looked up, her smile made her look years younger. 'You are a good man, too. Strong, I can tell. Sladana is very lucky girl.'

'Thank you. I think I am a lucky boy.'

They sat at a table overlooking the back garden; a small square patch of grass surrounded by larchlap fence panels that looked in danger of collapse. Sam decided he'd offer to do some jobs for them.

Sladana pointed to the dishes they had laid out. 'This is Sarma: pickled cabbage, mince and rice. And this is special treat, just for you, Gibanica - cheesy pie. And after, if you eat it all, mama says we can have a glass of Slivovitz.'

'I'm sure I will eat it all! What's slivo -?'

Marija laughed as he stumbled over the word: 'Slivovitz. We must teach you the language. Brandy made from plums. Very nice.'

'Sounds amazing, but I'm driving.'

Marija tutted: 'No, no, you must have tiny taste at least. For me, okay?'

Sam smiled and nodded.

They ate in silence; Sam relishing the flavours, especially the cheese pie. He cleared his plate before they'd made it halfway through their own, and Marija laughed again: 'I said you were good man. Good appetite, too.'

She sat by the window again while Sam helped Sladana clear away into the cramped kitchen.

He put an arm round her shoulder, keeping his voice low. 'Thanks for inviting me. I love your mother - sorry, mama.'

'I'm so happy. I can tell she loves you, too. You make her smile. Now, shoo!' She waved him out of the kitchen. 'Go and talk.'

Sam saluted. 'Yes, miss.'

Marija wanted to talk about painting, and Sam told her how Lindsay had helped him get started. 'I never thought I would be able to do it. I was so bad at school. But I feel confident now.'

She nodded. 'Confidence is important.'

Something in her voice spoke of regret. He cleared his throat: 'Erm, would you like to have a go, too? I could help, if you needed it.'

'I think you are busy, so maybe some time, but not yet, yes?'

175

He held her hand when it was time to leave and was puzzled by the look she gave Sladana.

Sladana whispered in his ear. 'I think it would be better to kiss on both cheeks.'

Sam bumped his face awkwardly against Marija's and she watched from the window as Sladana walked out to the car with him. She turned and squeezed his arm. 'So, you like each other?'

'I love her already.'

'Really?'

'Yes, really. I wondered if she'd like to come out with us somewhere, for a change, next time?'

She pursed her lips. 'Maybe. She is happier at home, but she might come if you are the one to ask. It's sad how she has become so, I don't know...'

'Afraid to go out?'

'Yes, I think. Papa loved being outside, and he would take us on trips, to the seaside, or to the park, and she liked that. But now...'

'She's lost her nerve.'

Sladana nodded earnestly. 'That's it, yes.'

'I promised myself I would paint her picture, get her back into painting, and take her out somewhere - maybe even just for a drive at first.'

'She would make a very good picture.'

'Yes, I know. I can't believe how young her skin is. I know she has grey hair and sometimes she looks older, but other times -'

'- Yes, she was beautiful as a girl. She tells me she has good skin because she puts her face in a bowl of cold water every morning and stays there until she has to breathe.'

'Wow! I should be ok then. It's the same for me when I have a shower and forget to put the heater on.'

He waved to Marija as they turned the corner; then kissed Sladana and told her he loved her.

She just wagged her finger at him and reminded him she was on night shifts the rest of the week.

He slumped into the car. 'Yeah, I know.'

176

She smiled and leaned in through the window. 'But you're coming for Christmas Day, yes?'

'Yeah, please. Try and stop me.'

She wrapped her arms round his neck and kissed him: 'Good. And Sam?'

'Yeah.'

'I love you too.'

It was a clear starry night when Sam drove home, and he felt lighter than air.

He went for a run next morning, and watched from the top of the hill as the fog rolled in from the sea to press down on Whistle Bay like a grey pillow.

Sam took a picture in case he decided to try and paint the scene, then the sun briefly picked out the bronze weather vane on the church tower piercing the fog. It was like the flash of a lighthouse, or, Sam imagined, a signal that only he could pick up.

But the memory of the confrontation with Karen kept coming back. It was there late last night as he assembled the parts for a work bench he was going to install in the shop he'd rented.

He kept telling himself to forget her, but the thought of what she might do wouldn't leave him.

He looked around. The sun had gained some height, but not heat, and Sam checked his watch.

He jogged carefully down the steep path, trying to avoid putting too much pressure on his knees. He stopped when he heard the cry of a gull and looked up. But the sun and the sky were already blotted out by the fog.

Rick was shrouded in a dark coat, his face half hidden by a scarf.

He hopped from foot to foot. as Sam opened the door. 'I hope you've got the heating on.'

'Nah, we just jump up and down to keep warm up here.'

'Sorry. My partner's always tells me I sound patronising.'

'That's ok. She's wrong.'

'He.'

177

'Sorry.'

'Don't let him hear you. He's never wrong. But can you let me in? I'm bloody freezing. Took ages getting here in this horrible stuff.'

'It's called fog.'

'Yes, thank you. We do have fog in otherwise civilised cities.'

Sam laughed: 'What, London? Call that civilised? I couldn't wait to get out.'

'Touche.'

Sam showed him into the living room and turned the gas fire up a notch.

Rick warmed his hands, agreeing to remove his coat only when Sam agreed to put the kettle on.

When Sam came back with mugs of tea and a plate of biscuits, Rick was spreading out his drawings on the sofa.

'Right, Sam. It's all good news.'

'What do you mean?'

'Apart from the fact that you'll have solar panels and a heat pump and a new heating system, you mean? Well, number one, we - sorry, I - have come up with a brilliant design you are going to absolutely adore. And two, the planners have told me they are just going to wave it through. All we have to do is allow a dull building inspector to poke a nose in now and again.'

'So…?'

'So, let me have a biccie and a slurp of this and I'll talk you through it.'

Sam dunked a digestive as he waited.

Rick carefully unfolded the plans. 'Before I stun you with my brilliance, you also need to know that we'll come in under budget. Am I good, or am I good?'

Sam laughed. He liked Rick and wished he had some of his self-confidence. 'You're amazing.'

It was easy to see that the design was going to transform the place, even though, as Rick said: 'No-one would notice anything much different from the front.'

He'd retained but widened the front door as the main entrance, bricking in the other doorway and fitting new double-glazed windows that looked like the originals. The back of the house would be knocked into one big space with full height sliding glass doors, but with two rooms knocked together to create Sam's studio.

'So all the heating and hot water will come from solar panels and this pump thing, will it?'

'Exactly right. And you've got a lot of roof to cover with panels, so you can sell any excess to the grid.'

'Grid?'

'National Grid. They're the ones who supply electricity. They won't pay you a fortune, but it'll bring in a bit of income. And think how virtuous you'll feel, living off free energy.'

Sam thought for a minute. 'Yeah, but it's not free, really, is it? It's going to cost me a fair bit to install.'

'Don't argue with your architect. It's not allowed.' He sipped tea quickly. 'But, yes, it will cost, and it'll be a few years before you recoup the cost, but the real point is that you're doing your bit for the planet, right?'

Rick said it would be a big and messy job at first. 'I would think seriously about moving out for a few weeks.'

'I hadn't thought of that. When will they want to start?'

'Our builder says he can get a team onto it first week of the New Year. How does that sound?'

'It sounds very soon.'

'A man of your wealth could just check into a hotel. How cool would that be?'

'I could, but I wouldn't be wealthy very long, would I?'

It was only after Rick had driven off into the slowly dissipating fog that Sam remembered he was supposed to be meeting Grace, and he was already late.

He sat on the sofa, spread out the big sheets on the carpet and tried to imagine what the house would look like. He began to wonder if he was making a mistake. It was so big.

His phone rang: 'Hi Grace, I'm sorry, I -'

'It's OK, Rick told me he was coming to see you, so I guessed you might have too much on your mind.'

'Honestly, I was just about to call.'

'Sam, relax... it's no problem. Anyway, your day is about to get even better.'

'How come?'

'Interest rates are going up, which means the value of your investments goes up, too. We reckon you're already about £10,000 better off.'

Sam held the phone away from his ear and stared at it, for some reason he couldn't explain. 'What? Dad would work a couple of years to earn that much.'

Grace was laughing. 'Yeah, I know, bless. Rick tells me he's coming in under budget, so it looks like you're going to end up with a new house with no mortgage, and around £150,000 in savings and investments tucked away. And that's without the money you're earning from art.'

'I should be celebrating.'

'You should. Invite me, though, yeah? Especially if it involves champagne.'

'Definitely. Thanks, Grace, for - you know.'

'It's a pleasure Sam. So...' The line went quiet.

'Grace?'

'Can I ask you something?' Her voice had changed.

'Yeah, course you can.'

'Hope you won't mind me telling you, but there's a story going round about you being abusive and threatening to a woman in Hightown.'

Sam stood and began pacing. 'Oh shit.'

'Is it true, then?'

'I lost my rag with Karen a few days ago because she'd been slagging off Sladana.'

'Yeah, I remember you saying ...You'll have to be careful. You know what this place is like.'

'I know.'

'Look, even if you raised your voice, or got in her face, there's a risk she could claim she felt threatened, and she could -'

'- go to the police, Yeah, I know. I've been lying awake worrying about that.'

'Why don't you go round and straighten it out with her? Apologise, if that's what it takes.'

'You reckon she'd listen?'

'I think it's worth a try. Take her a Christmas present, or something.'

'I know what I'd like to give her.'

Grace laughed but made him promise he'd think about it.

Tackling a new portrait was just the diversion Sam needed.

Aaron was as chatty as ever when it was over, and Sam bought him a coffee in Billy's place. Hard- faced June had been replaced by a smart lad by the name of Willy.

Aaron laughed so much he had a coughing fit. 'Billy and Willy! What a team!'

Sam nearly choked on his latte. 'Aaron! Anyway, come on. Is Billy still at it with DIY Dorothy?'

Aaron grinned. 'Nah, keep up - she gave him the elbow last week. We all thought you'd be her next victim. Anyway, what's the game?'

'What d'you mean?'

'Why do you wanna paint my ugly face?'

'It's not ugly, Aaron. You've always been a good mate, and you were close to my dad, so I wanted you to be the first.'

'First what? Idiot?'

'Shut up. I've decided to start painting people as well as landscapes. Places are nothing without people, are they? And I thought why not start with the traders. People like you, and Billy, and Jim -'

'And Dorothy - she'd be well up for it; probably strip off if you asked her.'

Sam snorted. 'I'm going to paint scenes with local people in them. I've got everything set up in that new shop. I'm going to paint some new pictures and have it as a sort of studio and gallery.'

'And put my mush in the window?'

'Definitely. You could be famous.'

'You must be mad. No-one'll come near the place if you do that.'

Billy came over to say hello and it was obvious that Aaron was building up to something. He twisted in his chair, looking round as if he'd lost something.

Billy rose to the bait. He gave him a puzzled look. 'What's up Aaron?'

Aaron could hardly get the words out he was laughing so much. 'I was just wondering... where's your Willy?'

Sam was still giggling like a schoolkid as he left Aaron on the esplanade and set off to meet Karen. It didn't last long. He remembered there was a time when he thought he and Karen might actually get together.

That set him wondering; was that the problem? Did she think that, too, and get angry because Sladana had come on the scene? Karen's mood changed after Sladana turned up at the wake.

By the time he turned into her street, he was psyched up; convinced Grace was right. It was just commonsense: when you mess up, apologise and make up.

Grace had suggested he should give her a Christmas card and a present. He decided not to: 'She'll probably throw it at me.'

He knew he was right the minute she opened the door and invited him in without even a smile. They sat across the table in the cramped kitchen. It felt so formal – and that was doubly weird after what they'd been through together.

He'd rehearsed his speech, but he knew he was rushing it. The sentences came out in a different order, and it sounded all wrong.

'I didn't mean to shout, Karen. I didn't want to upset you, I just wanted to let you know you'd upset Sladana. When I saw you outside the shop, I suppose I just lost it. I couldn't believe you said those things to her. I came to ask you to forgive me.'

Her voice was flat, and she wasn't giving anything away. 'So, what are you saying?'

'I'm saying sorry. I didn't mean to upset you.'

She sipped her tea slowly. Sam hadn't touched his. 'Right. But you did upset me. In fact, you did more than upset me; you threatened me, and at least four people who know me saw it.'

'I was angry. I know I was wrong.'

'Well, that's something. At least you're admitting threatening behaviour.'

182

Sam shook his head. 'No! Hold on, I'm not admitting anything.' He saw the amusement in her eyes. 'Why are you doing this, Karen?'

She stood and he felt vulnerable, just for a moment.

She laughed in apparent disbelief: 'Why am I doing this? We wouldn't be having this conversation if you hadn't lost your rag and threatened and abused me in the street, right outside my shop. Do you know how damaging that is, to me and to my reputation? I'm trying to build trade, not drive people away. Jesus! You just don't get it, do you? And look at the size of you. How do you think it felt, you in my face with your fist clenched, eh?'

'I know. I'm sorry.'

'Yeah, you said. But sorry doesn't help much does it?'

He looked up at her. 'So what do you want me to do? I've apologised. What else can I do?' He paused. Grace had said she was in debt. Maybe that's what this was all about. 'Do you need money?'

The sudden silence was brief, but long enough for him to realise his mistake. Her voice was cold. 'So, the rich guy writes me a cheque and the problem goes away. Is that the way your mind works now, Sam? You think it's all about money? Yeah, well done, big shot. I might have been prepared to let it drop, but not now. So, I suggest…' Sam flinched as she hammered her fist on the table. '… that you get out of my house now!'

'Look, you've got this all wrong, I didn't mean -'

'Oh just get out! You're pathetic. You thought you could pick on a defenceless woman and intimidate her. It hasn't worked, has it? And you know what, congratulations, you've just made it worse.'

She pointed to the door. She was breathing heavily but her voice was calm now. 'You say you're sorry, but it's nowhere near as sorry as you're going to be. I'm going to make your life hell.' Her smile was like ice. 'Close the door on your way out, will you?'

Sam walked quickly through the back streets.

The sleet was soaking into his clothes, but he was too pumped to care.

Each step felt like it was clearing his mind, and eventually the idea took hold that Karen was bluffing. Think about it…what could she actually do to make his life hell? He smiled bitterly. It had been pretty shit up until now anyway. Yes, that was it, she was trying to scare him to make herself feel better. She was getting her own back.

He stopped outside his shop. This place represented his new life, and it hurt to even think that he might have blown the whole thing because he lost his temper with Karen.

He knew what Lindsay would say: 'Just deal with it.' It had been Grace's idea to go round and apologise. Maybe he should have ignored her.

His fingers were cold, and he fumbled with the key, keen to get in before anyone saw him.

Inside, it smelled of new paint and new wood, and it was warm: the hour he'd spent on YouTube looking at boiler fixes had paid off. He locked the door behind him, left the blinds down and sat at his desk to scan through the photos of Aaron.

He hung his sodden fleece on the old hat stand and warmed his hands on a radiator, then flicked the desk lamp on and began sketching.

He'd only been working for a few minutes when his phone rang. He cursed himself for not putting it on silent. He didn't recognise the number.

'Hello?'

The voice was friendly. 'Mr Taverner?'

'Yes.'

'Oh hi, my name's Bill. I work for the Recorder.'

'Oh hi.'

'Hi. Yes. You are the Sam Taverner that I met at the launch?'

'Oh, you mean the Whistle Bay campaign. Yes, that's me.'

'Okay, good. Well, we're running a story next week - oh, by the way, I'm recording the conversation. It's what we always do these days. Okay?'

'Yeah, okay.'

'Great, thanks. The thing is, sorry about this, but we've had a few complaints about you - threatening behaviour. A few witnesses say they saw you in the street at Hightown, shaking

184

your fist and yelling at a woman. I just wondered if you could tell us about it.'

Sam stood and began pacing. 'I didn't threaten her.'

'So that confirms it was you then. Okay, but that's how it looked to people we spoke to. They recognised you from the poster campaign. And the woman, Karen Madeley, she was your brother's partner, right? The one who died recently?'

Sam sat down again. 'Yes.'

'So, as I say, we're running a story, and we wanted to hear your side of things. We wondered if you had anything you'd like to say.'

'No, I haven't.'

'Really? Are you sure? You realise how this is going to look, don't you?'

'No comment.'

'Okay, Mr. Taverner. I've written that down. My next call will be to the Council, to see what they think about -'

Sam put the phone down, picked up the sketch and tore Aaron into pieces.

He jerked awake just after 9am. The rain was machine-gunning the bedroom window.

He stared at the ceiling. Sleep had come sporadically; brief interludes between dreams, including the one that had just woken him …

The beach was full of people, but no-one knew where the beach hut was, and he was lost, whirling round, his bare feet gouging ruts in the sand that got deeper and deeper until the water began to bubble up and he began to sink. He shouted for help but everyone was busy painting; pointing at the view or hunched over their drawing pads. He screamed as the water level rose, up to his chest, his chin, his mouth. He began to choke, then someone put a hand on his head, very gently, and he felt safe again until the hand grew heavy and started to press him down into the soft muddy water. He twisted and tilted his head, spitting out salty water, gasping. Then he saw her face. It was Karen.

Sam kicked free of the sheets and sat up. The rain was heavier now; buckets of water being thrown at the window.

He forced himself to move. Still in his boxer shorts, he went downstairs and switched on the radio; but he wasn't in the mood for carols, so he turned it off and sat with a mug of tea listening to the rain.

He realised there was no-one he could talk to. Sladana was working extra shifts, and Lindsay and Grace were making up for lost time at the flat.

He used to come home crying after school because he wasn't making any friends. Mum held him tight and told him not to worry because he was part of a family that loved him. Now the whole family was gone but he'd kept going: honouring Dad's wishes by carrying on with the business; supporting Mikey through his last days.

But he was still alone – feeling sorry for himself, sitting alone on Christmas Eve, for God's sake,; dreading the next phone call; scared to go into town in case someone asks him about Karen.

He rinsed his mug and leaned on the sink. Was Karen right to be scared of him that day? He didn't often lose it, though he was red-carded twice last season for retaliation. And he'd snapped at Aaron for no good reason a few weeks ago and lost his rag with Potts and the others when they complained about the art class.

He sat down again, head in hands. There was only one person to blame for him being alone. He was the problem.

Lindsay and Grace had told him he needed to get away; but he wouldn't listen.

He'd become so obsessed with keeping the business afloat that he'd forgotten what it was like to enjoy himself. He'd given up playing football, stopped going out with the few people he still knew from school.

Sam walked down the hall into the living room, watching the tops of the trees bending in the wind. He'd been calling it mum's room for years, but it was his easel standing next to the window; his pictures leaning against the wall. The hut had always been Dad's hut, even though Sam had been running the place for a year.

He suddenly felt energized at the realization that he was in a trap that he'd set for himself. Sam tore off a sheet from the pad on the easel and sat at the kitchen table, pen in hand.

He drew two columns. On one side, he scribbled: *No family; no hut; Karen; newspaper story.*

And on the other: *Sladana; money; new house; art classes/painting - portraits, landscapes; Lindsay, Grace; Bay campaign.*

Maybe it was time to start appreciating what he'd got.

The forecast had said it was going to be torrential all day, but the rain was easing to a drizzle and there was some light in the sky.

Chapter 21

He was out early on Christmas morning, his breath a vapour trail as he ran to the esplanade.

He waved at the parents leaning on the railings, as they watched children wobble on Christmas bikes.

The hut was gone, replaced by whiteboards with red health and safety signs and keep out warnings. According to Michelle, the new arts centre would be open before the end of March, which meant the family business would be history; existing only in the memory: old photographs on new walls.

He walked onto the beach, tasting the freshness as he closed his eyes and gulped the air. The excited shouts of children mingled with the cry of gulls, and the sea came in with a slow drum beat. The soundtrack was timeless, familiar, and it was easy to imagine that he was ten years old again, standing here with Dad. His breathing slowed, and it took an effort to open his eyes again.

But when he did, he wasn't thinking about what he'd lost, he was remembering the Christmas Eve list he'd stuck on the fridge door. Mum's mantra - 'count your blessings' - suddenly meant something.

He turned away, shivering slightly as the sweat cooled on his skin, and took a few more breaths before setting off for the run back home.

He took one stride, then stopped. There was a gull on the sand on the corner of the hoardings; almost lost against the white background, until it moved.

'Gary?'

The gull twitched its head at an angle and pecked at the sand, and Sam saw the distinctive patch of grey.

He called out louder, laughing: 'Gary!' And took a few cautious steps nearer.

Gary waddled a few steps further away, keeping his distance, and Sam crouched down. 'Come on boy... it's me...come on...'

Gary gave him the eye and Sam held his breath, willing him to come nearer. But he suddenly sprang into the air, and, with a soft cry, flapped lazily into the wind coming off the sea, and was carried away towards the hill.

Sladana's mother talked all the way through the meal, educating Sam about the Serbian Christmas. She told him they used to celebrate it on January 7, until they moved to England.

She insisted on breaking bread - cesnica. 'Always made with coin inside, for wealth.'

Sladana winked at Sam: 'I bet he gets the coin, mama.'

But she found it, and, after roast pork, they sat on the sofa, whispering, while Marija napped in her chair.

Sladana kissed his cheek. 'Where's my present?'

'Where's mine?'

'I'm here.'

'You're not even wrapped up. I used to love opening presents.'

She giggled. 'You want me to take my clothes off and roll up in Christmas paper?'

Sam groaned. 'Oh yes please.'

'Maybe next year.' She rested her head on his shoulder. 'Anyway, mama likes always to save presents till late, so we have something to look forward to. But, I have something for you now.'

'Does it involve you taking your clothes off?'

'Shhhh! Definitely not! But mama has relative coming to stay, and I have swapped shifts, so I can come to you day after tomorrow, and stay.'

Marija grunted as she woke up. 'Why are you smiling so much over there?'

Sladana laughed. 'We're happy, mama. Happy to see you wake up so we can have our presents.'

Sam went out to the car and came back with a large brown paper parcel. She nudged Marija. 'I bet it's a painting.'

189

She knew she'd guessed wrong when Sam handed it to her. 'What is it? It's so heavy!'

Sam helped her lay it on the carpet and she tore the wrapping away. Sam smiled. 'It's a deckchair. I made it for you with wood from the hut.'

Sam set it up in the bay window, then Sladana moved in closer, pointing to a metal strip on the frame. She leaned over to read it: 'For Sladana, with love, Sam.'

She hugged him fiercely and turned away, dabbing her eyes on her sleeve, as Sam produced another parcel and gave it to Marija.

She unwrapped it carefully and smiled. 'My beautiful daughter.'

'It's the first proper portrait I've done, and I wanted you to have it, and to say thank you for making me feel welcome.'

'Thank you for this beautiful gift, Sam.'

They drank wine while Sam sipped apple juice and asked Marija if he could paint her portrait, too. 'I could take some photos of you now, and then I can work on it tomorrow.'

She looked pleased and unsure at the same time, then nodded. 'Yes, thank you Sam. I would like that.'

The blue skies gave way to Boxing Day grey.

Sam was up early, made scrambled egg and salmon pieces on toast, and left the washing up for later.

The sketch he'd done last night was on the kitchen table. He wanted to paint Marija in watercolour for the first time, using the dry on wet technique, and he was determined to do it today.

He started by wetting the paper on one side, then turned it over so it naturally flattened itself onto a plastic board he'd mounted on the easel. Then he moistened the other side, set the timer for ten minutes, and drank tea while he set out the colours he'd picked.

He'd painted Sladana's picture in oils, and she'd loved the result, but he wanted to get more atmosphere into this one. This technique would allow him to do it in one session, so he could show Sladana tomorrow.

He worked quickly, starting with the lighter shades of the face and neck, remembering to moisten the paper regularly and not overload the brush.

The paper was beginning to dry after half an hour, so he wetted it again, and carried on. The challenge was to capture the fascination of her face: the smooth pale cheekbones versus the dark sadness of her eyes; the ebony gloss of her hair against the faint lines of ageing on her forehead, and around her mouth.

Sam painted, sipped tea, wetted the paper, mixed colour, painted some more. He lost all sense of time and felt no pressure, even though he only had one go at it: the painting would be spoiled if he left it to dry out too soon.

Finally, he stretched and stepped back to view it. He'd been painting for three hours and there she was, Marija by the window, with a half-smile and eyes that were a mix of happy and sad. That was the thing about her; you couldn't pin down what she was feeling by how she looked.

Sam looked closer, frowned, and sat down again. The border between the darker background and the paleness of her face needed more definition. He picked up a small brush and set to work.

When it was finished his back and shoulders ached, so he walked into the back garden to stretch. He was wearing t shirt and shorts and it felt like the breeze was firing icicles at him. He jogged upstairs and changed into a tracksuit.

He'd just finished eating pasta with feta cheese and tomatoes when the phone rang.

Lindsay, shrieking: 'Sam! Happy Christmas and all that! I simply have to see you! Have you missed me terribly?'

'Yeah, course I have.'

'Liar! I'm coming round so don't you dare go anywhere!'

'What? Now?'

'No in 2050 - of course now! So, get the kettle on, okay?'

Sam half expected her to be at the door in five minutes, so he quickly carried Marija's portrait up to his bedroom. He wanted Sladana to be the first to see it. Time was, he wouldn't have dared show his pictures to anyone unless Lindsay had given her approval, or, more likely, told him what he needed to change.

She rang his doorbell ten minutes later and he staggered back as she threw herself into his arms.

'I need a hug!'

'What's wrong?'

'Grace has abandoned me. Gone into work. On Boxing bloody Day! Can you believe it?' She walked into the kitchen and sat down without another word, then exploded into laughter. 'Oh Sam, your face! You live such a quiet life. Sorry, I should…' She began to whisper. '…talk slowly, gently. Don't want to disturb the peace.'

Sam laughed. 'Too late, you already have. Anyway, have you just come round because you're bored?'

'As if! No, I wanted to see you.'

'That sounds a bit worrying.'

'Don't be so suspicious! I just wondered how you were. Anyway, you shouldn't be on your own at Christmas. Think of me as your Christmas angel.'

'I can't imagine you sitting on top of a tree.'

She smiled as Sam handed her a mug of tea. 'Oh, perfect, thanks darling. So, come on, what's happening in your life?'

Sam sat down, one hand holding onto his tea. He told her about the work he was doing on the new shop and gallery, and about Sladana and her family. It was obvious she was listening, but he got the impression she was waiting her chance.

It soon came. She took a big gulp of tea and put the mug down slowly. 'Sam? Can I say something?'

'Erm… yeah. Go for it.'

'This thing with Karen… No, don't look like that. I'm not going to nag you or criticise. I just want you to listen to my advice.'

Sam sighed - another day about to be spoiled by Karen. 'Go on then.'

'Grace told me what happened, and how the local paper is on the story.'

Sam nodded. 'Yeah.'

'Well, I know how these things work, Sam. If you're not careful, you're going to get damaged big time. As soon as the paper comes out, everyone will judge you - right or wrong, it won't matter. Michelle will read it, or be told about it, and you can imagine what she's going to do.'

'Ditch me.'

'Damn right she will! Don't expect loyalty or forgive and forget. And it's a small town. This is your home, Sam, and you can't afford to lose goodwill. Do you think people will want to buy your pictures? Come to your gallery?' She leaned forward, staring so intently he couldn't avoid looking into her eyes.

She spoke gently now. 'Sam, you have to make it up with Karen; stop this happening.'

'I tried that once and I just made it worse.'

'Why? How?'

'I asked if she wanted money and was that what it was all about.'

'Nice one.'

'Yeah. That's when she threatened to ruin me: I think that's what she said.'

'It's bad, Sam, but nothing is irretrievable. You must find a way to make the peace.'

'I don't know what else I can say. I told her I was sorry.'

'Ask her what she wants.'

'What?'

'Simple. She's upset. She's the one kicking up the fuss, worrying you to death. So just be straight with her. Tell her - I've said I'm sorry, what else do you want me to do? How can I make it up to you?'

Sam stared at his tea. 'You think that would work?'

'It might. It gives her the power; makes her feel she's in control. Puts the thing back onto her. It's like you're saying to her - okay, you're upset, so tell me what you want; what would make you feel better.'

Sam nodded slightly and Lindsay stared. 'Was that a yes?'

He looked up. 'Yes.'

She ran round behind him and wrapped her arms round him and kissed his head. 'Oh Sam, you're such a star. I hate to see you worrying.'

'I've been okay. Done a fair bit of painting, taken my mind off it.'

'Oh! Can I see?'

He was ready with his answer. 'It's all at the shop, but I'll show you next week if you're still around.'

They moved into the living room, and Lindsay said she was staying with Grace for a few more days, but then she'd been asked to do another week at the V And A, and after that she was building up to an exhibition in Marylebone.

'Do you think Michelle will want to carry on with you, even if she drops me?'

'Well, I hope so! She's bound to want me - the young beautiful one! Sam - I'm sure she won't drop you, but you can't just sit back.'

'I know! I'll phone Karen tonight.'

'Yes? Cross your heart?'

They talked about her residency, his new studio, and the building work, until Lindsay looked at her watch.

'Gotta go. My turn to dish up the grub tonight.' She turned as she opened the front door. 'Don't forget.'

Sam nodded. 'I won't.'

Karen answered on the third ring.

'Karen? It's Sam.'

'Christ! What now? I'm just going out.'

'Sorry. I won't keep you long. I just wanted to say again that I'm sorry.'

'Right.'

'I wanted to ask you... what can I do to make it up to you? What would you like me to do?'

'Seriously? Have you been reading books - like Teach Yourself Grovelling?'

'No, I -'

'Listen. What I'd like you to do isn't physically possible. So instead, why don't you just face up to what you did, accept what's coming to you, and leave me alone.'

'What do you mean, what's coming to me?'

'What's up, have I worried you? Just wait and see.'

'So, are you threatening me?'

'No. Informing you. Is that it? Can I go now, please sir?'

'Oh, for Christ's sake Karen, why won't you listen?'

194

'I'm listening, but you're not saying anything. Don't call me again, okay?'

The line clicked dead.

Sam threw his phone at the sofa.

Chapter 22

He was dancing with Karen. They were lost in the tunes, eyes closed, moving together like lovers, his hands on her hips. Then she twisted and was gone, and he was panicking, twirling round, eyes screwed up against the flashing lights, pushing through the crowd to find her, the beat pounding in his ears.

He woke to the sound of hammering on the door, and scrambled downstairs in his boxers and T shirt.

A man and a woman, about his age, in uniform. Sam rubbed his eyes and felt ridiculous, but he instantly knew why they were here.

'Morning sir, I'm Sergeant Willocks and this is Constable Parker. Mind if we come in?'

Sam just nodded, fighting down the dread in his stomach.

'What's the problem?' he said lightly, as he pulled the door open wider.

The sergeant looked him up and down. 'Do you want to get dressed? We can wait.'

'Yes! Erm.. ' Sam pointed to the kitchen. 'Do you want to sit in there?'

They glanced at each other. 'No, it's fine, thanks. We'll wait here.'

PC Parker nodded amiably.

'Right.' Sam ran upstairs, splashed water on his face and put on jeans and a sweatshirt. He smoothed his hair and took a few deep breaths, then walked down, trying to stay upbeat.

'Can I get you anything? Tea?'

Sgt Willocks shook his head. 'Shall we sit in your kitchen now, sir?' He sat opposite Sam, pulling a notebook from a side pocket. PC Parker stood at the door.

'Can you confirm your name, sir?'

'S-Sam Taverner.' Shit. The stutter was back.

'And this is your home?'

'It is, yeah.'

'Thank you. I have to tell you that we are investigating an allegation against you of threatening behaviour, contrary to the

Public Order Act 1986. The offence is said to have taken place on the main street in Hightown, and specifically relates to actions by you alleged to have caused fear, alarm and distress by way of threatening and abusive words and behaviour.' He looked up. 'You don't seem at all surprised, if you don't mind me saying, sir.'

Sam shook his head. 'I'm not, to be honest.'

The sergeant made a note, then frowned as PC Parker's radio crackled. She stepped into the hall. Sam waited, thinking fast. He knew this moment would come, and he'd had a long time to prepare for it. He'd spent hours doing web searches.

He felt ready, but the bubble in his stomach was still there. Or was that just hunger? He scraped his chair back. 'I need a biscuit. Can I get you anything?'

'No, thank you, sir. We had our breakfast a few hours ago. Early start today.'

Sam wasn't going to plead guilty to the crime of staying in bed a bit longer than usual. He attempted a smile. 'Right.'

He took a couple of digestive biscuits out of the tin by the cooker and sat down again. The constable came in. 'We're needed on a call out, Sarge.'

'What? Really?' He stood. 'Excuse us for a minute, sir.'

They moved out for a whispered conversation, then came back in.

'Sorry, sir. We have a call out on the other side of town. Could you come with us, please, so we can drop you at the station on the way for a formal interview?'

'Am I under arrest, or s-something?'

'No, however we do need to interview you in connection with the allegation. It's just a case of taking a statement at this stage. You can contact a solicitor, if you want to. We'll decide next steps after the interview, which will be conducted by a colleague in CID.'

PC Parker smiled: 'You'll need a coat, sir. It's chilly out there.'

'Thanks. I'll just go and get it.' Sam stopped as they followed him out into the hall. 'OK if I phone my girlfriend? She's supposed to be coming round this afternoon.'

The sergeant nodded. 'No problem. But you'll be back in plenty of time. This should only take an hour.'

Sam thought better of calling Sladana - she'd only worry. He sat in the back of the patrol car, hoping none of the neighbours had seen him, forming answers to expected questions as PC Parker drove to the station using back roads to avoid the morning rush.

She stayed in the car as Sgt Willocks escorted him to the reception desk. The smell was a blend of disinfectant, body odour and coffee.

'Right, sir, I'll leave you here.'

'Yeah. Err, thanks.'

The woman behind the reinforced glass stared mournfully and took his details. 'Wait over there, please. They'll be with you in a minute.'

He sat opposite a man with a long grey beard who was staring at the floor, muttering to himself and scratching the back of his hand. His hair was matted and his coat greasy and stained. Sam's first instinct was to give him money. But he reached for a four-year-old copy of Practical Motoring instead, and hoped he'd get offered a cup of coffee.

'There you go, Mr Taverner: white, no sugar.'

Sam nodded his thanks.

The detective wore a dark suit with an open neck blue shirt. He nudged a saucer of biscuits casually across the table. He looked and sounded totally relaxed: 'Help yourself... Right then, shall we get this done? Might as well while we're here, eh?' Sam nodded and smiled dutifully. 'As you know, we wanted to ask you about an allegation of threatening behaviour, said to have taken place at around midday on December the 10th. This is an offence under the Public Order Act 1986 so we want to hear what you have to say. Ok so far?'

Sam nodded.

'Ok, so... I'm DC Rooke, by the way. I'll ask a few questions, and I'll be writing down your answers, so please speak slowly. At the end, I will give you the opportunity to read through what I have written and then sign your name to confirm it is a true and accurate record. Just to be clear, you are not under arrest; you are helping us with our inquiries, and we want you to make a statement so we can decide what to do. Anything you say to me today could be used in evidence at some stage in the future, if it comes to that. Alright? Happy to proceed without legal representation?'

'Yes, I'm ready.'

'Grand. So, did you go to see Ms Karen Madeley at her tattoo parlour in Hightown on December the 10th this year?

'Yes, I did.'

'Can you tell me why you went to see her?'

'Yes, she'd upset my girlfriend, calling her a gold digger and making racist remarks. I wanted to tell her she was out of order.'

'Your girlfriend's name?'

'S-Sladana Ilic.' Sam told him her address, then took a deep breath. 'I was angry with Karen, and very surprised. We had been close, and I thought we were friends. I couldn't believe she could be so cruel, so I went to s-see her. She was locking up her shop to go for a run, so I spoke to her about it outside. I told her she should stop slagging off my girlfriend and upsetting her, but she said she meant every word and I was being a fool because Sladana was misleading me.'

'Okay, thank you. Just let me catch up before you continue… '

Sam stared over his shoulder as he wrote, holding onto the words he'd rehearsed.

The detective looked up. 'Right. So, did you threaten her in any way?'

'I just told her to back off.'

'Right. So would you describe it as a polite conversation?'

'No. I admit it wasn't. I was angry, and I did shout. She just wasn't listening. I did get close to her at one point.'

'Did you raise your hand as well as your voice?'

Sam paused, then spoke slowly. He knew this was they important bit. 'No, I don't think so… I always clench my fist when I'm angry, but I didn't shake my fist at her, or anything like that.'

'Can you describe the nature of your relationship with Karen Madeley?'

Sam talked about Mikey and how he and Karen had helped him through his last days.

'So, you were close friends, then?'

Sam hesitated. Would Karen have told the police about the time they first met, or the night he stayed at her place? He gambled. 'Yeah, we were good friends. Close, yeah. Well, I thought so...'

DC Rooke raised his eyebrows as if he understood, then carried on writing.

The questions kept coming, some repeated and phrased slightly differently, but Sam stuck to his story, and the more he talked, the more he felt like an innocent victim of a misunderstanding. He hadn't threatened her physically, though he did shout, and he knew there were people watching at the time, and he was sorry for losing his temper.

Eventually, DC Rooke checked his watch and wrote the time in his book. 'Right, Mr Taverner, I think that's as far as we can go now. Please read my notes carefully, and sign at the bottom if you're happy that they are an accurate summary of your side of the story. Take your time. You do that while I get you another coffee.'

'Thank you. What happens next?'

'I'll be consulting a superior officer, who will review the case based on the statements made by yourself and the complainant, and she will decide if there is a case to answer, and if charges are to be pressed.' He held up a hand as if in apology. 'I'm sure it won't take long. You should hear something in a day or two, and thanks for your co-operation. Now... coffee, yes?'

Sam shook the tension out of his shoulders, read the notes and signed his name.

Part of him wished Mum and Dad were here with him, but another part was thankful they weren't. The shock would have finished Mum off, and Dad would have lost his temper and done something stupid. Sam stared at the wall: that's exactly what he'd done, isn't it?

DC Rooke came back with coffee and a copy of the Mirror. 'There you are how's that for service? I'll come back and show you out, all right?'

Sam stood and scraped his chair back noisily. 'S-Sorry, but do you mind if I go now?'

He sighed. 'I wouldn't, if I were you, mate.'

'Why not?'

'There are a few women waiting outside, asking where you are. Having a bit of a demo. They don't look happy.'

'What? How did they know I was here?'

'No idea. It didn't come from us; I can promise you that. I guess someone must have seen you when you came in. Best to wait here for a bit. They'll soon get bored.'

Sam sat down heavily, his stomach churning. It would be all over town even before the Recorder ran their story. But he couldn't hide in here forever. In fact, the longer he stayed, the bigger and angrier the crowd could get. Better to face it now?

He stood again. 'I'd better get it over with, if that's ok.'

'Okay mate. It's your call. I'll ask one of the uniforms to come out with you, just in case, all right? But keep your cool. We don't want any trouble.'

Sam drank the lukewarm coffee in one go. 'Okay.'

The light hurt his eyes as he stepped outside. He couldn't tell how many there were, but the chanting was loud and angry: 'Lock him up! Keep women safe!'

The duty sergeant warned him there were a few reporters, and he could hear them shouting his name, trying to make him look at their cameras - 'Sam! This way!' But he kept his head down and tucked in behind the sergeant as he cleared a path, then blocked the way as Sam jogged away down an alley. The shouting seemed to bounce off the walls, until he turned a corner, and the sound was cut off.

He leaned back against the rough brick wall. He remembered Dad showing him the network of passageways, and how he used to play hide and seek there with Sean. This shortcut was a favourite: narrow and cobbled, and running behind the offices that fronted the main square . He met Sladana here after school sometimes.

All he wanted now was to get home, but he felt weighed down by worry. Would anyone believe his side of the story? Would he have to appear in court? Go to prison? Would Sladana, Michelle and Lindsay stand by him?

The bricks felt hard against his back as he slid down until he was squatting on the cold flagstones.

His phone pinged. Sladana on WhatsApp: *I just heard. How horrible for you. Don't worry. Love u and c u soon xxx*

She'd be on her way now.

He winced as he pushed himself upright. His knees felt worse in cold weather.

He walked slowly towards the square, trying not to make a sound. There was another back way he could cut through, next to the estate agent. If he moved quickly and kept his head down, he might get away without being seen.

He ran as fast as he could, coming out onto the esplanade by the harbour. The cold air cleared his head, and by the time he got home he knew what he had to do.

And the police - and Karen - could think whatever they liked.

Chapter 23

"The first step towards getting somewhere is to decide you're not going to stay where you are." —John Pierpont Morgan

They were lying on a blanket in the park when the Town Hall clock rang in the New Year.

Sladana's face was framed by the furry hood of her parka. 'I love you, Sam. But you are mad. It's freezing!'

Sam kissed her on the lips. 'I love the way you say luff.' She laughed and pushed him off. He pulled her up and hugged her. 'Come on, let's go and get warm.'

'How? You still have plastic sheet instead of windows in the living room.'

'Yeah, but I left the heater on in the bedroom, so…'

'Ah. I see.'

They looked up as rockets whined, tracing arcs on the black canvas of night, then exploded, sending cascades of coloured light showering down.

Sladana winced. 'I feel sorry for the dogs. They hate this.'

Sam pulled her close. 'Trust you to think of that. You're so nice. I don't know what I'd do without you.'

She touched his cheek with a gloved hand. 'Don't worry. It's going to be okay.'

'Yeah, I think so. Let's get inside.'

They sat in the kitchen and drank red wine. The heater blew warm air round their feet and the window began to mist up. They were quiet and Sam realised this was the first time in his life that the house next door had been empty. It was all his now.

He looked up as Sladana touched his hand. 'That was a nice thing you did for Karen. Do you think she will be happy?'

Sam frowned. 'Oh, I don't know. I did wonder. But it's up to her. I just wanted to do the right thing.

'It must have been a lot of money…'

'Yeah, but I forgot Mikey's boat was just sitting there. I told Mikey I thought she should have it anyway. I put the word round and a guy at the football club bought it. It was just about enough to pay off her arrears. Grace told me how bad it was, and I thought, why not? I promised Mikey I'd look after her, and if she takes it the wrong way…'

'Does she know it was you?'

'I doubt it. Not yet anyway. But she'll find out, I suppose.'

Sladana sipped her tea. 'She will. Did you hope it would make her change her mind?'

'No.' Sladana gave him a look. 'No, honestly. I just felt I should do it. I got the idea on the way home after the police interviewed me. After those people yelled at me, I decided I didn't care what anyone else thought. I'll take what's coming. Dad used to tell us we shouldn't drop our standards because other people do.'

'You remember a lot what he said. He sounds nice man. I wish I met him.'

'He would have loved you.' He reached for the bottle. 'Let's have one more before bed.'

'I have better idea. Let's have wine in bed.'

'I like the sound of that.' Sam leaned in and nuzzled her neck, breathing in her soft warmth. 'You know what? I don't care what people say anymore. All I care about is you and me. I just -' he pulled away.

'What's the matter?'

'It's the start of a New Year.' He hesitated.

'Yes, come on, Sam. Say it.'

The words came out in a rush. 'Will you marry me?'

The alarm went off at six and she drove off to her shift after mugs of tea and poached eggs on toast.

The house was empty again but he felt less alone.

Sladana had told him about the abuse she and her family suffered because they were from another country.

Shirley Sugar rang to wish him a happy new year and said she'd sold out of the Christmas cards he designed and was telling her customers not to believe everything they read in the newspapers.

Aaron and his wife sent a card saying he was welcome at their house anytime. 'You're a good lad so take no bloody notice,' was Aaron's advice.

The police had told him he'd be facing charges, but Grace put him onto a solicitor who said she could 'make this go away.' She hadn't been impressed that he'd paid off Karen's debts, though. 'That looks like a guilty man trying to buy someone off. Or maybe -' she smiled '- a good man fulfilling a promise to his dying brother.'

Sam dried the plates and put away the glasses. The more he analysed, the more he realized that the only thing that mattered was his new life with Sladana.

He tried to imagine Mum's reaction when he told her he was going to get married. He could picture her, laughing and crying at the same time.

Sam thought again about the family he'd lost, and wondered how life would have turned out if they were still here now. If Dad was still running the business, would Sam have gone to uni, or found work somewhere else?

It was cold and he ran quickly, taking a detour along the esplanade to see how work on the arts centre was shaping up. It was obvious that Michelle had been right about the timescale: the steel frame was more or less complete.

He thought back to her phone call a few days ago…

I can't believe I'm saying this, Sam, but I'm dropping you as an ambassador until further notice. I'm truly sorry, but I don't have a choice. The council can't be seen to be endorsing someone accused of abusive behaviour.'

Five minutes later, Grace had called to tell him that the posters had been defaced. *'They've sprayed you out, Sam, bloody idiots.'* Sam had surprised himself by staying calm: *'It's okay; Lindsay's better looking than me anyway.'*

Sam jogged slowly up to his shop, breathing heavily. At least there was no graffiti or damage here yet. He opened up quickly, locked the door behind him and left the blinds down.

The deckchair he was making for Lindsay was complete and looking good he thought. The frame just needed staining and polishing now. He'd wanted it to have the feel of a Charles Rennie Mackintosh piece - like the ones that inspired him at the V&A - so he'd shaped the frame differently, bowing the legs slightly, and extended the uprights. He'd added a rectangular

205

panel to form a headrest and carved it in the style of a Mackintosh he'd seen online. He flicked on the fluorescent tube lighting, levered the lid off the wood stain with one of Dad's old chisels, and got down to work.

He waited till it was dark, then ran home, detouring up the hill to make it more of a workout.

His mood flicked on and off as he ran: buzzing about Sladana and imagining living with her in the new house; worrying about being found guilty; excited about Lindsay's reaction to the deckchair; wondering if he should abandon art and concentrate on furniture making.

He remembered chatting with Bob at the builders' merchants when he went round to buy the wood stain. He'd made a brew and said he'd heard the news.

'Thing to keep in mind, Sammy,' Bob said as he dunked a biscuit in his tea, 'is not to dwell on things that have been and gone.'

'What do you mean?'

'What I mean is, nipper, you can't change it, so you've got to find a way to live with it. Don't waste time fretting. Decide how you're going to handle it, and then get on with your life. The people that matter will stick with you. And who cares about them that don't?'

He leaned back and studied Sam, his eyes like dark pinpricks under his shaggy grey eyebrows. 'I reckon your problem is you're on your own: too much time to think. You need to keep yourself busy, or, better yet, find yourself a girl: it'll do you the world of good.'

Sam smiled. 'You live on your own, Bob, and you're doing all right.'

'Aye, but I'm a stubborn old bugger. No woman in their right mind would shack up with me. Unless they were after my money.'

Sam slowed to a jog, warming down as he neared home, and Bob's words morphed into Karen's voice, which seemed to echo down the dark empty street... 'Unless they were after my money.'

Chapter 24

Sladana's face shifted from smile to frown in a millisecond when Sam said he wanted to take her to London to choose an engagement ring.

'Sam… wow!' Then, the frown:' Oh, no, I can't leave mum.'

'She could come with us.'

The smile again: 'Oh my God! Really? You know, I think she would like that. She always talks about London, the galleries, the buildings. And if you were there, too…'

'So, is that a yes?'

'Yes. I think!' She kissed Sam on the cheek. 'I will ask. Oh, but this is just for one day?'

'No way! I'll find us a hotel.'

Sladana laughed. 'Then she will definitely come.' She hesitated. 'But you are sure it's okay? We won't be alone so much.'

Sam winked. 'Yes, we will. We'll have our own room.' It was his turn to laugh as she threw herself at him. 'I love her, too, you know. I was thinking…when we get married, we could all live here. It'll be a big house: your mum could have her own rooms.'

Sladana's eyes filled with tears.

'What's wrong? We don't have to if you think -'

She wrapped her arms round his neck, sobbing and laughing at the same time. 'Nothing is wrong. I can't believe it, that's all. You and me… it's making me so happy, and mum will be so happy too.'

Sam stroked her hair: 'You know what? I'm happier than I've ever been.'

They made love slowly, gently, holding on so long that the climax was almost painful, and then they slept, wrapped together.

An hour later, they were talking sleepily about plans for the house; then sat up and flicked through London hotels on Sam's phone until they found the one they liked. It was within walking distance of Lindsay's place in Marylebone, and close to an Underground station.

Sam made hot chocolate while Sladana checked her shift pattern for January. They moved downstairs and sat on the sofa in the living room with the gas fire on full.

Sam's phone pinged, and he grabbed it quickly: 'Yes! We're booked in next week!' He laughed at Sladana's excited squeal. 'I just had an idea. Shall we go and see Lindsay while we're there? I made her a present and I'd love to see it in her flat. Would you mind?'

Sladana shook her head and wiped milky foam off her lips. 'She is your friend. Maybe she will be mine, too.'

'She'll love you. I made her a deckchair, so I was thinking I could get it delivered just before we go to London. What do you think?'

'Good idea. So now, clever man, maybe you can start new deckchair business as well as the pictures?'

'Hmmm…That's a very good idea, Mrs Taverner.'

Sladana was in the kitchen phoning her mother. Sam's phone pinged again: a text from Shirley Sugar: *Sorry Sam. Just walked past and your shop window is smashed in x*

Sam held up the phone to show her, and Sladana told Marija she'd call back. Sam had never seen her so angry. 'Bastards! Come on. I come with you.'

Sam held her close. Her anger seemed to cancel his out. 'No, don't. Whoever did it could still be there. It's not safe. Please, wait here.'

'You think I am scared? No way!'

'Please, for me… I won't be long. I'll get someone to meet me there.'

She pushed away. 'Okay, but I am going to call police.'

Sam nodded. 'Yeah, good idea. Hey. See you soon, okay?'

He called Bob and asked if he could deliver a few sheets of ply. He sounded angry, too. 'I'll do more than that, nipper. I'll come and help you.'

As soon as he saw the damage, he felt the anger growing, like a lump inside. The whole front window had gone; the shop floor was covered in glass and lumps of brick.

God knows how many they'd thrown. He checked the back room: at least Lindsay's chair was unmarked.

He switched the gas and electricity off and began sweeping. The cold was already seeping through his thin fleece, but the exercise warmed him.

Another text from Shirley: *Want some help? x*

Thank you x Any chance of coffee? x

No problem x

Bob turned up with one of his lads and told Sam to stay inside while they boarded up. 'Don't want you out here, losing your temper again.'

Sam swept the glass and rubble into a pile in the far corner, then cut off a sheet of bubble wrap, strapped it round Lindsay's deckchair and manoeuvred it into the back of his car.

He heard Bob's voice and found him sipping coffee and flirting with Shirley.

She smiled and held out a paper cup: 'One for you, too, Sam.'

'Amazing; thanks. How did you know to bring three cups?'

'Because I'm a genius. I looked out of the upstairs window and counted.'

Sam put an arm round her waist, and she leaned into him. 'Thanks Shirley. I owe you one.'

Shirley stood on tiptoes and kissed his cheek: 'You're very welcome.'

Bob drained his cup. 'Now then, you two. Behave yourselves. So, Sammy, what next, eh?'

Sam was still holding onto Shirley, and guiltily pulled his hand away. 'What do you mean?'

'You can't go on like this. When are you in court, d'you know?'

Shirley groaned. 'Oh God, yes: it can take months.'

Sam took a deep breath. 'Months? Jesus!'

Bob punched his shoulder. 'Why don't you cancel the rent on this place, empty your stuff out? You can store it at my yard as long as you like. Get your new place sorted and wait till it all blows over.'

Sam shook his head. 'Thanks Bob, but I'm not hiding. I haven't done anything wrong! Whoever did this can get stuffed.'

Bob gave him a bear hug. 'Come on, son. It makes sense to keep your head down. Avoid trouble. Just think about it, okay?'

'I've messed everything up, haven't I? What am I going to do?'

Bob pulled back and shook him by the shoulders. Sam felt his strength. 'I've just told you, you daft puddin'. You're going to get over it, double quick. Now, come on, get that lot cleared while we make sure these boards are fixed solid. There's a storm on the way.'

They drove away a few minutes later and Sam put the heating back on.

Shirley had brought some bags with her. She was wearing what looked like a short skirt and her coat looked new, but she held the bags open while Sam took off his fleece and shovelled in the debris. He felt drained but the exercise revived him.

He smiled: 'Sorry about all this, Shirley.'

'Can't blame yourself. The pillocks that did this should be locked up.'

'Thanks for helping and sticking up for me. I appreciate it. You're all dressed up too. Were you off out somewhere?'

'Nah. I like dressing up when the shop's shut. Nice to give my legs an airing. Makes a change from jeans and my Photo Shop hoodie. Anyway, how could I resist helping my favourite customer?'

'Well, you're my favourite shopkeeper.' He'd never spent time with Shirley away from the shop, and he felt the tension easing out of him. He gave a mock groan as he scooped up the last shovelful. 'My bloody knees!'

She put a hand on his back, her voice was teasing. 'You getting past it, Sam?'

'Not yet.'

Shirley turned away slightly. 'No. I didn't think so.'

'You should dress up more often. You're definitely not past it.'

She laughed as she tucked her hair behind one ear: 'Me?'

'What's funny about that?'

They looked into each other's eyes. She unbuttoned her coat and moved closer. Sam breathed in her perfume, and instinctively leaned in; then stopped himself. He put a hand on her shoulder. 'I'd better go, Shirley.'

She stepped back and spoke softly. 'Yeah.'

'Thanks again.'

'Yeah. See you around. Good luck.'

He watched as she walked towards the door, then strode after her. 'I meant it you know. You really are … it's just that -'

'It's ok. Am I allowed to give you a hug?'

'Any time!'

He held her, and the kiss he aimed at her cheek became a kiss on the lips as she turned her face. She pulled back, looking at him intently, then put her hands on the back of his neck and kissed him hard, her tongue pushing inside. Sam closed his eyes and responded eagerly, without thinking; tasting her, feeling himself harden as she moved against him, the pressure building inside as she moaned in his ear; her hand reaching down.

He couldn't stop himself. He lifted her off her feet and pushed her against the wall. Her skirt rode up her thighs as she opened her legs, and she moaned again as his fingers moved inside her. She took him in one hand and shuddered as he pushed into her, her breath coming in sharp gasps.

'Sam, Sam… oh Sam!'

Her voice became a whimper as he pushed again and again, until he couldn't hold on anymore, and they came together in a stifled shout.

'Shirley. I -'

'Oh God. Shhhh… don't say anything. Please. Stay inside me.'

Sam's breathing slowed. He rested his head on her shoulder, then felt her tightening against him, squeezing, sliding. He hardened again as she began to push, slowly, gently, sighing in his ear: 'Yes…yes…'

'Shirley…'

The squeal of tires and slamming of a car door made them flinch. He pulled away and they straightened their clothes.

Sam peered out through a gap in the window boards as he zipped up: 'It's the police!'

Shirley straightened her hair and smoothed her skirt over her thighs. 'It's ok. We're not breaking any law, are we?' She seemed calm, in control. She smiled: 'Better let them in then.'

Sam moved towards the door, then stopped as she grabbed him from behind, laughing: 'Might be a good idea to tuck your shirt in. Don't want to totally give the game away.'

'No. Right. Erm…thanks.'

He opened the door to a stout policeman who gave him a cheerful greeting: 'Mr Taverner, I presume?'

Sam gave a weak smile. 'Yes… that's me.'

'Right. We had a report of criminal damage at this property.'

'Yes, someone smashed the window.' He turned to introduce Shirley. 'Shirley has been helping me clear up.'

She smiled and put a hand on Sam's arm: 'I'm afraid we've put all the evidence in those bags over there. I hope that's okay. I suppose I'd better leave you both to it. All right, Sam?'

Sam nodded briefly, avoiding eye contact. 'Yeah, thanks, you know.'

The PC stood to one side to let her out. 'Hang on, miss…are you the lady who called this in?'

'No. Must have been someone else. I saw the window had gone when I walked past and just phoned Sam.'

He took her name and address and closed the door behind her, then turned to Sam with a grin.

'Right, then, Mr. Taverner. You have been keeping us busy lately, haven't you?'

He took his time over the questions, but finally, he left.

Thin streams of yellow light streaked across the room through gaps in the plywood sheets. Sam sat on the floor, leaning against the work bench, massaging his forehead. A couple of hours ago he'd been happier than he could remember. But now…how could he have been so stupid?

If he told Sladana would she ever forgive him? They'd spent the whole morning planning their future, talking about buying a ring. Sam groaned. And how quickly would the word get round if Shirley told anyone?

He knew what people would think: they'd say he couldn't control himself with women. And if that was the message, just before the court case, one -he was certain to be convicted, and two - Sladana would leave him. Even if she forgave him, she'd never trust him. And three - he'd had to move away from Whistle Bay.

He couldn't face Sladana, not now. The thought of deceiving her made him feel sick. But if she never knew, maybe it would blow over and they could carry on?

He had to do something though, so he sent her a message: *All ok. Still clearing up. Will be a while sorry. Have a good shift. Call you tmrw xx*

He waited, but there was no reply. Maybe she was already at work?

The streetlights were on, but it was dark where he'd parked the car. Sam sat with the engine running. as the first drops of rain hit the windscreen. He couldn't risk going home yet in case Sladana was still there. But where else could he go?

He felt the phone vibrate in his inside pocket, and stared at the screen: *Can we meet? We need to talk. You around tonight? Karen*

Chapter 25

Sam drove slowly down the esplanade, pulled in opposite Jim's arcade and switched the lights off.

The streetlamps added shades of orange to whitecaps that were flying like litter off the dark waves. Bob was right: the radio forecast was force 9. Sam reckoned it was already a 7.

Dad loved storms and helped Sam to conquer his fear. He remembered one afternoon, sitting in the hut, with the timbers creaking and windows rattling; the wind growling, He was curled up in the furthest corner by the shelves, as if the books would protect him from the terrifying ghosts that he imagined were swirling round outside.

Dad took his hand and lifted him onto the highchair so he could look out. He opened one eye, then the other as Dad put a heavy arm across his shoulders. The softness of his voice felt more powerful than the storm: 'Just look, Sammy. Isn't it beautiful? Look at the waves! And d'you see the gulls? Imagine being one of them. They're loving it. Don't you wish you could fly like that?'

Sam had become transfixed, watching the birds swoop, then hover; hanging motionless in the face of strong winds that were blowing dog walkers on the beach sideways.

Something frightening had become something magical, and he wished Dad was with him now.

Looking in the rear-view mirror, he could see that the hut had now become a steel skeleton. He shivered and turned on the ignition to get the heater going.

His voice sounded unnaturally loud as he talked to himself: *'The hut's gone, but so what? You're still here, and you've got your whole life ahead of you. Who cares about a few knock backs? Everybody has them. Think about what you've got…'*

'Yeah, what have I got? A court case for threatening behaviour; a girlfriend who'll leave me if she finds out what I've done; and people who smash my windows because they think I abuse women.'

The car was warming up. He let his head fall back against the headrest and closed his eyes, listening to the wind whistle like a boiling kettle, feeling the car rock as the storm gathered strength.

He pictured Gary riding the storm, his white plumage shining against the dark angry clouds. Sam had tried so hard to capture Gary's individuality on paper and he remembered the pride and sense of achievement when he finally did.

It felt like he'd become an artist at that moment, and no-one would ever take that away from him.

'Don't be afraid…Think about what you've got…'

Sam snapped his eyes open and got out of the car.

The wind slammed into him, but he fought against it, locked the car and walked towards Karen's flat.

He didn't know why he'd agreed to see her. Maybe anything was better than sitting in his empty house feeling guilty.

Whatever, he was here now, and what else could happen to make things worse?

All he had to do was knock on the door.

He raised his fist, then stopped. It felt as if something was holding him back: a thought, trying to get through. He tried to tune in, but it slipped away.

He rapped on the door.

She smiled politely and sounded formal but not unfriendly: 'Hello Sam. Thanks for coming.'

'You wanted a word, so…'

'Yeah. Well, come up.' She led the way up the stairs and pointed to the cramped sitting room: 'Don't worry; I'm not going to bite your head off, for a change. Tea or beer?'

'Tea. Please. Thanks.'

The room was warm and just as comfortably untidy as when Mikey stayed here. Sam draped his jacket on the back of the armchair and moved a couple of magazines onto the floor.

She brought tea and biscuits and sat leaning forwards, clasping and unclasping her hands round her knees. Sam sipped tea and chomped on a Nice biscuit, wondering what was coming.

He caught her eye and she smiled, and he began to relax. He felt awkward, but if she wanted to talk, she had to go first. She hadn't attacked him yet so that was a good sign.

Karen nibbled on a biscuit, then put it back on the plate. She cleared her throat: 'My landlord told me you'd paid off my rent for this place and at the shop, for a year. I can't believe you'd do that for me, after -'

Sam nodded and stared at his tea.

Her words came in a rush: 'I'm so sorry for everything, Sam. I just - I've been stupid. I don't even know why… jealous maybe. And then I found out you'd given all that money and I felt really bad. I couldn't work out why you'd done it; but then I realised, and it brought back a lot of memories. You and me… You made that promise to Mikey, yeah?.'

Sam looked up, a lump in his throat. He'd never seen her looking so vulnerable, and he had to fight down the instinct to put his arms round her. He swallowed. 'Jealous?'

'You and… your girlfriend.' She shook her head. 'I might as well admit it: I felt lonely after Mikey died. I thought maybe we … I think you did too. But, well, I'm over it now, so…' She wiped her nose on a tissue and sat back, crossing her legs. 'I'm sorry I put you through all this. I just wanted to say thank you and to let you know I've dropped the charges.'

'What? Really?'

Karen nodded. 'Not because of the money, if that's what you're thinking. Because I was wrong. I'm big enough to look after myself so…' She smiled: '…threatening behaviour just doesn't fit. I'm a tough girl who runs a tattoo parlour. Why would I feel threatened? I can stand up for myself. Not great for my image, right?'

'Yeah, I know, but - I don't know what to say.'

'So say nothing. It's okay. I knew it would be a shock. Anyway, I don't need you to make a speech. I'm going to tell everyone I made it all up to get back at you because I was jealous. I've already told that jerk at the Recorder and he said they'll do a story this week. They'll be slagging me off instead of you before you know it. But I can cope with that; they'll soon get bored anyway.'

Sam sat back: 'Bloody hell!'

216

She stretched out her hand. 'Forgive me?'

'Yeah, course I do. I know I lost my rag a bit, but that's all it was. I know how tough you are, so I couldn't believe it when I found out you'd reported me to the cops. And it's fine about the money. I did promise Mikey I'd keep an eye out for you. Someone I know is friends with your landlord, and she told me about the rent that was owing, so I thought, why not? I just didn't want you to think I was trying to buy you off or something. All I did was sell the boat, and I wanted you to have that anyway.'

'Buy me off? You'd be lucky.'

Sam smiled and Karen squeezed his hand. 'Fancy a beer now?'

He hesitated: 'Thanks, but I should go.'

'Okay. Well, if we're friends again, maybe we could go for a run sometime.'

'Yeah, I'd like that. Do you think you could keep up with me?'

'Cheeky sod.'

They stood at the same time, so close they were almost touching.

Sam leaned down and kissed her cheek lightly. 'I'm glad we're friends.'

'Yeah, me too. I'll text you.'

'Yeah. See you.'

The night air was like a cold shower as he stepped outside; the flagstones glistening under the lights. He stopped and watched Mikey's boat rocking in the choppy water as the incoming tide crashed against the outer harbour wall.

He zipped up his fleece and walked on, round the corner onto the esplanade, and staggered as the wind slammed into him once more.

Three in the morning, and the emptiness of the house felt oppressive.

Sam lay on the sofa, hoping his exhaustion would end in sleep. But his mind had other ideas again, nudging him as his eyelids were drooping… what to do about Sladana, and Shirley; should he still go to London; what to say to people about the charges being dropped; seeing Karen again, and feeling the same desire, despite everything.

He just wanted to stop thinking. But the voice inside was trying to make itself heard. Sam rubbed sleep from his eyes and sat up…

Everyone thinks of you as this sensible, reliable, guy; the Chair Man. NIce S-Sammy. But it all goes out of the window as soon as a nice-looking girl comes along. You just can't say no. You would have done it with Lindsay, and Grace. And then you did do it with Karen the first time you meet. Sladana reappears and you're all over her straight away. Then Shirley gives you a look and there you go again. What's the matter? Are you sex mad? Or just pathetic and weak?

Sam walked into the kitchen, leaned against the sink and drank a glass of water.

Maybe that was the problem. If so, could he trust his own feelings anymore? He couldn't even be sure he loved Sladana now. Was he marrying her because she was the only one who wanted him? Had he convinced himself he loved her because Lindsay, Grace and Karen weren't available?

After all, he'd always felt a bit depressed about the idea of being alone -

No, that's not right.

He loved Sladana when they were at school. They were right for each other; that's what Mum would have said…

He drank more water. He walked through to the other downstairs rooms that used to be the house next door. The only sounds were the wind roaring; his own footsteps on the bare floorboards; and the voice in his head…

So are you going to tell Sladana or keep it secret and hope she doesn't find out? Could you live under that pressure? Are you really going to marry her, or do you fancy Karen too much? Or is it all about Shirley now? She obviously fancies -

Sam punched a sheet of plasterboard and shouted: 'Leave me alone! I love Sladana and I'm going to tell her what happened!'

He stopped. Where did that come from? His voice was so loud it sounded like someone else's.

He took in a few deep breaths and let them out slowly.

218

He was on his own: the voice was gone.

He lay in bed as the storm ghosts swirled round the house, and the first streaks of dawn made patterns on the bedroom wall.

Chapter 26

It had begun as they ate breakfast. She'd come round, tired at the end of a night shift and he felt worn down by nervous energy. There was no easy way to say it, so it came out in a rush of words.

Sladana's eyes were wide with disbelief and wet with tears.

Sam's voice was hoarse: 'I'm sorry. It was just once. It didn't mean anything. I just thought -'

She sniffed and turned away. 'You thought you get away with it because you know I love you.'

He put a hand on her arm. 'Sladana -'

She pulled roughly away. 'Don't! I can't believe you do that and then expect it to be all right; that I just forgive you. We were going to get married. Then you do… that, with her? Now I know why you didn't want me to come with you.' Her voice cracked. 'I thought you loved me… now I can't trust you.'

'Yes you can! It will never happen again.'

She turned to him, wiping her eyes with the back of her hand, but her voice sounded stronger. 'No. It won't.' She stood. 'I'm going.'

'No, don't. Let me try again.'

'We shouldn't have to try! Maybe you won't do it again, but how could I ever be sure?'

She snatched up her rucksack and moved to the living room door. She stopped, and when Sam looked up, he could see her eyes had hardened: 'I don't want to see you again.'

Sam flinched as the front door slammed shut.

He sat there, lifeless, rewinding their conversation.

The ping of his phone broke into his thoughts, but he left it on the arm of the sofa and moved away to look out through the new sliding doors.

The storm was heading north now, and the builders had been making up time. They said they'd be back later in the week to replace the upstairs windows, and then they'd be rewiring, and plumbing in the new heating system. They'd already set up the ground source heat pump, and installed solar panels on the roof.

This was meant to be his big moment: creating a new home to share with Sladana and Marija. They'd talked about it excitedly, making plans, imagining living somewhere big and bright and new.

Part of him felt he should be slumped on the sofa, crying his eyes out; another part knew it could never work and that Sladana was right. How could she trust him after what he'd done?

He picked up his phone. It was a message from Lindsay... *How r u? Send me some pix of your latest paintings! You ARE still painting?! You'd better be xx*

He walked into the kitchen. Dad's chair was still in its place, as if it was waiting for him to come back and drink tea and read the paper. Sean would laugh at him because he always turned the pages so carefully, folding them back neatly so the edges lined up.

Sam heard their voices as clearly as if they were still with him. This house was soaked with memories, and he was wiping them away with all this new stuff. Soon this room would be history; converted into a glossy white utility room. Was that when he'd stop hearing?

Out with the old...in with the new: Dad used to say that every New Year's Eve.

Soon there'll just be me and your chair, thought Sam; playing country music, remembering the times we spent together.

He made a mug of tea and sat at the table; listening to the kettle as it slowly fizzled out.

He whispered into the silence: 'I'm okay, Dad. The storm has blown over.'

'Good to see you, Chair Man!'

'You too Billy Whistle. How's it going?'

'Never better young man. And I bet you're a happy chappy.'

'What d'you mean?'

Billy slapped Sam on the back. 'That bitch dropped the charges, didn't she?'

'Hey, come on, Billy. Don't call her that. It's not nice.'

221

'Bloody hell! Listen to you. She wasn't nice, was she, taking you to court, you getting treated like a criminal, windows smashed in an'all?'

'Yeah, I know. Anyway, everything's okay now, so...' He looked over Billy's shoulder. 'Looks busy in there, for a wet day in January.'

'I finally realised people would come if I stopped my stupid whistling, see? Now I get all the best customers, don't I?' Billy laughed. 'Seriously, Sammy, it is good to see you out and about again. What are you up to?'

Sam told him about the work on the house and replacing the shop window. 'I'm going to start making my own deckchairs.'

'What? No more pictures? You gotta keep up with that. You're getting good at it.'

'Really? Ta, Billy!'

'You know what I mean... Did I tell you a customer offered me a few hundred for that picture you gave me?'

'No way!'

'Straight up. Just before Christmas, too. I was tempted, but then I thought, if he's offering me that much now, it must be worth more.'

Sam laughed. 'You wish! Anyway, got to get going, loads to do...'

'Cheers, my boy. You must be mad, running everywhere. Be good.'

'You should come with me.'

'You what? I can't even run to the toilet, me.'

Sam smiled as he jogged down Marine Parade. Billy was right, it was good to be back. But he missed the whistling.

He put his head down as he passed Shirley's shop. She hadn't been in touch since that day. He'd thought about her, wondering if it was just a one-off, or whether she hoped they'd get together. He'd come close to asking if he could see her again. They'd always got on well. He decided it was just desperation, so he didn't bother.

He slowed to a fast walk as he neared his shop. He still had no regrets about confessing to Sladana. He'd known how she'd react, and he couldn't blame her.

222

He opened up the shop, switched off the alarm, and raised the blinds for the first time since the protests had started. People were nodding at him in the street again.

Bob had given him a few metal shelving units, and he began stacking them up with timber, tools, nails and screws, tins of wood stain, and pictures and art supplies he'd moved from the house.

He tapped out a text to Lindsay: *Thinking of coming to see you. Got a present for you. When are you around? X*

She replied immediately: *A present??!! Get over here now!! Any day is good this week and next. Excited!! xx*

How about day after tomorrow? X

Definitely! Want to stay over? xx

Definitely! Thanx. See you soon! Sx

'Oh my God Sam! That is so fab I could die!'

'So, you like it then?'

'Very funny. I totally love it. It's better than anything in the V&A. And you made it, just for little me.'

Sam sipped beer and smiled. Lindsay was completely over the top, as usual. She'd grabbed the parcel the minute he walked in and ripped the brown paper off like an over excited kid at Christmas.

He was pleased with the chair, but he'd been nervous on the train, wondering how she'd react.

Now she was all over it and making a mess of setting it up.

'Here, let me have a go.'

She put on a girly voice. 'Oh Sam, it's just like the old days: you're so masterful!'

'Yeah, I know. So, ready? Just do it like this…' He set up the chair in three moves and Lindsay hugged him.

'Sam, it is beautiful. How the hell did you manage to make this? I'm going to call it my artdeco-chair. See what I did there?' Sam nodded patiently. 'Right. You sit in it right now. I must have a pic of you, and then you simply have to get one of me, when I've done my hair and lippy… ready? Well, smile for God's sake!'

She cooked fish pie and garlic bread and opened a bottle of Chardonnay, and they sat on the squashy sofa and talked.

She raised an eyebrow when Sam told her about Shirley and how Sladana walked out on him. She said: 'Jesus, Sam! I said you could pull the girls. But you were going to get married for crying out loud. What goes on in your head? You really blew it, didn't you?'

'Yeah, I did. I've always been good friends with Shirley, so I've probably messed that up, too.'

'Come off it Sam! You have led a sheltered life, haven't you? Sounds like she got what she wanted, so why feel bad? It happens all the time. And, you weren't even engaged to Sladana, were you?'

Lindsay stared at him for a moment, then finished her white wine and asked if he'd seen Grace lately.

'No. I was thinking on the train that I hadn't heard from her. Why, haven't you?'

'No. I blew it, too.'

'What?'

She pulled a sad face: 'I finished with her. It was hopeless. We live too far apart, and we ended up having separate lives. I haven't met anyone else. I suppose it was inevitable: sad, but, hey ho - that's life, eh? Anyway, does this mean you and Shirley are a thing? Or was this a cunning plan to get rid of Sladana so you could make out with Karen again?'

Sam laughed. 'Cunning plan? Me? I don't know what that is. I just mess up every time. I'm sorry about Grace; I like her. But, God, I don't know what it is with me and girls.'

She touched his arm. 'You know what I think?'

'No, but I wish you'd tell me.'

'Oh Sam… You must remember you've lived an unreal existence. All you've ever really known is your family, and you've lost them, one by one. You've been on your own for so long, it's unbelievable. And the result is that - sorry, Sam - you don't know how to handle relationships. That's not a criticism - '

'No, it's okay; you're right. What do you think I should do?'

'Learn to relax and stop feeling you have to impress people. You try too hard because you feel a bit inferior, don't you?' He nodded. 'But look at you! Talented artist, maker of amazing deckchairs, and owner of a bloody mansion! And you can now travel to London like a veteran!'

She laughed and bounced up off the sofa. 'Let's have one more glass together. Two singletons, eh? We should be celebrating our new lives.'

Sam drained his glass. 'Definitely!'

Night came and they sat on the squashy sofa in the warm glow from a streetlamp.

Lindsay stretched out and leaned back on Sam's shoulder. Her hair smelled of flowers.

She yawned: 'It's probably bedtime.'

'I know. Trouble is, I can't move.'

'You'll have to soon, otherwise I'll fall asleep on you.'

'That's okay, I'll just throw you off.'

Her voice was so sleepy he strained to hear. 'No, you wouldn't. You're a gentleman.'

After a while, Sam wondered if she really had fallen asleep. He whispered: 'Lindsay?'

She sat up, rubbing her eyes. 'Hmmm?'

'Best go to bed.'

'Yeah. I'd love to fall asleep in your arms tonight, but life is complicated enough. I've put you in the spare room. Try not to dream about me, okay?'

Sam leaned in and kissed her on the cheek. 'I'll try.'

He drank a glass of water, walked unsteadily to his room, and didn't wake up until Lindsay tapped on the door: 'Breakfast, you lay about!'

Sam spread marmalade on his toast as she poured more coffee.

She was wearing mustard-coloured leggings and a grey sweatshirt. 'Good to see you making yourself at home.'

Sam smiled: 'That's thanks to you. I still remember the first time I saw you. You were in really bright coloured clothes.'

'Really? What colour?'

'Erm…'

'Ha! Liar, you can't remember, can you?'

Sam sipped coffee deliberately slowly, put the cup down: 'Yellow jacket and red trousers.'

225

Lindsay scoffed: 'You could say anything! How am I going to remember?'

'You'll just have to trust -' Sam stopped and looked away.

Lindsay quickly caught on. 'You and Sladana?'

'Yeah. I asked her if we could try again. She said she could never trust me.'

'She was probably right.'

'Oh, thanks!'

'You're welcome. Anyway, come on. Finish your breakfast. Are you staying or going back today?'

'I'd love to stay, but I've got the builders in, so...'

'Okay. I'll come and stay at your mansion next time, as long as you don't tell Grace I'm coming.'

'That would be great. It should all be finished in about six weeks.'

She reached for her iPad and turned it so Sam could see. It was her Instagram page, with a picture of her posing next to Sam's deckchair. She pointed. 'Check that out.'

Sam squinted: 'Is that 1,200 likes? Since last night?'

'Since this morning. Brace yourself Sam. Simply everyone has messaged me asking where I got it, and I'm going to do a reply today giving them your details, if you're happy.'

Sam leaned back in his chair and laughed. 'God, yes, I am! Thanks!'

Lindsay moved behind him and kissed the top of his head. 'It's only what you deserve. Now pack up and bugger off; I've got masterpieces to paint. And you've got a zillion chairs to make.'

'Sorry. Shall I wash up?'

'Oh Sam! No! You're such an angel. Come here!'

He hugged her fiercely again as they said goodbye on the doorstep, and she waved and called out as he reached the corner of Marylebone High Street: 'Bye Sammeeeee!'

Four hours later, he was replying to another email enquiry about deckchairs, as the train rolled gently to a halt at Whistle Bay station.

Chapter 27

His days were full: running to the shop in the morning; working on designs for deckchair commissions; measuring and cutting out wood; keeping customers informed; updating his accounts; running back home in the darkness to grab dinner; then settling down to paint.

Aaron was a regular visitor. Today, he'd abandoned the Liverpool football shirt in favour of a gaudy sweater his wife had knitted for Christmas. Sam told him it made him look like a Christmas tree, and Aaron grimaced. 'If you don't shut up, I'll tell her you want one as well.'

They drank tea and Aaron grabbed the last chocolate biscuit: 'It's good to see you back at work but it's funny not seeing you on the beach.' He spoke through a mouthful of crumbs. 'Oh, yeah, and have you seen the arts centre? We can't believe how quick it's going up. They reckon it'll be open in a couple of months. I hope you're going to the opening.'

'They won't want me, not after all that stuff with Karen.'

'They dropped the charges, didn't they?'

'Yeah, but they'll just say it was a fix, and I'm still guilty. Anyway, it's the council's place now, and they won't want anything to do with me.'

Aaron went quiet for a moment, then pronounced his verdict: 'They're pillocks.'

Sam smiled. 'I can't blame them. And it'd just feel weird, being there. I'd be thinking about me and Dad selling deckchairs, and all those people staring at me, thinking I'm a misogynist.'

'Mis-what?'

'Someone who treats women badly.'

'Bollocks to that. You're a good lad and I think you should go. Get in their faces. If you don't get an invite, you can come with me. My missus wouldn't want to do it. She hates making conversation. Even with me.'

Sam laughed. 'Thanks Aaron, that's nice of you.'

Aaron looked thoughtful, then spoke hesitantly. 'Sam, hope you don't mind, but you haven't stammered lately. Has it gone?'

'I hope so. I think it has.'

'How come?'

'I don't know. Mum and Dad used to say I'd grow out of it, but I thought I'd be all over the place when the police interviewed me. I was all right though. Maybe I was thinking so hard about what to say that I forgot to stutter.'

Aaron smiled and raised his mug: 'Well, cheers: at least something good came out of it.'

Loud Louise was being extra nice later that morning, too. She shouted from the kitchen as he ordered a sandwich: 'Well, look who it is! Welcome back my love- it's lovely to see you. No charge for this gorgeous man today!'

The girl serving him giggled as she started packing a bread roll the size of a rucksack with tuna and tomato. Sam was trying to think where he'd seen her before, until she turned, and he saw the name badge.

'Hi June. You used to work at Billy Whistle's cafe, didn't you?'

She looked up and blushed slightly. 'Yeah, I did. It's much better here, though.' Sam smiled and she smiled back. 'I didn't enjoy it very much.'

'Well, I can tell you're happy here.'

She wrapped the roll and handed it to him. 'Aww, thank you, that's nice.'

'Thanks. And keep smiling. It suits you.'

He was back at the workbench eating his roll when his phone rang. It was Shirley.

'Hi Shirley, how are you?'

She sounded different. Maybe she hadn't expected him to answer. 'Yeah, fine. You okay?'

'Not bad. Busy, you know…'

There was a pause. 'Sam, there's no need to avoid me -'

'I'm not!'

'I bet you are… But it's fine.' She was laughing. 'Don't worry, I haven't told anyone and I'm not expecting you to

228

propose marriage, or even take me out to dinner. Though, dinner would be nice! Only kidding… I just think it would be a shame not to see each other, just because…'

'Yeah, I know. You're right. I'm glad you phoned. I don't suppose you've heard that me and Sladana have split up?'

'Oh God! Really? Because of us?'

The lie came easily. 'No, no… nothing like that. We both just thought it was time, so, there you go.'

'Right. Well, I'm sorry. You must be upset.'

'I'm over it now. To be honest, I'm too busy to think about it.'

'Well, that's good. I was wondering, do you fancy meeting up for a coffee?'

'Yeah, great. As long as it's not Billy Whistle's place.'

'God, no! Imagine the gossip! Let's go down the coast. There's that nice place about a mile down the road… oh, what's it called? That's it, The Shack. Or you could just come here if you like. I can shut the shop for an hour.'

'Yeah, I'll come to you. I was going to knock on your door anyway. I've got loads of commissions for deckchairs, and I need help getting fabric designs done, if you could take it on for me.'

'Definitely! Come round tomorrow morning then, yeah?'

'Yeah. Thanks Shirley.'

'No problem. See you.'

'Yeah. And now you mention it, maybe we could go out for dinner one day.'

'I'd like that.'

Aaron was right about the arts centre. The roof and solar panels were on, the cedar cladding was finished, the windows were in, and the stainless-steel flue for the wood burner was glittering in the weak sunlight.

Sam walked down onto the beach to see it from that angle. It looked ten times bigger than the hut, and the glass frontage and upper and lower-level decking looked cool. He nodded, impressed. It was true to the plans Michelle had shown him, and still had the feel of a beach hut. He was glad they'd decided not to paint it. He told Michelle at the time it would look much better in a natural wood finish.

He was sure Dad would be proud. Maybe Aaron was right; he should go to the opening to represent the family; show people he had nothing to be ashamed of.

He took a picture on his phone to send to Lindsay and set off for the run home.

It was good to feel that he belonged in Whistle Bay again. It was as if the town had welcomed him back. The story in the Recorder about the case being dropped had probably helped. It had made page five, and Karen had meant what she said about taking the blame:

I regret bringing the charges against Sam. All he did was lose his temper because of the way I was behaving towards his girlfriend. He was right. He didn't threaten me. I was out of order, and I'm sorry I put him through this, and for wasting everyone's time and causing so much ill feeling. There's only one person to blame, and that's me. I hope we can all move on now.

The run cleared his head temporarily. But as soon as he sat down with a mug of tea, he realise he'd fooled himself into thinking he was fine on his own. Now he was questioning whether he should have kept quiet about what happened with Shirley. Sladana would never have known, and they'd still be together. She'd be here with him now…

But would it have worked, and could he have been strong enough to keep the secret from her forever?

He knew the answer to that; he'd been right to tell her the truth. He was on his own yet again; but that was nothing new.

He sipped his tea. His life lately seemed to revolve round fanciable women. He was still good friends with Lindsay and loved being with her. Hopefully it would be the same with Shirley. And then there was Karen.

He'd fantasised about all of them. Did that mean he wasn't capable of just being a friend to any of them?

He turned to the ring binder on the table. His first deckchair commission had come from a woman in Dulwich, who wrote: 'I really want a matching pair that will fit with my antique

230

furniture collection, so if you can come up with something that combines ornate carving, dark wood, and lush fabric, that would be fab!'

He'd already started on the carving, after she sent a few photos, but he spent the whole evening looking up fabric pattern ideas so he could talk it through with Shirley in the morning.

It was only when he looked through the rest of his emails that he realised how much pressure he was going to be under to keep pace with the orders. He'd updated his website with a minimum six week turn round for new orders, and he already had seven confirmed bookings, with £100 deposits paid.

He thought most people would be happy with a standard frame with a few frills that would be easy for him to add in, but half the enquiries were asking for bespoke frames.

Bob was laid back, as usual: 'They all want something unique. Just shout if you need a hand. I know a few joiners who'd jump at it, especially at this time of the year.' When Sam said he'd think about it, he went on: 'Aye, but don't think too long, Sammy. You can't afford to cut corners when you're making a name for yourself. Nobody wants a rush job.' He winked: 'Especially at your prices.'

He sat at Shirley's kitchen table, sipping coffee and eyeing up the dish of sweets she'd brought in.

The conversation had been easy, as if nothing had happened, but Sam still felt on edge. He couldn't trust himself if she made the first move.

She smiled. 'They call me Shirley Sugar, but you're worse than me. You always grab the best ones off my counter, and don't think I hadn't noticed.'

Sam laughed. 'I know. I'm sorry. It's the ones with the purple wrapper that get me.' He paused. 'Oh! Speaking of colours, can you find someone who could do fabric printing for me, really quickly? I thought maybe we could work together on the deckchairs, like we did on the cards.'

He told her about the orders and showed her the designs he liked. She took her time looking through them, then went into the shop. 'Hang on. I've got an idea.'

231

She came back looking pleased. 'Consider it done. I'm in regular contact with a company in mid-Wales who would be just the job for this. They're a small family firm, and I know they'd love the work. Here, take a look…'

Sam slowly turned the pages of the brochure and nodded. 'We did okay with those Christmas cards, so do you fancy coming in with me on this?'

'Bloody right, I do.' Sam turned away. 'What's wrong?'

'Oh it's just me. I sometimes think I don't deserve it.'

Shirley put a hand on his shoulder. 'Deserve what? Me taking a cut of your earnings?'

'No, because you've been so nice, since we… Oh, I don't know!'

'Listen. I'm not going to lie; I've fancied you for a long time. But whenever I thought I might have a chance, I'd see you with a gorgeous looking woman. So, what chance did I have? Then, last week, I wanted you to notice me.' She smiled. 'And you certainly did… It was great, Sam, but it's not like I'm going to make a habit of leaping on you every time we meet.'

'Oh, really? Why not? -' He stopped suddenly, the smile freezing on his face.

Shirley spoke softly. 'Relax. It's okay. I'm happy as I am. We're both single; these things happen. Having great sex with someone isn't that unusual, is it? And it's not illegal. I'm just trying to say there's no need to feel awkward, or guilty, or whatever, okay? We'll carry on being friends, but that doesn't mean I'll never want you again. Yeah?'

Sam nodded. 'Okay.' He opened his laptop. 'Shall we work out some percentages?'

His phone rang, while he was stretching canvas onto the Dulwich deckchair.

An upper-class voice, female: 'Hi, am I speaking to Sam?'

'Erm… who is this, please?'

'My name is Becky, I'm a researcher for The One Show. Long story short: we've heard about your amazing deckchairs, and we'd adore it if you could come in for a chat.'

'On TV?'

'Yes, that's right. We'd need you to come to the studio tomorrow. Don't worry, we'll sort out a train ticket and a taxi for you. No expense spared! We'd just love to hear your story. You used to rent out deckchairs, didn't you?'

Sam struggled to keep the stutter away. Maybe it is stress related. 'Y- yes, I did. How, how did you -'

'Find out about you? Oh, that's easy. We monitor social media and there's a real buzz about you on Insta and Twitter. You're becoming a bit of a celeb. Isn't that awesome? So, we just want you to come in, sit on our lovely sofa and have a chat with our gorgeous presenters. They're really nice…'

'Oh, right. Tomorrow. Erm, what time?'

'We'd want you with us by 5. Get you made up etc. Give me your email and I'll send you the info, and a train booking, of course.'

'Right. What sort of things will they want to know?'

'Oh, just the usual. A bit about your story, you know, renting out deckchairs, how you discovered your talent for making, where your inspo comes from -'

'Inspo?'

She laughed, and it sounded like Lindsay: 'Sorry! London speak. Inspiration… So, all good?'

Sam chewed his lip, then nodded to himself. If he was serious about making a name for himself, he had to do it. 'Yes, I'll be there.'

'Right, fab!'

'Just one thing, what should I wear?'

'Oh, don't worry about that. Just be like you are, dressed for work.'

'So, hoodie and jeans, okay?'

'Absolutely perfect. We don't always want guys in suits. Can't wait to meet you. Just ask for me when you get here. And look out for the email. I'm on it right now. Byeeeee!'

Click, and she was gone.

Sam leaned back against the workbench, scrolled through his contacts, found Michelle and sent her a message: *Hi. Hope you're ok. I'm on The One Show tmrw. Will do my best to give WB a good plug. Sam*

Her reply came quickly: She replied: *Wow Sam! Thanks for letting me know. Is this about your art? Amazing opportunity for you, and us! You must mention the arts centre. Will send info. Come and see me when you get back. Got an idea. So glad all that stuff is out of the way. Mx*

Right, thanks. Nervous and excited! See you soon then! Sam x

'

Chapter 28

He followed Becky onto the set, blinking against the lights; his face feeling stiff under the make-up.

Cameras the size of sheds floated into position like silent Daleks as she led him to a green sofa.

She was nice but he wished she'd shut up so he could take it all in. 'It all looks a bit weird at first, doesn't it? Anyway, you'll soon settle in. So just chill. We've got a bit of time because there's an OB on air now, for…?' She peered into the darkness that circled the set and a voice said: 'Three minutes.'

She explained as Sam gave her a questioning look: 'OB, outside broadcast.'

She nodded to the presenters, who looked up briefly as they checked through their notes. 'This is Sam. Sam this is Fiona, and Dan.'

Fiona put a hand on his arm. 'Nerve wracking, isn't it? First time?'

Sam nodded. Dan laughed: 'Feels like the first time, every time, for me, mate. Relax, just be yourself.'

Fiona kept her eyes on her notes as she talked: 'Yes, just forget all the stuff around you. Focus on us, and we'll have a chat about your amazing deckchairs; just us three, alright?'

'Yeah, that's fine. Erm, thanks for having me.'

Still reading: 'Awww, bless. You're welcome. Okay, sit yourself down and Geoff will clip your microphone on.'

Becky had disappeared, and he suddenly felt alone. His stomach lurched, so he concentrated on the presenters, hoping some of their confidence would rub off on him.

Geoff clipped a tiny microphone onto the neck of his T shirt and poured water into a glass. 'Grab some, mate. It's hot in here and you don't want your mouth to dry up, yeah?'

'Great, thanks.'

'Good.' He checked something on his tablet. 'Just say a few words for me, so we can check sound levels. Your name and where you live.'

'Right. Erm… I'm Sam Taverner and I live by the sea in Whistle Bay.'

Geoff grinned, gave him a thumbs up, and disappeared behind a camera.

It was quiet, apart from the rustle of papers, and Sam began to relax. Then he noticed the presenters were listening intently to something, and watched as they gave a thumbs up to someone off to Sam's right.

Dan winked: 'Ready in about 30 seconds, Sam. Okay?'

Sam tried to smile. 'Yeah, okay, thanks.'

'Come on mate. You can smile more than that. It's a great way of relaxing you. Give me a big grin, like I was about to give you a hundred quid.'

It helped, and when the interview started, Sam somehow forgot all where he was. The questions were easy to answer, and he managed to get in a mention of the new arts centre.

Fiona nodded: 'Okay, tell us about that.'

'Like I said, my Dad and me used to rent deckchairs from the hut on the beach, but the council asked me if I'd sell it to them so they could build a new arts centre.'

'That's amazing. How come?'

Sam told them how Lindsay's arrival helped Whistle Bay become a magnet for artists, and how she encouraged him to take up painting: 'It was because of her that I went to the V&A and saw amazing pieces of furniture. That's what gave me the idea to try and turn deckchairs into proper furniture.'

Dan chipped in: 'Thanks for that great link, Sam! We've got a few pictures to show you of Sam's art, and one of his deckchair creations.' Sam looked at a monitor. They were showing one of the paintings of Gary, and the Dulwich deckchair.

Fiona whistled: 'That's beautiful. No wonder you're still getting orders.' She turned to the camera: 'Well done to Sam. He's a great example of young people who make a difference, if they try. If you want to find out more about this talented young man and his work, check out the links on our website.'

She turned back to face Sam, and Sam began to realise how slick and precise they were with every movement: 'So Sam, finally, tell us about Whistle Bay. It sounds great.'

'Yeah well, I've been there all my life, and I love it. The beach is fantastic, and the hills around are pretty spectacular, too. The people are like friends, especially the local traders. They really helped me when I took over the business after Dad died.'

Fiona smiled: 'Don't tell me: I bet they thought you were too young, and you'd never cope.'

Sam laughed: 'How did you guess?'

He was early for the train and sat alone in first class, feeling pleased with himself.

His phone was alive with emails and texts: a mix of new orders and well done messages from Lindsay, Grace, Karen, Shirley, Bob, Michelle, Aaron, Jivin' Jim, Billy, Louise - and one that made his heart beat faster: *You were so good on tv. Mama loved it. She wants to meet you. Will you come? S*

He replied straight away. *Still buzzing about it! I'd love to come. Tell me when is best. It would be so good to see you and M again. Sammy x*

There was no time to dwell on the thought of how he would handle meeting Sladana again. Michelle copied him into her appointment calendar for a 9am meeting the next day, and by the time he reached Birmingham, he'd taken down the details of another 25 orders for deckchairs.

The rocking of the train was making him sleepy, so he put the phone on silent and tried to switch off, feeling the adrenaline seep away. He stared at moving landscapes and caught glimpses of cars waiting at level crossings, cars at superstores, cars at traffic lights.

He closed his eyes, and Sladana was there...*They were sailing away, bobbing gently in the boat he'd made for Mikey, watching Whistle Bay get smaller. The big red sun was sinking below the horizon and a seal pup floated a few feet away, gazing at them with black eyes. Then the sun was gone, and the circle of warmth in the sky switched off. The wind began to howl and the dark shapes of gigantic ships surrounded them.*

He swung round to avoid hitting one of them, but the boat pitched and swayed as the waves got higher. Sladana began to cry and Sam held her closer; then a towering wave smashed into them and washed her away. Sam dived into the sea. It felt warm under the surface and all he could hear was the distant thunder of the waves. He swivelled, searching frantically. He opened his mouth to call for her, forgetting he was under water. He spluttered and choked and felt the icy water running through his body, up to his brain ...

He opened his eyes, gasping for breath, as the train slammed into a tunnel.

A steward pushed a trolley to his table. 'Are you alright, sir? Can I get you anything?'

'No, I'm okay, thanks. Nodded off. Forgot where I was.'

'I do that all the time. Where are you heading today?'

'Whistle Bay.'

'Do you live there?'

'Yes, I do.'

'You're a lucky man. It's a lovely part of the world. Used to go there for holidays when I was a lad. Happy days.' He glanced at his watch. 'We'll be there in about half an hour. Let me know if you need anything.'

'Thanks.'

Sam looked out at the blur of houses and trees. It was hard to distinguish detail in the fading light. He closed his eyes again but sleep wouldn't come.

It felt good to be so busy when he got home.

He called Shirley to offer her a part time job taking on fabric design and sourcing, and admin. Bob the Builder had recommended a newly qualified carpenter called Derek, and he accepted a six month contract; and Grace put him onto a friend in Hightown who signed up to a monthly retainer in return for managing the website and social media.

Next day, Shirley brought him a coffee and sat with him at the work bench. 'You're a whirlwind wheeler dealer. What are you eating for breakfast? Three Shredded Wheat and Red Bull?

'I got an egg and bacon roll on my way in.' Sam checked his watch and nearly spat out his coffee. 'I'm supposed to be meeting Michelle in quarter of an hour.'

'You'd better copy me in on your appointments so I can be your personal organiser. So, are you going to run there as usual, or shall I get you a cab? I'll have some designs to show you for that Edinburgh order when you get back.'

Sam gulped his coffee. 'It's okay, thanks; I'll walk. It'll do me good.'

He was five minutes late, but Michelle was friendly enough: slightly more formal but he expected that.

She shook his hand. 'I'm sorry we had to drop you, Sam, but you know how it is. We have to be so sensitive these days' It's hard to know what to say or do in case someone gets offended. But I'm glad it's over for you.'

Sam accepted the coffee, which tasted better than Shirley's, and said he was glad, too.

They chatted about the deckchairs and art, but he could tell she was building up to something.

She put her cup and saucer on the coffee table and leaned back in the armchair. 'I've talked to the Leader and the Mayor, and a few colleagues, about the new arts centre, and we agree that you would be the best person to do the official opening.'

Sam couldn't help laughing. 'What, really? Me? I mean, wow! But isn't there -'

Michelle leaned forward. 'Sam, you were the one who inspired us. You changed your life through art, reinvented yourself; went from a shy, amiable boy to a successful, charismatic and confident man. Not only that, but you also represent a family that has generations of Whistle Bay history. Even now, I don't think you understand just how much you've achieved: the odds you've overcome. Listen, Sam: there's no-one more qualified to do this than you.'

Sam thought for a moment, before speaking: 'It's nice of you to ask, but all I've done is gone from renting deckchairs to painting them and making them.'

Michelle laughed briefly but carried on as if he hadn't spoken: 'We'll be opening a couple of weeks earlier than expected, in early to middle of February. The contractors say

239

the fitting out is going quicker than expected. You'll love it, Sam. Please don't be shy. Please say you'll do it.'

Sam sipped coffee that had gone cold. He'd been expecting an invitation to be an ambassador again, and he would have refused it, because he was sure it would go down badly after what happened with Karen. But now, this… his emotions were a replay of his reaction when Becky asked him onto the tv show: disbelief, then fear, then knowing what it could mean for his business; and finally, the buzz of excitement.

He met Michelle's gaze. 'Thanks Michelle. It would be an amazing honour. I'll do it. But I'd like Lindsay there with me.'

'No problem at all. We're inviting her anyway.'

'Okay, and can I invite a couple of other people, too?'

'Of course. If you give me the names in an email, I'll make sure they're on the list.'

'Right, and could you give me some notes that would help me. I'm no good at public speaking.'

Michelle laughed: 'Says you, straight after appearing on the telly.' She scribbled in her notebook, then looked up. 'You must stop underestimating yourself. You're so confident, and more than capable of doing this speech. I got the first hint of that when we unveiled the big poster, remember? But I will send you an email, promise.

'You'd only need to speak for a few minutes. The Mayor and the Leader will do the boring bits, thanking everyone, but we'd like you to talk about the importance of art, and what the centre means to you personally, as well as the Bay. It's a showpiece building, and people will be stunned when they see it. But it's important they know it belongs to the Bay; to them. It's not like a yacht club. It's open to everyone. That's why we feel your family history is so important here.'

Sam nodded: 'I'll do my best.'

'I know. Just one more thing. When the rush dies down, the council would like to commission you to produce 50 of your deckchairs, using designs of your choice - something that represents the history of the Bay and your own unique journey. We'd like to put them out on the beach terrace.'

240

They shook hands, and Sam walked back to the shop. Shirley hugged him when he told her the news. He whispered: 'You'd better let me go before anything else happens.'

'Yes, sir. Sorry, sir. Will that be all, sir?'

'Get back to work, slacker.'

Work on the house was going quickly, too. His new kitchen was such a bright shade of white he felt dirty. He'd even started taking off his shoes at the front door.

The biggest transformation was in what Rick called the garden room, with sliding glass doors silently opening onto a teak verandah, and blinds that slid down at the touch of a button.

But he loved being in the study. One wall was panelled with timber from the hut, and Dad's paperback Westerns were lined up on the same old shelves. His home felt like a gallery, but this was more like a nest.

On the easel, a pen and ink drawing of Sladana and Marija, both of them looking straight at him. He wanted to give it to them tomorrow, but it wasn't ready yet.

Sam picked a country album from his Spotify list, sat on the high chair he'd saved from the hut, picked up a pen, and got to work.

Chapter 29

'Live as if you were to die tomorrow. Learn as if you were to live forever.'
-Mahatma Ghandi

He sat next to Marija by the window.

It was drizzling gently, but Sam could see a neighbour hosing a car, while a gang of lads kicked a ball against his garden wall.

The light that filtered through yellowing net curtains cast a warm glow on Marija's face.

Sam shifted slightly on the hard backed chair: 'I didn't think you'd want to see me after what happened. I'm sorry…'

She leaned forward. 'I don't want to hear sorry.'

'Okay… erm…'

'She told me and I tell her: her father went with another girl before we were married.' She saw the surprise in Sam's eyes. 'Yes, it's true. She never knew this. Like you, we were not … erm… do you say, committed?'

'Engaged?'

'Yes. I cried, but I forgive him. Like I say to Sladana, he didn't belong to me then. But I loved him, so…' She shuffled forward in the faded red armchair; her face so close Sam could feel her breath. 'Sladana loves you. I tell her she must-'

Sladana walked in, carrying a tray. Sam jumped up and took it from her. Marija pointed: 'The table please. Thank you.' She stood and Sam noticed she seemed stronger, steadier, as she walked across. 'Please, come. I shall be mother, yes?'

Sam glanced at Sladana, waiting to see where she was going to sit, but she didn't look at him; just pointed to the chair next to Marija, unsmiling. The only word she had spoken to him since he arrived was hello.

He told them about his trip to London, what it was like in the tv studio, and about the orders for deckchairs. Marija was doing all the talking, but suddenly, she stood: 'Now I will wash the dishes, if you will carry the tray for me, Sam.'

Sladana stood quickly. 'No, it's okay, Mama. I'll do it.'

'No, you must stay here with our guest.'

She whispered in Sam's ear as he put the tray by the sink. 'She is nervous, so you will need to be patient.' She patted his hand. 'Now, leave me.'

Sladana was still at the table. Sam pulled his chair nearer, and leaned forward, elbows on his knees.

'Sladana, I - I'm sorry. Can we get back together? I can't stop thinking about you. I was so stupid, but - I just want you to know that I love you.'

It was impossible to read her expression. Then she frowned, and he felt certain that Marija had got it wrong. He sat back, feeling the optimism draining out of him.

She got up and walked to the window, then turned, still not looking into his eyes: 'I haven't slept very well. Mama says it's because I made a mistake walking away from you. It didn't feel like a mistake. I was so angry.' Sam stood and walked towards her, but she held up a hand, and he stopped a few paces away. 'Please. I was angry. I wondered how could you do that to me on the same day we were planning to go to London to buy a ring. I was like this for days, then Mama told me about her and Papa, and I start to feel a little stupid.'

Sam took another step: 'No, you're not -'

'Yes, stupid... I see that I am unhappy; and I begin to think Mama is right. I should forgive, forget and everything will be okay between us again. The school friends becoming husband and wife. Like fairy story.'

She laughed and moved closer. He could feel his heart pounding as he tried to work out how to react. Then he put his arms round her and held her tight against him and breathed in the scent of her hair and spoke without thinking: 'Sladana. I have always loved you. Will you marry me? Let's go to London and buy that ring now.'

Her body was shaking and when she pushed away from him, he saw the tears. She pulled a tissue from a pocket in her cardigan and slowly opened it: 'This is Mama's engagement ring. Papa gave it to her. She wanted you to put it on my finger. When she finishes washing up, she will hope to see me wearing it. That's what she wants; why she wanted me to send you the message.'

Sam's voice was a whisper. 'That is so beautiful. Can I put it on now?'

She shook her head: 'It is too soon. I'm sorry.'

He sounded more certain than he felt. 'No, it's okay. You don't need to be sorry. This is all down to me. We need time. I'm in too much of a hurry, as usual.'

'Yes, maybe.'

'Can I see you again?'

'I think so.'

'Why don't you and Marija come to the house to look round? You'll love it.'

'No, no, I think maybe we could come to your new shop?'

'That would be great. I'd love to show you round. I'm working on a new picture... and you can see the new deckchairs, too.'

She looked up. 'Yes, that would be nice.'

Lunchtime; the day of the arts centre opening ceremony. The place was full, and the chatter was deafening.

Michelle attached herself to Sam as soon as he arrived, showing him the gallery of old photos, including one of him and Dad outside the hut, and one of Sam's paintings of Gary perched on a deckchair, next to a landscape by Lindsay - the one she'd sketched out on her first deckchair session.

Michelle linked his arm and steered him towards the sliding doors that led out onto the terrace, and pointed out the plaque:

This arts centre is dedicated to the Taverner family, who rented deckchairs from this site over four generations; and especially to Sam Taverner, who gave permission for this redevelopment. His emergence as a nationally famous artist and furniture maker symbolises the regeneration of Whistle Bay of which this building is a part.

It was supposed to be the biggest day of his life, but Sam told Aaron he wished he was somewhere else. Aaron said: 'I know what you mean, mate. This is your place. It must feel weird, just being here. But you're with friends, remember that.'

244

So Sam smiled, laughed, listened and nodded dutifully as one familiar face after another loomed in front of him: Billy with DIY Doris on his arm; Builder Bob, looking chipper in a suit; Loud Louise, tucking into the buffet; and Jivin' Jim in his dinner jacket, and his wife in evening dress.

He checked his watch. Sladana said she'd be there as soon as her shift finished, but that was an hour ago, and he was due to give his speech in ten minutes.

Sam listened patiently to someone else telling him how much they loved the old hut, then locked himself in a cubicle in the gents, and tapped out a message: *Where are you?! x*

He waited, listening to the noise levels going up. Either more people were arriving or they were all getting merry on the free prosecco.

Sam shook his head. Why did he agree to this? He didn't need the publicity:business couldn't be any better. The deckchair orders were still coming in, and he was getting requests from locals to do portraits. His accountant told him last week he needed to get some advice about wealth management, whatever that was.

The shrill chime of his phone echoed off the tiles. Sladana: *I can't come x*

Why what's happened?

I'm not sure about us anymore I'm sorry Please let's leave it for a while.

Sam stared until the screen went blank. The words disappeared as if they had never existed, then were replaced by the calendar alarm he'd set weeks ago. It was time for the opening ceremony.

He heard someone pushing the door open. Then a voice he didn't recognise: 'Sam, are you in there? Michelle says it's time to get started, okay?'

Sam cleared his throat: 'Yeah, give me a minute.'

'Great, thanks. I'll tell her to hang on a bit longer. No worries.'

Sam's hand was shaking as he unlocked the cubicle door.

In the few seconds it took him to check in the mirror and splash water on his face, he was feeling that familiar pressure; the pressure that pushed him into taking on the family business;

245

the pressure to be a friend to the traders; to provide for Karen because it's what Mikey wanted; to –

Michelle smiled as Sam stood with her on the raised platform near the terrace doors.

'Ladies and gentlemen, let me introduce the star of the show, Sam Taverner!'

Sam had rehearsed his speech over and over, but he kept one hand in his jacket pocket, hanging onto the notes in case he dried up. It felt like a real possibility; his throat was dry and he felt hollow, despite all the mini-Danishes he'd eaten.

'- and so without further ado, let me ask Sam to say a few words before he officially opens this beautiful space.' Michelle turned to him: 'Sam.'

He waited for the applause to die down, pulled the speech out of his pocket, then put it back.

He took a deep breath as he scanned the faces in front of him.

'Dad's hut was never as busy as this.' The laughter was like an explosion that released something inside. Suddenly, he felt free, and he smiled.

'I did write a speech but I'm just going to say what's on my mind instead… I've lived in Whistle Bay my whole life. I know most of you and you know most of me.' He caught Lindsay's eye, and she gave him a thumbs up.

'I reckon I was asked to do this because of a little hut that stood on the beach for years and years. All my family did was rent out deckchairs. And all I can remember is how happy it made us; how happy people were to sit on the beach; how much they loved Whistle Bay; and how all the traders were a team, that got on with it, helping each other, even when things started to get difficult.'

He saw a few heads nodding and pressed on.

'Quite a few people thought there was no way a young lad like me would be able to take over the business. And those that did, reckoned I'd soon get bored and move somewhere else. Well, here I am!'

The applause was loud, and Sam took the chance to sip water.

'I feel proud and sad now. Proud that I kept my promise to Dad, proud that this place will always have a plaque on the wall that reminds people of my family. Proud that our little business made so many people happy. Proud of Lindsay, who came to Whistle Bay and changed my life, and the whole town with her beautiful art.'

He stopped as the applause started again.

'But I'm sad that my family aren't here to see this, and to see the new life I've made.

'None of this would have happened – to me, or to Whistle Bay - without Lindsay, so I really think there should be another plaque here with her name on it.'

He turned to Michelle during the applause, and she nodded.

Sam called Lindsay up and hugged her, and said: 'And now, we declare the Whistle Bay Arts Centre officially open.'

'

Chapter 30

Sam leaned on the chrome rail, looking at the khaki brown of the sand, and the blue grey of the sea; at the bright gulls that swooped and swirled, their sad song mixing with the dull rhythm of the waves.

Behind him, the faint chatter of the last few guests filtered through as they said their goodbyes, and then the clink of glasses as staff cleared away the debris.

He heard footsteps. Lindsay put her arm through his and leaned into him: 'Feeling sad and thoughtful?'

'Yeah. Liking the view, though.'

'You going to paint it?'

'I mght if Gary was there. The colours are great in this light.'

She squeezed his arm. 'I love that: you sound just like an artist. I miss this so much. London's colourful, but not like this. Anyway, why are you sad?'

'It just feels weird. Been in that hut all my life, It's like something ended.'

'The hut, you mean?'

'Not just that…'

She gave him a knowing look. 'Okay… Sladana?'

He nodded.

'Well, when something ends, something else has to begin.'

'Yeah, I suppose.' He turned to her. 'I reckon I'm ready for something new. What about you? Are you and Grace together again?'

She paused. 'Yep. We're going to give it another go.'

'That's good. Come round to the house, have a tour, while I'm still there.'

'We'd like that, Sammy, thanks. What about you and Sladana? If I had to bet, I'd say that's the something that ended, right?'

'Yeah. She's had enough of me.'

'Is it ending as in terminal?' She stopped, and her eyes widened. 'Hang on, what do you mean, while I'm still there? Are you selling the house?'

Sam nodded. 'Yeah, I am. Feels like a good time after what's been going on.'

'Where will you go?'

'No idea.'

'Well, that's good news, though. You're free at last. Don't fret. You'll find someone else who appreciates you almost as much as I do.'

'Maybe I'm just meant to be on my own.'

'Nah. I'm not having that. You just need to get out there. Come and see me in London town whenever, all right? Now, chin up... I've got to go and rescue Grace. Someone's tapping her up for inside info on property prices or something equally dull. Take care Sammy.'

She kissed his cheek and turned as the doors slid open, shouting loud enough to be heard down Marine Parade: 'Call Grace about the house, and keep painting!' Then her scarlet jacket vanished into the interior shadows.

He hugged Michelle on his way out. She smiled up at him: 'So, can I tempt you to come back and be our ambassador?'

'I don't think so, sorry. Everything's a bit mad at the minute.'

She nodded and patted his arm: 'Yeah, I'm sure. Anyway, thanks for today, Sam. You were a star. And don't be a stranger, okay?'

He loosened his tie and sat on the beach. The setting sun was daubing crimson in the clouds.

He didn't recognize her until she was just a few yards away; silhouetted against the brightness of the lowering sun.

'I haven't got sweets, but can I join you anyway, boss?'

'Shirley?'

'You look like you're waiting for a bus.'

'I was hoping Gary might show up, but I reckon he's moved on.'

'Ah well. It's lovely, isn't it? We should make the most of it.'

249

'Yeah. Come and sit down. Sorry, I'm out of deckchairs. But it's free to sit on the sand. I could never work out why more people didn't do it.'

She laughed. 'You're not out of deckchairs; your new ones are the best in the world.' They heard doors slamming and shouted goodbyes behind them. 'So, which do you like best - sunset or sunrise?'

'Erm ... sunrise.'

'Why?'

'New start, new day.'

'Yeah, fair enough.'

'You?'

'Both. Sunrise, new day; sunset, new day coming.'

Sam nodded: 'I like that.'

A lone gull pecked at the water's edge as the sun added an undercoat of red to clouds that hugged the horizon.

He felt Shirley shiver. 'Beautiful colours... Looks like it's going to be a great day tomorrow.'

Shirley rested her head on his shoulder. 'Do you want to come back to mine tonight?'

Sam watched the gull lift off and glide across the bay towards the open sea. 'Thanks, but I'd like to spend some time on my own.'

'You're not working, are you?'

'Nope. I've got to try to paint this amazing sunset.'

Milton Keynes UK
Ingram Content Group UK Ltd.
UKHW020643260923
429409UK00015B/879

9 781916 596818